YANKEE TWANG

MUSIC IN AMERICAN LIFE

A list of books in the series appears at the end of this book.

YANKEE TWANG

COUNTRY AND WESTERN MUSIC IN NEW ENGLAND

CLIFFORD R. MURPHY

UNIVERSITY OF ILLINOIS PRESS
Urbana, Chicago, and Springfield

Publication of this book was supported by a grant from the L. J. and Mary C. Skaggs Folklore Fund.

Manufactured in the United States of America
C 5 4 3 2 1
∞ This book is printed on acid-free paper.

Library of Congress Cataloging-in-Publication Data
Murphy, Clifford R., author.
Yankee twang: country and western music in New England / Clifford R. Murphy.
pages cm. — (Music in American life)
Includes bibliographical references and index.
ISBN 978-0-252-03867-9 (cloth: alk. paper)
ISBN 978-0-252-09661-7 (ebook)
1. Country music—New England—History and criticism.
I. Title.
ML3524.M87 2014
781.6420974—dc23 2014012436

To the many women and men of New England country and western music: this book is for you, that the world should know you, your music, and your contribution to the character of New England community life.

To the memories of those who contributed so generously to this work and who have traveled on before seeing their names in print: Wendell Austin, Angelo Boncore, Vinny Calderone, Bill Chinnock, Jerry Devine, Doug Garon, Flo Cody Hooper, Gene Hooper, Clyde Joy, Herb LeBlanc, Paul Roberts Metivier, John Penny, Rusty Rogers, Jim Senter, Johnny Smith, Rex Trailer, John Lincoln Wright, and Richie Zack.

To the memory of my late father, Gordon D. Murphy, Jr., who always dreamed of publishing a book: this one's for you.

To Mom and Peter, for always encouraging me to follow my muse.

And, finally, to my wife, Monica, without whom my life would be so very empty. You are profoundly beautiful by every measure. I love you so much.

CONTENTS

ACKNOWLEDGMENTS

My ethnographic and historical research was informed by—and shaped by—my having been a resident of New England from 1978 until 2008, my family heritage in Massachusetts and Maine that stretches back in parts some two centuries, and my having traveled extensively throughout the region as an itinerant rock and country and western musician from 1988 through 2003. Formal research for this project began in 2004. As a bi-musical participant-observer, I carried out ethnographic fieldwork with country and western musicians and fans in the states of Rhode Island, Massachusetts, New Hampshire, and Maine, as well as in the Canadian provinces of New Brunswick, Prince Edward Island, and Nova Scotia. I conducted oral histories with performers active (and formerly active) in all six New England states and with pertinent persons who now reside in the states of Tennessee, Colorado, Oklahoma, Florida, and Ohio and in the Canadian province of Nova Scotia. Oral histories were all conducted under the auspices of the Maine Folklife Center, the Massachusetts Cultural Council, and the American Folklife Center. Copies of fieldnotes, sound recordings, photographs, transcriptions of interviews, and signed release/consent forms have all been deposited in those archives as noted.

Research in historical primary sources—field recordings, commercial recordings, photographs, oral histories, print media, radio transcriptions, recording contracts, show posters, advertisements, fan mail, and business documents—was conducted in the archives of the New England Country Music Historical Society in Watertown, Massachusetts; the Maine Folklife Center at the University of Maine, Orono; the American Folklife Center at the Library of Congress; the Folklife and Heritage Archives of the Massachusetts Cultural Council; the New England Folk Music Archives at the Passim Center; the Country Music Hall of Fame and Museum; and the John

Edwards Memorial Foundation (JEMF) Collection of the Southern Folklife Center at the University of North Carolina, Chapel Hill.

The archives of the now-defunct New England Country Music Historical Society are maintained by Gordon "Country Gordy" Brown of Watertown, Massachusetts; Mr. Brown and his archive contributed the bulk of historical materials (rare radio transcriptions, photographs, regional commercial and noncommercial recordings) used in this work. A series of oral histories and field recordings conducted by folklorist Edward D. "Sandy" Ives and his anthropology students and interns (Greg Boardman, Lisa Feldman, and Debora Kodish) at the University of Maine in Orono between 1975 and 1980 with musicians, fans, and radio executives active in country and western and hillbilly orchestra music in Maine and the Canadian Maritimes between the 1920s and the 1980s proved an invaluable resource. These materials are housed in the Northeast Archive of Folklife and Oral History at the Maine Folklife Center at the University of Maine, Orono. Other items located in the archives of the Maine Folklife Center and utilized in this work are a series of oral histories, field recordings, and rare radio transcriptions of Maine country and western musicians collected by folklorist Jeff "Smokey" McKeen. I am most grateful to Maine Folklife Center director Pauleena MacDougall for her ongoing support of this project.

The New England field recording collections of Phillips Barry, Helen Hartness Flanders, Alan Lomax, and Eloise Hubbard Linscott housed at the American Folklife Center and the Vermont Folklife Center were valuable in providing historical context for this work. The Linscott collection was particularly helpful as—unlike the recordings of Barry, Flanders, and Lomax—it contained a wide variety of styles and reflected a far more elastic definition of "vernacular" or "folk" music worthy of recording in the 1930s and 1940s. Linscott's collection includes several recordings of radio broadcasts made in 1942 by Massachusetts cowgirl yodeler Georgia Mae, as well as the only known recordings of Maine performers like the Katahdin Mountaineers, the Singing Smiths, and other early Maine string bands experimenting with proto–country and western sounds. Finally, the archives of the Country Music Hall of Fame hold several high quality rare commercial recordings of New England artists unavailable elsewhere, as well as songbooks from the 1930s through the 1950s of New England artists. The archives also include oral histories conducted with Bradley Kincaid and Grandpa and Ramona Jones (which cover their brief tenure in Massachusetts and New Hampshire in the 1930s and 1940s) by Douglas Greene and with Kenny and Bettyanne Roberts by John Rumble.

Beyond those persons mentioned above who extended gracious and insightful assistance above and beyond the call of duty, I would like to thank the mentors, colleagues, and friends who helped to bring this book along: Jeff Todd Titon, Maggie Holtzberg, Jennifer Post, Rose Subotnik, Pauleena MacDougall, Pamela Dean, and Millie Rahn. And a most grateful thanks goes to my wife, Monica, and to my friends Eric Chalek, Baynard Woods, Nate Gibson, and Elaine Eff for offering so much editorial insight and moral support along the way. Thank you, too, to Terry Chinnock for sharing biographical details about her father, the late, great Dick Curless. Thanks to Alyce Ornella and Andrew Jawitz of Rockhouse Mountain Productions for their generosity and enthusiasm for all things Al Hawkes. And thanks to my team at the University of Illinois Press: my editor, Laurie Matheson, for her calm and patient guidance; and my copyeditor, Mary M. Hill, and managing editor, Jennifer Clark, for their indefatigable dedication to quality and good cheer. I must also add a thanks to my friends and musical colleagues, the late, great Say ZuZu and Hog Mawl: those thousands of hours of conversations on tour, in living rooms and at truck stops, about all that is righteous and good and devastating about playing music for a living—those led me to this, and your insights and hard-won wisdom fill these pages.

PROLOGUE

FIELDNOTES ON THE DICK PHILBROOK AND THE FRYE MOUNTAIN BAND SHOW

Place: Thompson Community Center, Union, Maine

DATE: AUGUST 4, 2007 The drive from Waldoboro to Union, Maine, was as beautiful as I remembered it from two years before when I attended the Dick Curless Memorial Scholarship Fund concert. Old coastal Colonial houses and clam huts gave way to rolling fields of blueberries and small dairy farms. I arrived in town around 5:30, which was the time I had arranged to meet Yodeling Wade Dow for an interview and to make a recording of his virtuosic cowboy yodeling. I went inside the Thompson Community Center—a wonderfully dusty old basketball court with high rafters, a stage, a kitchen, an ancient scoreboard with orange bulbs, and dim, rusty-red overhead lighting. I approached the first man I saw in a western shirt with pearl buttons to ask Wade's whereabouts. This was—it turned out—Dick Philbrook, the leader of the Frye Mountain Band, with whom Wade was to be playing that night. Dick is a solid man of short stature with white hair slicked back in a 1960s trucker style, a thick Down East brogue, a wide smile with a front tooth cut at a sharp angle, and big, strong hands.

Dick told me that Wade had been given the night off, and he was chagrined to find that I'd traveled all the way to Union only to be disappointed. Dick and his girlfriend, Evelyn, tried to call Wade repeatedly, but to no avail, and we talked awhile about country and western music in Maine. I stepped out to look for a bite to eat, perused the snacks at the Mic-Mac Convenience Store and a small grocery store, and took a look at the Union Fairgrounds and the warehouses that serve as the center of Union, Maine's blueberry industry. I went back into the Thompson Community Center, paid the eight-dollar cover, passed on the fifty-fifty raffle, ordered a couple of hot dogs and a Moxie, and sat down next to Evelyn while the band began to play.

During the second song, Dick waved me over to the stage and told me to grab my guitar out of my trunk and sit in with the band for at least one set.

Being the youngest person by a good twenty years at least in a room (the gymnasium in this case) full of a hundred or more people is not a feeling I am comfortable with. Young people—particularly young people in their twenties through forties—are so rare at these events that the regulars can't help but be curious about the "youngster." I figured if I was going to stand out that much, I might as well be playing and not sitting. So I went out to the car, tucked in my shirt, and got my guitar.

The Dick Philbrook band wears matching white western shirts and black pants. Dick plays electric bass and has two men playing electric guitar (both lead) and a woman on drums. The group was very loose, and band members traded off songs, with the singer starting the tune and the others joining in halfway through the first verse or so. I plugged in my acoustic and played rhythm guitar. I knew most of the songs without having ever played some of them, and I sang lead on about one in every four or five songs—mostly Hank Williams, Lefty Frizzell, and Merle Haggard songs. I got a good hand each time, and Dick gave me high praise at the end of each song on which I sang lead. That felt good.

For me, personally, this was a milestone performance: though I have been playing this music now for over ten years, this was the first truly country and western gig I'd ever been on. Shows I had been playing with my own band for the past seven years either were for rock crowds or were in diverse rooms where some patrons were serious country and western fans, but most people were socializing to music that happened to be country and western. And though most of the songs we played that night originated in Nashville or Bakersfield, what we were doing at the Thompson Community Center did not feel attached to those places at all. The heady commercial country music world of Nashville—where I had spent considerable time in the past knocking on doors, making commercial recordings, playing at record label showcases, meeting with music industry professionals, lawyers, and songwriters—felt very far away from Union, Maine. Here at the Thompson Center, people in matching cowboy clothes were dancing, and we had to play mostly slow or midtempo songs for them. This was a challenge for me, as I like to push the beat, and—instinctively as someone who grew up playing rock music first—I think of "dance" songs as fast songs. This is not the case when you are playing traditional country and western for a room full of Mainers who grew up two-stepping, polkaing, and square dancing to country and western music.

The stage sound was not good—the drummer had trouble hearing the band and would occasionally drop the beat when the phrasing fell behind or ahead of the established rhythm. This is part of the country singer's job—

to keep a steady rhythm on guitar while falling *around* the beat with the vocals. This is particularly true at a dance in Maine for a room full of Dick Curless, Lefty Frizzell, and Merle Haggard fans. So a muddy stage sound that causes a drummer to be thrown off by this kind of vocal technique is a bit of a liability. But no one seemed to mind, and I found myself watching the feet of the dancers in order to keep time when the drummer's beat was unclear. This visual metronome was like nothing I'd ever experienced before as a musician.

At one point the drummer teetered on reversing the beat of the song, and so she dropped out entirely for about two measures. During this gap, the swooshing of the dancers' feet as they grazed the dance floor was fully audible: no conversation in the room could be heard, just the swooshing of the dancers' feet in time to the music like a set of brushes on a snare drum. The sound filled the gymnasium in balance with the reverberating music, and the engagement of the band with the audience—and the audience with the band—was fully palpable and audible if just for a moment before the drums kicked back in. The nature of the relationship between the country and western group and its audience appeared revealed in that moment—where the musicians and the audience serve as alternating engines that drive the country and western event.

I wound up playing three sets with the band. The material covered songs by Gene Autry, George Jones, Buck Owens, Hank Williams, Ray Price, Merle Haggard, Willie Nelson, and other "traditional country" songs. There were no songs from the Maine country and western pioneer repertoire (meaning, no songs written by Mainers), though we played a number of traditional instrumentals, and I sang Doc Williams's "Roses Are Blooming," to the surprise of the band members and the audience. During a set break, the other players in the band each told me stories about playing with Dick Curless at some point in the past.

We played a couple of tunes that I just never would have ever played otherwise, including "Tiny Bubbles" (Don Ho), "Chattahoochie" (Alan Jackson), and "Margaritaville" (Jimmy Buffett). The audience wanted to hear them, so we played them. I had gone nearly twenty years playing gigs while successfully avoiding ever playing a Jimmy Buffett tune. No longer.

After the third set, Dick Philbrook kicked me out: he knew I'd hoped to find a motel room up by Belfast, and he told me that it'd be too late by the time they finished the fourth set. So I packed up to leave. Dick told me that anytime I was back in the area, I was welcome to sit in with the band. He was very enthusiastic about this. Evelyn handed me her cell phone, too, as Wade Dow was on the other end of it. Wade, too, felt bad that we'd crossed wires, and he invited me to come by on Sunday to his house to meet up for an interview. We decided on 3:00. Dick pulled me aside and suggested I stay at a motel that's just on the other side of the bridge in Belfast. "It's got a good rate, and it's where I used to take my girlfriends back in high school." I made a mental note not to stay there—not because I didn't trust Dick, but because I took him at his word and didn't want to get a room next to a couple of high school kids. With that, the band thanked me for my help, the crowd gave me a hearty round of applause, and I was on the road down Route 17 toward the coast, having finally played a real country and western gig. It was not the first time I had benefited from the inclusiveness so pervasive among audiences and musicians at New England country and western events, but it was certainly the most personally rewarding.

YANKEE TWANG

INTRODUCTION

REINTRODUCING NEW ENGLAND TO THE COUNTRY MUSIC WORLD

New England country and western music has been buried under a mountain of corporate propaganda that wants you to believe that country music is an exclusively southern cultural export. This process began in the late 1950s, when corporate music industrialists in Nashville orchestrated a union between record companies, song publishers, and radio DJs that effectively swept the nation's copious and colorful regional subsets of country and western music off the airwaves and truncated the music's commercial moniker to "country music" (without the "western"). In this new Nashville-based and corporate-controlled order, country music became virtually anything sung with a southern accent. And as country and western music makers outside the South had ever-decreasing access to broadcast mediums from the late 1950s onward, the ensuing decades of southern-"branded" country music have served to erase much of the living memory of the rich country and western legacies of those regions whose misfortune places them outside of the vaunted southern United States. The subsequent popularity of the new corporate country music among working people in the North has led industrialists, scholars, and cultural purists to alternately celebrate and lament this illusory triumph of southern culture in the North.

In New England, many have come to misunderstand the music's popularity as a new phenomenon, unaware that New England country and western music has a long and storied history, convinced instead by Nashville's chokehold on broadcast media that country music is and always has been a white, Anglo-Saxon, Protestant, southern cultural export. Up until the formation of the Country Music DJ Association (later to become the Country Music Association) in 1958, the country and western music heard on the airwaves in New England was mostly made by New Englanders (and not just any New Englanders, but predominantly those of an ethnic and religious heritage different from that of their southern counterparts). That would begin to change radically in 1958, and by the mid-1960s nearly all New England country and western music making had been removed from the airwaves in New England.

At the very same time (1965), New England's greatest and most iconic country and western figure—the eyepatch-wearing Dick Curless of Bangor, Maine—scaled the barricades of corporate country music with a song inspired by and written and recorded in Maine for Mainers. The power of the song—"A Tombstone Every Mile"—propelled it up the national country music charts in 1965 with the help of fiercely independent truckers who delivered the local release to truck stop jukeboxes up and down the eastern seaboard. Curless's recording captured the raw energy of a region grappling with life along a rugged frontier in a multicultural region largely forgotten in the national consciousness and proud of its legacy of stubborn persistence in the face of great odds. "A Tombstone Every Mile" is a rightfully proud moment in the minds of many of New England's working people. This work exhumes the still-living body of New England country and western history and tradition that produced Curless's great flash of brilliance and shows "A Tombstone Every Mile" to be a significant mile marker on a cultural journey that continues today, however much ignored and misunderstood.

This book explores what local working-class New Englanders often refer to as "traditional country music" and what I will refer to consistently throughout this work as "New England country and western music." The practitioners of and participants in this regional form of country music use live, local music to drive community events, and they are active stewards of the music's regional history and traditions. New England country and western music, history, and sociability is—has been for nearly a century—interwoven with national and international forms of commercial country music. This book also examines how the national and international commercial country music industry's diminishing interest in showcasing country music as a regional, working-class music has negatively impacted the vibrancy of New England country and western and has both threatened and fortified the region's sense of inheritance to the mantle of country music authenticity.

This work explores what the community's ground rules are for establishing authenticity in New England country and western music. This exploration reveals that New England country and western performers self-consciously position themselves in real and imagined American frontier regions as possessors of real or imagined ethnic, religious, socioeconomic, and geocultural inheritances that ostensibly create a more "authentic" frontier experience for the audience. As such, it comes as no surprise that New England country and western music is particularly resilient in and evocative of northern New England. Nor is it surprising that New England's most influential country and western musicians accentuate their Maine roots. Understanding this requires a basic orientation to the region of New England and its cultural, political, and industrial history.

Understanding New England

New England is comprised of six contiguous states in the northeastern corner of the United States of America: Connecticut, Maine, Massachusetts, New Hampshire, Rhode Island, and Vermont. For a brief period of time prior to the American Revolution, New York and New Jersey were included by colonial rulers as part of New England, but New Englanders, historians, and geographers do not consider those states a part of New England. Originally, the New England colonies were bounded to the north by what was the French-controlled region of New France (the modern-day Canadian provinces of Quebec, New Brunswick, Prince Edward Island, Newfoundland, Labrador, and Nova Scotia) and to the south by what was the Dutch-controlled region of New Netherlands (which included the modern-day states of New York and New Jersey, as well as coastal parts of Connecticut, Pennsylvania, and Delaware). Today, New England is bounded to the north by the country of Canada, to the east by the Atlantic Ocean, and to the south and west by the state of New York.

Within the borders of New England, a wide range of geographic phenomena can be found: the Appalachian Mountains stretch from western Connecticut and Massachusetts (the Berkshire Mountains) up through eastern Vermont (the Green Mountains) and northern New Hampshire (the White Mountains) and into western Maine before arriving with grand finality at the Atlantic Ocean in the midcoast Maine region near Bar Harbor. The rocky coastline of Maine and New Hampshire, combined with harsh winter climates, caused early European explorers to surmise that the inland regions of these states were inhospitable, and so with the exception of some small fishing outposts, settlement was concentrated along the coasts and inland rivers of Connecticut, Rhode Island, and Massachusetts where the soil was fertile and the winters slightly more tolerable. Today, these southern New England states remain the most densely populated of the New England states.

New England is an historical, geographical, political, cultural, and imaginary region of North America in what is the traditional homeland of the Massachusett, Wampanoag, Narragansett, and Abenaki peoples. The six New England states have a long-standing political and cultural affiliation with one another dating back to their origins in the seventeenth century as British colonies of mostly British (English and Scots-Irish) immigrants who practiced a form of Christianity influenced by Calvinism (mainly

Puritanism). In colonial times and during the early days of the republic, New England Puritan theologians trained at New England colleges exerted a powerful force in New England—culturally, spiritually, and politically—and provided formidable resistance to other faiths (primarily Native) and other Christian denominations (particularly Roman Catholic and Quaker). The political-cultural affiliation of New England began with the New England Confederacy in colonial times (organized to do battle against Native Americans, French, Dutch, and Spanish) and was solidified during the creation of the United States of America, when the New England states tended to vote as a block, and again during the War of 1812, when New England Federalists considered secession from the Union in the face of financially crippling embargoes. By this time period, New Englanders had developed a national reputation as economically and culturally aggressive "Yankees": a religiously stringent and highly literate (and self-assured and self-absorbed to the point of parochial) people who smugly viewed their pastoral Puritan/Pilgrim past as the birthplace of the republican spirit of America (Temin 2000; Nissenbaum 1996, 47).

In the face of a foundering economy due to diminishing returns from the maritime trade after the War of 1812, and in an effort to maintain political relevance within the larger United States, moneyed New Englanders transformed the New England landscape with the creation of textile mills centered in planned industrial cities along the region's ample waterways. The industrialization of New England coincided with revolutions in transportation and the New England farmer's inability to compete with the newly booming agricultural business of the Midwest. The creation of the textile industry in New England first spurred an influx of former farmhands (mostly women) into the mill cities, followed by an unprecedented wave of immigrants from the British Isles, Continental Europe, and French Canada (Quebec and the Canadian Maritime provinces). Of these "new" ethnic groups, the Irish, Italians, Portuguese, and Quebecois were the largest and most powerful in the ethnic transformation of New England that followed in the wake of industrialization (Lewis 1980; Temin 2000; Hareven and Langenbach 1995; Conforti 2001; Feintuch and Watters 2005).

Large planned industrial cities like Springfield, Massachusetts, Manchester, New Hampshire, and Pawtucket, Rhode Island, grew up along New England's most powerful waterways: the Connecticut, Merrimack, and Blackstone Rivers. Smaller and midsized rivers like the Salmon Falls, the Penobscot, and the Winooski produced smaller mill cities like Dover, New Hampshire, Bangor, Maine, and Waterbury, Vermont. In northern New England, the rivers functioned as highways for the region's lumber industry in the mid- to late 1800s. An extractive industry whose market was largely the construction, power, and paper demands of urban southern New England, the lumber industry was seasonal work whose fierce workers were drawn from farms throughout the North Country and Atlantic Canada. These working men developed a robust repertoire of folk music depicting the oft-gruesome tales of bravery and death during the epic river drives that brought lumber downstream to insatiable processing mills for export elsewhere in the region.

For laboring people—excepting agrarian, maritime, and woods work—life revolved around the mill. For nearly a century, mill owners colluded on wages and controlled most aspects of mill town life, and workers struggled to establish their voice in the labor marketplace. Until just after World War I, this struggle was compounded by the absence of interethnic solidarity; working-class churches, schools, neighborhoods, and workrooms at the mill were segregated by ethnicity. Country and western music grew up in these New England mill towns and cities and fostered an environment where multiethnic socializing flourished beginning in the 1920s. Country and western music also provided mill town and city musicians the option of nonmill work with the relatively unusual opportunity of traveling extensively into New England's more scattered agricultural centers, providing an important place of Yankee-immigrant sociability and cross-cultural learning (Temin 2000; Lewis 1980; Hareven and Langenbach 1995).

New England mill owners refused to modernize facilities, proved stubborn in raising wages, and were steadfast in maintaining a significant profit on their industries (Temin 2000; Lewis 1980; Hareven and Langenbach 1995). The Great Depression proved an enormous stress on the textile industry in New England. Tense strike conditions and inefficient facilities hastened the departure of industry from New England for the American South, though the complete departure of mill work was staggered somewhat on account of the (lucrative) demands of World War II and the Korean War. Following the Korean War, most New England mills were abandoned, and corporations completed their migration into the less-unionized Southeast. Following the industrial collapse, New England fisheries were dangerously depleted by industrial trawlers (so-called factory ships) from Russia and Asia. Since the 1970s, New Englanders have relied primarily on the education, high-tech, biotech, service, and tourism (and its extension in the creative economy) industries for employment (Temin 2000; Lewis 1980; Hareven and Langenbach 1995).

New England is conceptualized by its residents and by scholars as a region consisting of two parts: southern New England (Connecticut, Massachusetts, and Rhode Island) and northern New England (Maine, New Hampshire, and Vermont). Southern New England is the more urbanized, multiethnic, politically powerful, partisan, bureaucratic, and affluent of the two regions. (Ironically, it also houses two of the nation's ten most impoverished cities—Providence, Rhode Island, and Hartford, Connecticut.) Northern New England is the more "Yankee," "natural," touristed, libertarian, nonpartisan, agricultural, and impoverished region of the two. In the popular—or the tourist's—imagination, minutemen come from southern New England, and mountain men come from northern New England. For contemporary New Englanders, the imaginary heart of New England identity is in the region's maritime, agricultural, mountain/lake, and old colonial areas (virtually anywhere but its multiethnic postindustrial urban sections). Northern New England has a particularly strong hold on the imaginations of New England country and western musicians and fans, especially the "North Country" (northern New Hampshire), the "Northeast Kingdom" (northeast Vermont), and the "Great North Woods" (northern and western Maine, particularly Aroostook County), where stalwart Yankees are imagined to be (and imagine themselves to be) actively—albeit silently—resisting modernity and change.

Ethnomusicologist Jennifer Post and historian Joseph Conforti both show that when a broad range of New Englanders (scholars, tourism professionals, working-class laborers and farmers, middle- and upper-class tourists, magazine publishers, poets, landscape artists, etc.) discuss the location of the "real" New England, they refer to northern New England and more specifically to the North Country (the least populated and most mountainous, forested, and agricultural regions just south of the Canadian border) (Conforti 2001; Post 2004). Artisans like Andrew Wyeth, writers like Robert Frost, northern New England tourism boards, print magazines like *Yankee* and *Down East*, and folklorists like Phillips Barry, Helen Hartness Flanders, and Alan Lomax all have promoted the idea that the "real," unspoiled, or frontier Yankee New England is to be found in northern New England and the North Country. Prominent contemporary New England fiction writers Howard Frank Mosher (e.g., *Where the Rivers Flow North*), Stephen King (e.g., *The Body*, made into the film *Stand by Me* in 1986, and *Rita Hayworth and the Shawshank Redemption*, made into the film *Shawshank Redemption* in 1994), and Richard Russo (e.g., *Empire Falls*, winner of the 2002 Pulitzer Prize and made into an HBO miniseries in 2005, filmed in Skowhegan and Waterville, Maine) have based their most well known work in the imaginary heart of New England (Mosher's work tends to be set in Vermont's Northeast Kingdom, King's in northern Maine). And, most pertinent to this work, while many New England country and western musicians pretend (or have pretended) to come from the West or the South, those who publicly embrace their Yankee identity tend to come from the North Country—and particularly from the state of Maine—or claim it as part of their heritage. Maine contains New England's most vibrant country and western community, and New England's foremost country and western musicians—Dick Curless, Yodelin' Slim Clark, and Hal Lone Pine and Betty Cody—have made the rugged frontier identity of northern Maine the centerpiece of their press materials.

Northern New England is, perhaps, a good place for New England country and western to be holding out. The historical arc of the music—as outlined in chapter 2—shows that New England country and western's vibrancy correlates directly with the health and subsequent decline of working-class industry in New England. To live in northern New England today is a choice of inconvenience, a struggle to maintain community memory in the face of declining population and "brain drain," and a prioritization of social over economic capital. Whether it is the origin of the term or not, the idea that resources have "gone south" fits the story of industry in mill town New England as well as it does the story of country music. New Englanders, by and large, are expected to be consumers of goods manufactured elsewhere—including their country music. This work explores the idea that country music—while assumed by many to be a cultural import to New England—is one of New England's long-standing cultural resources, despite Nashville's desire that you believe otherwise.

About Community Memory

It is important to note that contrasting cheerful and elegiac tones emerge from much of the community memories documented here: misleadingly cheerful with regard to ethnic and racial relations, elegiac with regard to where community tradition is headed. Much of this has to do with nostalgia for the past, a reluctance to bring up unpleasantness, a commitment to remembering ourselves and our communities the way we wish them to have been, a confusion about a world in change, and a profound sadness that future generations may simply never know all that is beautiful about who we were and what we have witnessed, created, and experienced.

This working-class inclination toward nostalgic remembrance of tough times is acknowledged in country music lyrics, and nowhere so poignantly as in Tennessee country singer Dolly Parton's song about "the good old days, when times were bad." Indeed, there is much evidence to show that a defining characteristic of working-class New England community—past and present—is a rich social capital, much derived largely from the circumstances of hanging tough together through consistently difficult economic hardships. And working-class and country music culture is not without its own pitfalls. I have written extensively elsewhere of gender and familial conflict inherent in the country music profession in New England (Murphy 2008). Indeed, in conducting the oral histories that serve as the bedrock for this book, I discovered that the body count of musicians felled by drinking, drugs, and reckless living, as well as the number of musicians who self-medicated their way through PTSD following active duty in World War II, Korea, and Vietnam, is nothing short of staggering. And yet, however forthcoming participants might be in discussing issues of insobriety and infidelity, they were uniformly tightlipped when pressed to discuss the ethnic and racial conflict that is well chronicled in social histories of the region.

Such silence on social conflict is not unusual in community memories that intersect with America's so-called roots musics. Anthropologist Aaron Fox theorizes that this silence is based on the idea that racial conflict resides somewhere "outside of the Utopian space of musical practice itself" and that the absence of social conflict from roots music narratives is "instantly bothersome" when comparing historical to nostalgic recollections of community (2005, 181).

Indeed, the sociopolitical evolution of the New England working class from a highly insular, fractious place of multiple ethnicities bound, by and large, to specific social, residential, professional, and religious spaces into a multicultural place in which ethnic boundaries (if not race) have largely been knocked down can be read as rather pedestrian stuff when cleaned of its stains of social conflict. In removing the soft lens of nostalgia, we can better see that New England country and western musicians and fans were participating in radical social change, intermixing with people of different (and often forbidden) ethnic—and sometimes racial—backgrounds for the first time in the region's history.

Social historian Roy Rosenzweig summarizes life for the working class of Worcester, Massachusetts, in the late nineteenth century thus: "Generally speaking, the owners of the city's factories came from native American or Yankee backgrounds, while the workers in those factories were predominantly first- or second-generation immigrants" (1987, 215). In a mill city such as Worcester, where the city population grew over 200 percent from 1870 to 1890, there was rampant illness in overcrowded immigrant neighborhoods, working conditions in factories ranged from difficult to harsh, and available recreational space was alongside open sewers, public dumps, and smoke-spewing factories. Public health officials and city planners saw to it that middle- and upper-class neighborhoods populated by native stock were clean and beautified. This same native stock only comprised about 6 percent of the labor force while controlling the parks, the factories, and most major political offices. Ethnic groups—social clubs, mutual benefit societies, churches, and fraternal orders—would periodically mobilize to gain political ground in matters of public health. But solidarity was fleeting.

Working together for periodic, incremental political gain was not the same as building trusting, long-term partnerships (let alone mixing socially). Ethnic boundaries remained solid in New England mill towns and cities through the early decades of the twentieth century (Rosenzweig 1987).

Ethnic and kinship ties drove immigration patterns, which in turn drove the character of ethnic neighborhoods in mill towns and cities. In such places as Providence, Rhode Island, ethnic mutual aid societies provided a range of monetary and nonmonetary insurance to members, ranging from unemployment benefits to assistance with meals following the loss of a family member. In 1919 both the Italian and Lithuanian Jewish communities each boasted about a hundred mutual benefit societies whose organization mimicked provincial boundaries in their respective homelands. Such groups did not tend to intermix, even within a shared faith such as the Roman Catholicism practiced by Irish, French Canadian, Italian, and Polish communities. Different customs of worship varied greatly—Irish priests were reluctant, for instance, to embrace the vibrant customs of saint worship practiced by Italian immigrants, causing significant friction. The neighborhoods, schools, churches, social clubs, and mill rooms inhabited by New England working-class people were defined by ethnicity—which at times extended further into language, faith, race, and other heritage factors—from the mid-1800s until World War II. Studies show that ethnic neighborhoods had begun to grow more diffuse by the 1930s and that ethnic mutual benefit societies grew increasingly focused on New World traditions (rather than maintaining Old World traditions) but that families still tended to stick together, living in all three levels of the triple-decker houses that are so ubiquitous in urban southern New England (Smith 1987).

Even with the social mixing that country and western music played a part in facilitating, and even though ethnic boundaries have broken down considerably since the early twentieth century, divisions remain. It is not unusual to find young couples in New England whose parents oppose engagement or marriage to someone of another (or a particular other) ethnicity. Such issues were typically left unspoken in many of the oral histories collected for this book. Some participants chose to speak guardedly about interethnic tensions. And issues of racial tension were not addressed, with the notable exceptions of several Maine musicians who performed in interracial groups (predominantly white with some African American, black Canadian, or Native/First Nations members). Many musicians spoke of race in relation to their purposeful eradication of blackface minstrelsy from country and western musical performance and broader community practice, and all of these were—without exception, and somewhat surprisingly—persons from Maine. With regard to the role nostalgia plays in cleaning up racial conflict from community memory, this is significantly absent from narratives collected in southern New England, where the racial climate of Boston helped to shape two of the most iconic voices of black nationalism in the twentieth century—Malcolm X and Louis Farrakhan—while its universities also helped shape four of the nation's most visible progressive integrationist leaders—Dr. Martin Luther King, Jr., brothers John F. and Robert Kennedy, and protest singer Pete Seeger. The violent race-based clashes that took place in the 1970s around Boston's bussing program (bussing students from disadvantaged—a coded word for African American—neighborhoods into area schools) helped catapult people like James "Whitey" Bulger into prominent places in urban New England's ethnic underworld and caused community fissures that continue today. So it is somewhat ironic that the racial and ethnic conflicts so prominent in pop culture treatments of Boston, such as Martin Scorsese's 2006 film, *The Departed*, are part of the unspoken backdrop to the story of New England country and western.

With regard to the elegiac tone of many of the participants documented herein, much of that can be attributed to a festering frustration held by many in the New England working class (or of working-class backgrounds) that their story is forgotten or not included in the mass culture that is flashed back at them on the radio and on television, movie, and computer screens. At times this blends with an overriding frustration that the needs of working-class, rural, and impoverished peoples are ignored by a mainstream culture that resides closer to power and money. And yet perhaps the greatest source of frustration can be attributed to shifting conditions and tastes of many in the working class: working-class jobs in New England tend to be unionized and tend to pay better than their working-class counterparts in the American South that feature so prominently in the music of Nashville. And a great many New England working-class people today prefer hard rock and metal to country music. All of this frustration is magnified by a mass culture that prefers to market its country music as southern.

The elegiac tone can also be attributed to the fact that life has changed and that something beautiful is disappearing. And sometimes—however difficult it may be to watch—it is okay that traditions die out, as it represents the fact that change—even positive change—often demands a different form of expressive culture. Change has brought a great many comforts and increased choices to working-class New Englanders—choices symbolized, perhaps, by roads leading out of northern New England. As such, we have been determined here to document New England country and western music while the tradition is still living so that we can better understand who we are through who we once were.

1

NEW ENGLAND COUNTRY AND WESTERN MUSIC AND THE MYTH OF SOUTHERN AUTHENTICITY

Some readers may find the subject of this book somewhat perplexing. To many, country music and its various offshoots are inherently southern in style and cultural origin. If you have a pulse, there is a good chance you've learned exactly this in a book, at a concert, in a film, on TV, or in a derisive joke about rednecks. Few cultural sounds are so thoroughly tied to a specific geographic location in the imaginations of North Americans as country music. Indeed, modern country music musicians go to Nashville in order to claim they come from it.

New England country and western musicians and fans do not need me or anybody else to justify their cultural authenticity to anyone. And yet for New Englanders reading this work, odds are good that you, like me, grew up entirely unaware of your home region's country music heritage. In looking back on my own life, I feel as though I should have known better: I grew up in a house in New Hampshire where we listened to country radio every morning, I was a professional musician who played in an alternative country rock band for fourteen years, I fronted a traditional honky-tonk band for five years, and I plundered record stores (as both customer and employee) for the best music I could find. For as long as I can remember, I was interested in where American music came from. Yet my explorations of the roots of American music never led homeward, and I did not hear the extraordinary country and western music of Maine's Dick Curless until I was twenty-three. Even then, I thought Curless was an anomaly. After all, I had dug through a mountain of evidence that said quite convincingly that country music came exclusively from the South. The sad feeling in my gut—and the guts of my fellow working musicians in New Hampshire—was that our region was a place that was largely devoid of homegrown, living musical traditions older than a quarter century. It took me over ten years—and dozens of interviews, field recordings, and archival hunts—to develop an informed picture of my home region's musical heritage and to understand how that heritage had become obscured and undermined by powerful and remote corporate interests.

And so, in the event you are skeptical of the existence of such a thing as New England country and western music—or think that if such a thing exists, it can't possibly be good, authentic, or important—you've got plenty of company. What you will learn here is that New England radio's relationship with live, local music enabled local country and western traditions to flourish from the 1920s until the late 1950s and that the local tradition suffered when radio shifted away from live, local music to national playlists of music recorded elsewhere. This shift toward the playing of records on radio skewed the public's perception of where country music came from, replacing local music with that produced in Nashville and obscuring the music's local history and traditions. This book sets down a narrative of New England country and western history and illuminates some of the musical and cultural factors that make this deeply community-rooted music distinctive to the region. The point of it all is not to convince you that the best country and western music is from New England. Rather, it is to introduce you to extraordinary everyday New Englanders, to document the full participation of the New England working class in the story of North American vernacular music, and to celebrate that community's remarkable contributions to New England folklife.

Community history and memory is a temporal thing, governed as it is by the nostalgia triggered by the changing of generations and the values and memories they hold and share. Musical memory is stunningly short-term, always shifting and expanding forward, shedding stylistic phrasing, repertoire, and tastes like the many skins of an undying yet ever-traveling snake. Northern musicians active in the folk revival of the 1950s recall encountering the southern hillbilly and blues records of the 1920s and 1930s as though they came from an ancient, unreachable past, despite the fact that fewer than three decades stood between the revival and the time of those recordings' first release (Stampfle 1997). In New England, the same imagined gulf between today and the heyday of regional country and western music is accentuated by the fact that so few local musical performances were ever recorded. And so this work aims to set part of this community's tale down in writing while some of these practitioners and their traditions are still living.

This work also aims to revive the notion that country music is, at its foundation, a traditional social music that, nationally, encompasses many regional styles. New England—indeed, much of the North American continent—has a long, rich history and tradition of country and western music that dates back as far as that of its famous southern counterpart. Some regional scenes, styles, and communities have been documented from the Canadian Maritimes (Rosenberg 1988) to the Southwest (Boyd 1998) to Kentucky (Davis 1998), and the New England portion of this missing history is chronicled for the first time in this book. It is my hope that other regions will follow suit. After all, New Englanders have produced their own deeply community-based form of country and western music since at least the 1920s. From the advent of radio until the late 1950s, local music and musicians were well supported by regional radio and early television. Since the late 1950s, when the country music industry became a nationalized industrial triumvirate of broadcast, publishing, and recording based in Nashville, Tennessee, non-southern forms of country music have become marginalized, and their perceived authenticity in their home communities has been called into question by those generations who never witnessed an era in which local musicians played a significant role in regional broadcast media. In short, popular country music and its supporting industries have done a very effective job at promoting authentic country music making as an exclusively southern cultural export.

This book aims to reorient the compass of country music authenticity not just geographically but in its social wellsprings as people's music (Keil 1985), in the basic dialogue between musicians and audiences. Regional musicians and their fans outside of the South have soldiered on through decades of self-aware disenfranchisement and have come to view themselves as stewards of "traditional country music." It is a decidedly community-based form of what popularly passes as "country music," where its primary function is to facilitate social dancing, and it retains—counter to its pop brethren on contemporary radio—a homegrown regional accent in both vocal and instrumental delivery.

This history and ethnography of New England country and western musical traditions serves as a consolidation of community memories, an examination of cultural meaning, and a celebration of a musical history that has nearly become fully displaced. History is typically written by conquerors, and social history less so; ethnography is something altogether different. Ethnography demonstrates that multiple narratives of history and cultural meaning coexist within any society, folk group, or community. When well written, ethnography can help show how these multiple narratives inform, resist, and even rely upon each other. Again, ask anyone living in North America today where "authentic" country music comes from, and invariably you will be told the South. This is as true for New Englanders and Atlantic Canadians as it is for Tennesseans and Texans. Worldwide, people who parody or denigrate country music affect a southern accent while doing so.

And what of New England's domain of cultural authenticity? That domain is made up of anything you can attach variations of the word "high" to as a prefix: high society, higher education, high-tech, high-grade seafood, high-range mountains, and indulgent high times enjoyed by students in exclusive boarding schools and private colleges. Yet drive through New England and look around, and you will find that most places you travel through are untouched by high-rolling lifestyles. The towns and cities that feature prominently in this work—like Bangor, Ware, Waterbury, Manchester, Nashua, Lewiston, and Providence—are filled with the grandsons and granddaughters of workers wooed from near and far by thundering industry, only to be abandoned in that industry's rotting mill town corpse. What are the stories of New England's working-class people, and what is—and what was—their music? The answers are, of course, myriad, but one prominent thread among New England working people from the 1920s through the early 1960s was country and western music, no matter what language they spoke at home. Deindustrialization and the resulting destabilization of the working class in the decades following the Korean War plus the generational rifts of the Vietnam Era chipped away at country music as a family commonality. But the biggest change in the relationship of New England working-class families and country music was the rapid erosion of local people's voices and music in broadcast media. This erosion produced a significant rupture in community traditions, and Nashville turned that rupture to its advantage. Country music is popular today in New England, but it is a specific southern brand with exclusive access to mainstream broadcast media. This music and the community that rallies around it is not devoid of its own culture, but it is noteworthy for a cultural compass that points decidedly south.

Jimmy Barnes of Mariasville, Maine, believes that regional resources are harvested for the profit of outsiders and to the detriment of locals, a point he makes in the liner notes to his CD *Country & Eastern*:

> Country music was originally built around the lives of hard-working country folk who believed in family, honesty, and a simple rural life. That concept was embraced by the music industry and sold as a product. It's my belief that over the years, we, the public, have been robbed of our local music heritage and independence, in part, by being told that if you're not from a certain geographic location or sing with a certain accent, you're not country. I also believe that the

> woodcutters of the Maine woods, the farmers who grow blueberries to potatoes, the fishermen of the rockbound coast, the truck-driving diesel cowboys who truck Maine products all over the country and all those other independent Maine folk, beg to differ. Whether you're from country or town, North or South, mountains or seashore, country is a state of mind and a value system rather than a specific location. (2000)

Barnes's statement is a powerful one. What it claims is that local values and local musical heritage have been mined as a resource, moved south to industrial production plants, and resold to New Englanders as a cultural import.

So how did we get here? Essentially it comes down to three key developments: the radio industry's shift away from live, local entertainment programming toward nationalized playlists of commercial recordings in the 1950s; the creation of nationalized country music playlists generated by the Nashville-based Country Music Association; and the development of a body of country music scholarship in the wake of these changes that focused almost entirely on commercially recorded southern country music. The absence of New England—and Atlantic Canadian—country musicians and accents on modern country radio in New England today marks a stunning reversal of cultural history and signifies the extent of the conquest of the Nashville brand of country music as southern music that swept across New England and other regions beginning in 1958. Up until that point, local and regional acts dominated country music broadcasts and live performances in New England. That is unfathomable today.

So to understand why we have not heard—or heard of—New England country and western, we'll need to take a look at how radio developed in New England, why the country music industry formed a powerful coalition in Nashville, and what the cultural and intellectual ramifications of these changes have wrought in country music scholarship. The end result is a worldwide impression that "authentic" country music is, as Jimmy Barnes observes, an exclusively southern cultural export. And, as Barnes also observes, the absence of nonsouthern regional forms of country music on modern country broadcasts calls into question its cultural authenticity. Although authenticity is a cultural concept that has largely been dismissed by scholars, it retains great significance in the world of musicians like Jimmy Barnes: country music is one area where the notion of authenticity still holds sway among musicians, fans, and even detractors. To understand how New England country music became obscure at best and "inauthentic" at worst requires a trip into the respective histories of the New England radio industry, the Country Music Association in Nashville, and country music scholarship.

A Brief History of the Radio Industry in New England and Country Format Radio

New England was home to one of the nation's first regional radio networks—the Yankee Network (and its sister network, the Colonial Network), owned by John Shepard and founded in 1930 in Boston, with WNAC—founded by Shepard in 1922—as its flagship station (Halper 2007). By 1936 the Yankee Network came to encompass thirteen stations in five of the six New England states (Vermont was the only exception) (Kroeger 1968), and while most of its stations were either news-only or "free format" (meaning programming varied, from drama to news to religious services to various styles of music), its stations hosted hillbilly and country and western talent as early as 1930 (Little and Little interview 1975). New England's first national radio network preceded the Yankee network by nine years (1921) in the founding of WBZ at the Westinghouse factory in Springfield, Massachusetts. The Westinghouse Corporation had launched station KDKA in Pittsburgh, Pennsylvania, in 1920 (it remains the oldest surviving commercial radio station in the nation) and founded a network of stations in the North and the Midwest, stretching as far as Chicago. Westinghouse launched WBZA in Boston in 1924, and by 1931 the two Massachusetts stations (WBZ and WBZA) had switched call letters. By the middle 1930s, WBZ (Boston) broadcast at fifty thousand watts, and its signal could at times be heard as far away as Oklahoma (Westinghouse 1943).

Both the Yankee and Colonial Networks and the Westinghouse stations had reputations for developing strong local talent and programming. With the dawn of NBC and CBS network programming in the 1920s, Westinghouse stations and Yankee and Colonial Network stations often preempted network broadcasts for locally made programs. John Shepard, owner of the Yankee and Colonial Networks, saw radio as a means to amplify regional and individual expression (the FCC's first act of censorship involved silencing Shepard's anti–Roosevelt / New Deal editorials broadcast on the Yankee Network in 1938) (Halper 2007). Networks were friendly toward hiring and developing New England hillbilly and country and western talent. It was primarily on these networks that New England country and western music blossomed from the first-known broadcast of local hillbilly music (the Crockerville Mountaineers on WNAC in Boston in 1930 [Little and Little interview 1975]) until the advent of television and the arrival of Top 40 and country format radio in the late 1950s.

To the listener, the shift away from live music to DJ-style broadcasts of commercial records was somewhat gradual. Beginning in the late 1940s and taking hold by the mid- to late 1950s, major New England country and western on-air radio performers began spinning records during their programmed time slots. Performer/DJs generally had a great deal of control over what recordings they played during their shows. In the case of the duo Jerry and Sky, their show came to encompass far more than country and western, making them regionally famous among third-shift workers for their all-night radio broadcast, during which they interviewed major performers passing through Boston such as the Mills Brothers and Frank Sinatra (Snow 2006). By the 1960s, live in-studio performance had mostly been phased out of New England radio programming; performers either moved into television or became full-time DJs who only spun records.

This shift toward a format where DJs played songs primarily provided by major labels was strictly financial and logistical. The emergence of television caused radio to appear instantly as an outdated form of technology and caused the radio industry to be caught in a financial (and identity) crisis in the 1950s. Radio's key "selling" point for advertisers had been the radio play (essentially an audio extension of vaudeville skits), which was adapted more successfully for television. Though many people continued listening to radio for news, sports, and music, the ability of radio stations (large and small) to secure lucrative advertising was compromised by the emergence of television (Hilmes 1997). As a result, radio stations had less money to work with, and playing prerecorded music and network broadcasts was cheaper and easier than employing the larger stable of audio engineers and personnel needed to manage and develop live talent. In a sign of the times in 1956, WCOP's *Hayloft Jamboree*—New England's only barn dance–style radio program—went off the air the same year the station switched to a Top 40 format (Halper 2007; Senter and Senter 2004; Brown 2004; White and Albro 2004). By the middle 1950s, most radio stations in New England had shifted away from live entertainment and toward Top 40 formats.

Into this breach stepped Nashville. In addition to the arrival of television and radio's subsequent shift from live to recorded music was a confluence of other changes—the growing popularity of rhythm and blues and rock and roll had prompted the U.S. government to investigate key industrial participants in those musics' market successes (recording companies, publishing companies, radio stations, and DJs) for conspiring against the musical tastes of the public (Pecknold 2007, 6). The country music industry consolidated (geographically) most of its production operations in Nashville during the emergence (and subsequent success) of commercial honky-tonk and rockabilly music (roughly the World War II period through 1956) and adjusted its branding image accordingly. The origins of this branding can be traced to 1952, when the music publishing company owned by Fred Rose and Roy Acuff—one of Nashville's first powerful song publishers, which controlled the songwriting catalog of Hank Williams and Felice and Boudleaux Bryant, among others—invited a collection of radio DJs from across the nation to Nashville for a convention (Kingsbury et al. 1998, 149). The purpose of this meeting was to respond strategically to the changes sweeping the worlds of radio, music, and television.

Nashville-based country music song–publishing companies like Acuff-Rose made a regular practice of promoting (or "pitching") their copyrighted material to as many record agents and recording artists as possible. It was not unusual in the 1940s and 1950s for competing recordings of the same song to be released by multiple artists on multiple labels concurrently. Acuff-Rose also made a practice of promoting recordings of their copyrighted material to radio DJs across the nation. DJs who played Acuff-Rose's songs were invited to the Nashville convention. At the convention, the DJs formed the Country Music Disc Jockeys Association (CMDJA) (Kingsbury et al. 1998, 149), marking an early industrial shift away from the term "western." In 1958 a group of powerful Nashville-based corporations, performers, promoters, and songwriters took control of the CMDJA and reorganized it as a trade union geared toward the promotion of country music. The new trade union was called the Country Music Association (CMA), and it jettisoned previous monikers (hillbilly, western, country and western, etc.) and officially rechristened the genre "country music" (Kingsbury et al. 1998, 100, 149). Ostensibly, this was done with the intention of creating a less confusing "brand" (the irony of the cowboy origins of the term "brand" notwithstanding) at a time when those corporate interests at play were seeking to develop a more urbane and cosmopolitan (or "countrypolitan") recorded sound product as a means of moving beyond the "hillbilly" image (Peterson 1997, 263) and as a rallying point in the face of rock and roll (Kingsbury et al. 1998, 100; Peterson 1997).

In the wake of this industrial shift, national playlists originating from Nashville became the norm on stations nationwide, regional artists in New England began disappearing from local radio, and cowboy music dropped off the country music charts almost entirely. The term "country and western" was rendered archaic. In 1964 western musicians and promoters accused the CMA of geo-industrial favoritism (Peterson 1997, 263) and organized a separate trade union (the Country and Western Music Academy) geared toward the promotion of western-based artists like Buck Owens, Johnny Bond, Merle Haggard, and Roger Miller (Kingsbury et al. 1998, 4; Peterson 1997, 263; Academy of Country Music 2007). By the early 1970s they had renamed themselves the Academy of Country and Western Music and dropped "Western" from their name shortly thereafter, becoming the Academy of Country Music (ACM) (Peterson 1997, 263; Kingsbury et al. 1998, 4; Academy of

Country Music 2007). They claimed that the inclusion of "Western Music" in their title created the false impression that they were a school for classical music (i.e., Western art music) (Academy of Country Music 2007). The CMA remains the most powerful trade organization in country music, and through its offshoots (the Country Music Hall of Fame and Museum and the Country Music Foundation) and its financial backers and founders it exerts a powerful hold on public and scholarly perception of what "is" country music and what country music "is" (Sanjek 1998). Virtually all major museums, encyclopedias, trade organizations, and popular and scholarly histories produced in the past thirty years devoted to the music formerly known as "country and western" have used the CMA trade brand "country music."

Popular music scholar Diane Pecknold marks 1958 as the birth of country format radio and 1959 as the year it began to take hold nationally, noting that "even Bing Crosby, who had deplored the condition of popular music in 1956, acquiesced to the rule of consumer democracy over cultural guardianship. In 1959, KFOX, Bing Crosby Enterprises' major outlet in the Los Angeles market, switched to a full-time country format and became a pioneer in developing the form" (2007, 132). Pecknold attributes KFOX's success as the blueprint for the national success of country format radio, as it "became the model and marker of the genre's economic recovery and cultural rehabilitation" (132).

Between 1958 and 1975 country format radio stations—and small stations with designated country broadcast hours—sprang up across New England. Playlists remained flexible enough so that occasional local records received airplay (on both Top 40 and country format stations) if callers demanded it. However, the national industry trended increasingly toward maintaining nationally standardized, genre-based formats, much to the detriment of local and regional musicians of all genres. In 1975 country and western musician Doc Williams of Wheeling, West Virginia, wrote a letter of complaint to Richard Wiley, chairman of the FCC. Williams had been the star and host of the *Wheeling Jamboree* on WWVA for decades and had owned his own radio station. Williams explained that he was troubled by developments in radio that consistently excluded local and regional musicians:

> I refer to the fact that almost *no* local music input is included on *most* radio and television stations; as a result we have super-super stars operating out of Nashville, Detroit, Bakersfield, New York, and so forth. (I have nothing against super-stars. I'd like to be one myself). Modern recording technology and mass communications should help the local musician, not destroy him. . . . Radio stations use music tapes put together by syndication groups thereby shutting out the local-regional performer. I strongly suggest that radio and television stations should be requested not only to program local news events, sporting

> events and otherwise, but also should present recordings and musical programs on radio and television by local-regional artists. (1975, 1)

Williams lamented the lack of regional music found on radio stations in the Pittsburgh/Wheeling region, a region that had been historically rich in regional radio music, writing, "This presents a terrible and discriminatory disadvantage to the local-regional musicians and performers." The legendary singer concluded his letter to the FCC commissioner with the modest suggestion of requiring between two and five hours of local musical programs per week, depending on the size of the market (1975).

Such requirements never came to pass. In fact, the opposite was true: by 1976 country format stations had moved into every New England state but Vermont (Massachusetts, four; Connecticut, four; Rhode Island, one; New Hampshire, four; Maine, eight) (Peterson and DiMaggio 1975; Russell and Pierce 1976). In the 1970s and 1980s these stations employed several New England country and western "stars" as prominent DJs who actively promoted local country and western recordings on their programs. But with the arrival of computerized and satellite broadcasting in the 1980s and 1990s came a proliferation of automated country format stations in every state in New England. Independent, local musics were not integrated into automated broadcasts. Local and regional country and western recordings do continue to be played on small stations, particularly college radio stations (WHRB—Harvard University's radio station—has featured a program called *Hillbilly at Harvard* every Saturday morning since 1948), on some low-power AM radio stations, and on community or public radio stations like DJ Phil Briggs's *Country Stew* on WBLQ in Westerly, Rhode Island, and Doc Morrill's *Downhome Country* program on WERU in Blue Hill, Maine. (WERU actually features four blocks of programming time dedicated to either "downhome country," "independent country," or "truck stop" music in addition to multiple "Americana" blocks in which these "traditional" styles of country music are frequently played.) It is on these small-scale stations that New England country and western music still finds a home—a reality that says as much about its role as a social community music as it does about its marginalization in the mainstream.

Country Music Scholarship in the Wake of Country Format Radio

Country music scholarship arose in the wake of the formation of the CMA and country format radio. A group of prescient scholars in the 1960s—

mostly folklorists, historians, and serious record collectors—considered country music and its various offshoots (bluegrass, gospel, hillbilly music, cowboy music, etc.) to be a style and form of working-class community expression worthy of serious inquiry. Writing seriously about country music at that time was an act of great professional courage, and the field owes an enormous debt to these scholars. The perspective of scholars such as D. K. Wilgus, Archie Green, and Norm Cohen lacked a southern bias—Wilgus, in fact, characterized the South's claim to country authenticity as a "myth" (1965, 196). Nevertheless, their scholarship was primarily restricted to those artists who had made commercial recordings (most of whom were southerners), helping to shape a distinctly southern worldview in scholarly discourse about the music (Cohen 1965; Green 1965; Wilgus 1965).

Folklorist Bill C. Malone emerged as the foremost of this first generation of country music scholars and published the first scholarly history of country music, *Country Music, U.S.A.*, in 1968. Malone's book is a work of astounding depth, breadth, and historical precision, and his empathic literary eloquence is drawn from his roots as an East Texas farm boy whose parents were tenant cotton farmers. Malone achieved what most scholarly writers and country music producers only dream of: a certified crossover hit. *Country Music, U.S.A.* has been a foundational text for both scholars and serious fans alike for over fifty years (see Malone 2002a). In *Country Music, U.S.A.*, Malone developed what has become known as the "southern thesis," by which country music is understood to be a southern white form of musical and cultural expression. In Malone's view, country music's popularity represents the cultural triumph of the South (the South may have lost the Civil War, but it has won the battle to define the American character), as well as the superiority of southern country music to any and all variations.

Malone's work, which has set the tone for country music scholarship for a half-century now, explicitly sets down ground rules for the creation of authentic country music, limiting its sphere of authenticity to the American South:

1. a rural agricultural population composed of white Protestant Anglo-Celtic inhabitants,
2. a basic isolation because of rough topography, deficient education, widespread poverty, and poor communication,
3. a commitment to and preservation of traditional cultural values, summarized as basic conservatism, and
4. a socioeconomic system resting on a base of slavery (Malone 1968, viii, 3–5)

Malone's work provided a prodigious framework for scholarly discourse and set the stage for historians like the prolific Charles K. Wolfe.

I would not argue that Malone's treatment of country music is wrong, just that his portrait of the music is incomplete, as it leaves so many regional variations of the music out of the picture. A dedicated few scholars since have worked to develop a broader portrait of country music in America. Within a few years of *Country Music, U.S.A.*'s publication, some scholars began to challenge the southern thesis with examinations of country music in Canada (Taft 1974; Klymasz 1972). Most significantly, sociologists Richard Peterson and Paul DiMaggio published a study in 1975 showing sociological evidence that country music was a fundamentally working-class—rather than exclusively southern—music. Their quantitative analysis focused on country music makers, fans, and radio stations in the mid-Atlantic and New England regions. Other studies quietly gave some credence to the notion that country music had more to do with working-class values than with a white, southern worldview. Malone (2002a, 2002b; Malone and Stricklin 2003) amended his thesis in subsequent works to say that country music is white, southern, *working-class* music.

In 1976 folklorist Paul F. Wells published a brief history of Maine fiddler Mellie Dunham, whose short-lived fame predates the accepted "birth" of country music in 1923. In 1978 folklorist Elaine Eff examined trucker culture—including singing truckers, trucker broadcast radio, and so forth—in mostly northeastern truck stops. Other works followed suit in the North: Rod Roberts's (1978) and Simon Bronner's (1978) work on country music in New York and James P. Leary's (1983) work with "ethnic" country music on the south shore of Lake Superior. Not too long after, folklorist Neil Rosenberg (1985, 1988, 1993) began fleshing out a history of country and bluegrass music in New England and Atlantic Canada. These works helped develop a lean and important body of work on country music making outside of the South.

Significantly, Leary's work on "ethnic country music" on the south shore of Lake Superior—which built on ethnomusicologist Robert Klymasz's groundbreaking work with Ukrainian country music in British Columbia—helped develop a body of work examining country music making by North Americans of non–British Isles heritage. And Bronner's essays of the 1970s and 1980s, which culminated in his book *Old-Time Music Makers of New York State* in 1987, put forth a direct challenge to Malone's southern thesis, stating that Malone "is wrong in claiming that these conditions and the old-time music associated with them are unique to the South" (Bronner 1987, 41).

Bronner's work seeks to open up the scholarly discourse of country music to the notion that country music is a regional form found throughout the nation, shaped in different ways by conditions specific to each region (a point with which I agree). In an attempt to bring Malone's and others' southern vision of country music into proper alignment, he writes: "Using the example of New York's old-time musical legacy, I find the background of country music to be a more complicated story than the outline that has been previously drawn in works such as Malone's of a national musical foliage growing from a single southern root. Looking into the old-time music of regions such as New York State reveals the varieties of development and the fullness of the cultural reservoirs that fed the later popularity of a national country music" (Bronner 1987, xv). Bronner's work was, without a doubt, the biggest salvo against the southern thesis since Peterson and DiMaggio's study in 1975. In 1993 George Lewis contributed a scholarly essay entitled "A Tombstone Every Mile: Country Music in Maine." Rather than taking Bronner's tack of challenging Malone's idea of the "southern root" of a national flowering, Lewis sought to meet Malone on his own terms, adapting Malone's ground rules of authentic country music making to Maine and concluding that "Maine fits Malone's pre-conditions for the development of country music probably *better* than many of the regional areas of the South from which the model was constructed" (1993, 105).

Lewis's article cites many of his scholarly predecessors who used Malone's rules for authentic country music making to authenticate country music from other regions. Bronner, too, had applied this paradigm successfully to country music making in upstate New York. New England proved a tough fit for Lewis: the trickiest turn in this respect was navigating around the significant impact of Franco-Americans and other Mainers of Roman Catholic orientation to the Malone paradigm. Lewis's work is an important starting point for documenting the story of country music in New England, but the application of Malone's rules for authenticity is misguided. A foundational principle of ethnomusicology and folklore is that each community has its own ground rules for authentic expressive culture. Malone's work outlines rules that are perhaps appropriate to one region but too ethnocentric to apply nationally (Bronner 1987, 47).

The scholarly works of Lewis, Bronner, Rosenberg, Wells, Taft, and Leary did not win Maine, New York, Nova Scotia, Newfoundland, or Wisconsin widespread acceptance into country music's inner circle of authenticity. Instead, the fans and scholars who paid attention pointed to the southern origin of the overwhelming majority of commercially recorded country musicians as proof to the contrary. Another narrative that emerged in the work of Malone and others began to gather widespread acceptance—that country music's popularity in the urban North was the direct result of the deployment of musical southerners in northern military bases and the arrival of waves of migrant southerners in northern factories. Such claims were—in Bronner's words—"tossed about loosely" (1987, 46).

Indeed, such claims—while rooted in fact and flowering in songs about working life in booming Rust Belt cities like "Detroit City" and the "Streets of Baltimore"—are overblown, as they overlook the marriage of one regional style to another. Depression-era southern Appalachian migrants to Baltimore and the northeastern Maryland/Pennsylvania border region, for instance, recognized that locals had what they called a "New England" style of playing and singing, favoring plucked banjos over the clawhammer and three-finger styles of the mountain South. Incoming migrants adopted aspects of the repertoire of the region, just as the region adopted stylistic elements of the newcomers (Whisnant and Camp 1977). With regard to New England, this work presents a mountain of evidence to show that southerners may have participated in New England country and western music, but they by no means birthed country music making in New England.

Rosenberg and Bronner write that country music occupies dual strata in society: as folk music and as commercial music. The folk form becomes country music (the music industry term) when it gains access to national or international commercial recording companies. For New Englanders, the folk form of country music—what I call here New England country and western music and which makes up the bulk of this work—is deeply rooted in community and reflective of that community. Its national commercial successes are few and far between. But this fact is more telling of how the music business has succeeded in establishing its southern brand—and the nation's centuries-old romantic bias toward southern musical styles and themes of an imagined agrarian past—than it is of the heritage and authenticity of New England country and western music. The heart of Malone's southern thesis resides in the premise that country music is inherently southern, and—in reviewing his work and the vast body of country music literature (history and ethnography) produced over the past half-century—indeed it is when reduced merely to the prism of those musicians who have become enshrined in wax, silicon, and binary code by the Nashville-based recording industry. So this work takes a different approach and documents a regional folk form of country and western music with a few significant national commercial triumphs interspersed along the way.

Such a treatment of country music is somewhat out of step with current scholarly trends. For the past twenty years, country music scholars have tended toward examining the rules by which the country music industry—and its artists—establish authenticity among their fans nationally and internationally. Sociologist Richard Peterson—who had firmly established himself as the chief foil to Malone's worldview by the 1990s—set the tone for this with his seminal 1997 publication *Creating Country Music: Fabricating Authenticity*. Peterson's book, while profound, groundbreaking, and an important foundational piece for parts of this work, examined issues of authenticity through the lens of the international country music industry. His treatment, and those that have followed in its stead, continued to place the center of country music discourse in Nashville.

With the notable exceptions of anthropologist and ethnomusicologist Aaron Fox's revelatory work *Real Country* (2004) and Jennifer Post's staggeringly thorough *Music in Rural New England Community and Family Life, 1870–1940* (2004), Ivan Tribe's *Mountaineer Jamboree* (1996), Amy Davis's 1998 work on local oprys in Kentucky, Tex Sample's *White Soul* (1996), and folklorist Jim Leary's Wisconsin-based *Polkabilly* (2006), scholars have focused on the international country music industry and the products it produced while devoting significantly less attention to local country music makers and the communities that produced them. In short, scholars have focused on the popular form of the music at the expense of the living traditional folk form, all while carefully mentioning the pop version's early folk roots.

If scholarly writings about country music and the opinions of country music fans seem incongruous, the two are more entwined than you might think: Malone's work has been endorsed by major country music stars as well as Nashville's industrial powers that be. This can be seen on the walls of the Country Music Hall of Fame and Museum, whose grand narrative of country music mirrors that of Malone's book. So while barn dance programs like the *Wheeling Jamboree* were central to the country music experience of generations of working people in the Upper Midwest, mid-Atlantic, New England, and Atlantic Canada, it is barely a footnote in the Country Music Hall of Fame and Museum. I have counted four nonsoutherners on the walls of the Hall of Fame, and one of them is a Ukrainian-born rodeo tailor. The *Encyclopedia of Country Music*—produced by the Country Music Foundation, which operates the Hall of Fame and Museum—is more inclusive, as it contains entries on those nonsoutherners who made a significant number of commercial country music recordings. But, again, it chronicles the lives of only those artists who have gained commercial success in (or access to) the recording industry (Kingsbury et al. 1998). What an ethnographic view of country music—and an historical analysis of New England country and western music—helps to show is that country music "success," at least in its folk form, cannot be defined in the terms set forth by Nashville and the music industry.

Understanding New England Country and Western Music and Style

Anthropologist and ethnomusicologist Charles Keil writes that style—or "a deeply satisfying distillation of the way a very well integrated human group likes to do things"—is a reflection of class forces (1985, 12). In the case of New England country and western music, these are decidedly urban multicultural working-class forces with a nostalgic remembrance of an agrarian past that may or may not be located within the United States. Style is an important indicator of close community—or of a community that is working toward commonality across differences. In his treatment of the working-class Texas-Mexican style of *conjunto* music, ethnomusicologist Manuel Peña describes the emergence of style as "a cultural solution to a social problem" (1985, 8). For Keil, style indicates "an intense sociability that has been given shape through time" (1985, 122), and, indeed, New England country and western music is primarily the music—or at least *a* music—of working-class sociability (southern New England's strong polka heritage is an example of another). More to the point—and echoing Keil's assertion that twentieth-century musical style "is almost entirely an ethnic working class phenomenon" (123)—New England country and western is reflective of multiethnic working-class sociability (again, southern New England polka exemplifying a parallel working-class social music encompassing a smaller constellation of ethnicities). A community's musical style is the result of a process, like the dance I played for in Union, Maine, with Dick Philbrook's band, or the social dynamics of blues and polka, described eloquently by Keil: "It is in constant response to the expressed and implicit needs of the dancers passing before their eyes that tunes are chosen, tempos fixed, and the broad stream of musical style subtly elaborated from weekend night to weekend night" (123). It is through nearly a century of this process that New England country and western has become both a regional style of country music and a people's music.

So what is New England country and western music? Is it alive, or dead? And how does it differ from the stuff heard across New England on country format radio today? New England country and western music is larger than a single identifiable sound or image, yet it does contain a sound and style distinct to the region. It is still alive—though barely. And it is different from the stuff heard on country format radio in both real and imagined ways.

In New England and in much of eastern Canada, there is a community of musicians and fans who look to the precentralized days of country music (pre-1958) for inspiration and song selection. These musicians and fans mix "ethnic" material and newer selections—either composed by the performers themselves or pulled from well-known recordings—whose musical style or message falls closely in line with the community's aesthetic sense, which tends toward pre-1965 country and western music. This is not a hard-and-fast rule, although there are exceptions, such as Bob Fuller's Hillbilly Night at the Wheel Club in Montreal, Quebec, an open mic backed by a live band with the caveat that singers can only perform songs recorded prior to 1965.

By and large, New Englanders describe their music generationally: younger generations call it "traditional country," while older generations who have been active as early as the 1930s call it "western." Notably, this older generation favors yodelers and reserves the term "hillbilly" for mountain-style country music. This differentiation likely has something to do with New England country and western music having emanated primarily from long-urbanized centers. In upstate New York, however, which holds a great deal in common culturally, historically, and geographically with New England, country musicians were adamant about characterizing their music as "hillbilly." Floyd Woodhull—accordion player for Woodhull's Old Tyme Masters of Elmira, New York—told folklorist Simon Bronner that their music and image was decidedly that of a Yankee hillbilly, "not country and western" (1987, 54). Not so in New England.

Nevertheless, "country" is a gentrified "hillbilly," and in New England the musicians and fans alike have always gravitated toward country songs and cowboy songs. "Country and western" is a term popular with many older musicians and self-described "traditional" country fans in New England and also describes the name the genre held just prior to the formation of the CMA in 1958. Country music fans in New England—both dedicated and casual—can be divided generally into two camps: those aware of the music's localized history, and those not. It is the former community on which this book focuses—those stewards of community memory who consider themselves "traditionalists" who were involved in New England country and western musical events prior to 1958, as well as those who remember them or have sought out the history, the players, and the recordings of this bygone era. In this respect, traditionalists view Harold Breau (aka Lone

Pine, Hal Lone Pine, or Lone Pine Mountaineer), Betty Cody, Dick Curless, and Yodelin' Slim Clark as the defining figures who tower over the historical landscape. And, significantly, these traditionalists participate in community activities at which New England country and western is the main performative event. And so, ironically, the music one heard at the New England Country Music Festival in the summer of 2010—when Keith Urban, Taylor Swift, Tim McGraw, and other Nashville superstars filled the Foxboro, Massachusetts, football stadium where the New England Patriots play—will not be found in this book.

Stylistically, New England country and western music is distinct from its other North American regional counterparts on account of the influence and prominent participation of immigrants of Continental European heritage: French, Italian, Greek, Portuguese, Armenian, German, and Polish in particular. Herein is the ultimate incompatibility of Malone's theory: New Englanders of primarily orthodox Christian backgrounds (Roman Catholicism and Greek, Russian, and Armenian Orthodox rites) have played the most substantial role in the New England country and western community since the early twentieth century. Of these groups, persons of French heritage—particularly those of French Canadian extraction—have exerted the most resilient and audible stylistic influence. Indeed, Canadians of all heritages—African, First Nations, French Irish, and British Isles—have proven an equally lasting influence on New England country and western music. Additionally, the prevailing fiddle style of New Englanders of British Isles ancestry at the turn of the twentieth century was a more precise single-string melodic style with clearly accentuated (or less "loose-armed" or slurred) notes—as was the case throughout the Northeast and upper Midwest at the time—so as to meet the specific stylistic demands of dancers and regional dance callers (Bronner 1987, 49). This may be on account of the relative racial homogeneity of the region, though New York has had several historically significant African American country fiddlers. Nevertheless, in fairly vernacular terms, New England country and western music sounds more Canadian and less African American than its southern counterparts.

Most distinctive is the New England vocal style, which is identifiable by its use of the soft palate. In the case of some, like Richie Zack of Providence, Rhode Island, this is applied throughout, providing a sound akin to Lawrence Welk or Guy Lombardo with a steel guitar accompaniment. Others, like Dick Curless of Fort Fairfield, Maine, alternate between hard nasality and use of the soft palate on vowels and low notes. For those unfamiliar with Curless's sound, the singing style of Hank Snow, originally of Nova Scotia, would be the closest comparison.

Instrumentally, New England country and western music has distinguished itself through its accordion players and lead guitarists. The accordion—on account of its ability to hit notes precisely and to the liking of dance callers, and due to its widespread popularity among persons of Continental European ancestry—gradually replaced the fiddle, though it has greatly diminished since the 1960s. Guitarists have exerted the region's strongest influence on continental country music making. New England country and western music has produced a number of virtuosic guitarists of note: Johnny Smith, who left Portland, Maine, in the 1940s to fame and success in New York with an electric jazz guitar original called "Walk, Don't Run"; Ray Couture, who accompanied Maine greats Lone Pine and Betty Cody before settling in Wheeling, West Virginia, as the lead guitarist for Hawkshaw Hawkins and the house guitarist at the *Wheeling Jamboree*; Lenny Breau, son of Lone Pine and Betty Cody, student of Ray Couture, sideman for Dick Curless, and eventual Chet Atkins protégé; Dick Dale, son of Lebanese immigrants to Massachusetts who went on to become a founder of "surf guitar" when the family relocated to California; Clarence White, born in Maine, the son of a devoted fan of Lone Pine and Betty Cody, and future virtuosic flat-picking guitarist in the Kentucky Colonels and the folk-rock band The Byrds; George Moody, born and raised in Bangor and periodic sideman to Dick Curless but who relocated to Alberta, where his furious electric fingerpicking and stringbending were a primary influence on Merle Haggard sideman Redd Voelkaert; and, most recently, Johnny Hiland, born and raised in Woodland, Maine, legally blind from birth, a Toby Keith sideman with a taste for chickin-pickin' and heavy metal that has made him a darling of experimental rock guitarist Steve Vai.

The stories and contributions of these individuals and more are chronicled in chapter 2 of this book. While research for these chapters was exhaustive, it is by no means comprehensive. There are many more stories to tell. Nevertheless, this work represents a starting point—a framework upon which future discussions of New England country and western music history can be built—and a small piece of the continental puzzle of the folk strata of country music.

The personal histories of musicians chronicled in this work are likely the sorts of stories that many readers will initially be drawn in to read. And the stories of these musicians' exhausting life on the road, chronicled in chapter 5, perhaps provide some idea of why a tradition such as this is so challenging to sustain over generations. But most noteworthy and distinct to New England—more so than any regional stylistic variations, repertoires, individuals, and so forth—is the structure and meaning of the live performance event, what I call here the New England country and western event. At the risk of belaboring the point, this highlights the power and potency of the folk form of country music in its ability to drive and transform working-class community while underscoring the commercial music industry's utter inability to capture and commodify "folk" music at its most fundamental community level.

The New England country and western event—examined in detail in chapter 3—was generally something musicians and fans of the midtwentieth century called a "personal appearance." This latter term was not unique to New England. But what was distinctive about the personal appearance in New England was its binary structure—it was a show and a dance and was formally divided as such, with musicians charging the audience money for the show and playing a dance afterward for free. Musicians played what they wanted during the show, and they played what the audience wanted during the dance. This, combined with the country and western stagecraft, dress, décor, and stage names, explored in chapter 4, engendered a sociability adept at transcending ethnic barriers and drawing diverse communities together into a larger social circle. This, unto itself, was a dance between the performers and the audience and an embodiment of how the country musician walks a line between innovation and tradition, self-expression and community expression.

This last concept—that of community expression—is ultimately why this book and others like it are so critical. They are not an attempt to wedge New England artists into the country music canon nor to see the Dick Curlesses of the world enshrined in the Country Music Hall of Fame and Museum; rather, they want to show that country and western music—at the community or folk level—is a powerful and beautiful thing unto itself and tells us a great deal about what communities think and feel, who they are, and what they imagine themselves to be.

Threads of Remembrance and Resentment: Nostalgia and the Imagining of New England's Heritage

These days, New England country and western musicians and fans are nostalgic not simply for the days when good local country and western musicians could be heard on local radio but also for what those days symbolized: an era they know never really existed—the era of the self-sufficient community. This imagined community takes on many shapes, often blending into pure fantasy. An example greets travelers arriving in New Hampshire on I-95: a bilingual Welcome/Bienvenue sign featuring a rendering of a colonial New England village nestled in the center of an idealized old mill town ringed by fertile farms, forests, and waterways. These symbols once sustained New England's working people in powerful and interconnected ways, yet human geography in New England has historically shifted with technological, political, and industrial changes tied to each of these symbols, following a centuries-old cycle of abandonment of community centers and their subsequent reclamation, preservation, gentrification, and reimagining. The resulting image—whether of the traditional colonial New England village green (with requisite white steepled church and immaculately landscaped common), or the relatively recent phenomenon of abandoned mill complexes being converted into expensive condominiums—creates an idealized (and considerably cleaner) portrait of old New England self-sufficiency. New Englanders have been at this active reimagining of self-sufficiency for nearly three hundred years (Conforti 2001), and at times it produces distortions—on billboards produced by the tourism industry, as well as in country and western songs like John Lincoln Wright's "That Old Mill" (1990), an homage to the town of Sanford, Maine, where he spent his adolescence:

> That Old Mill—you supported every family in this town.
> You worked us too hard yesterday,
> But we could use your work today
> Now we don't ever work no more.
> (© John Lincoln Wright, lyrics)

There are obvious limitations to such an idealized (or entirely imagined) portrait or symbol of New England life—limitations to the actual democracy of the town hall event (which often excluded women, persons of color, persons of minority faiths and denominations, and nonlandowners), and limitations to the notion that the mill was more of a provider than an opportunist (or, in some instances, a parasite), which many of the state's older inhabitants remember all too well. The kind of idealized symbol of self-sufficient, democratic old New England rendered on the Welcome to New Hampshire interstate sign—a place where farm, forest, village, and mill coexist in harmony—is the kind of tourism-driven rendering of New England that causes some locals to blanch. And yet the power of such symbolism is heartily embraced by even the most cynical native New Englanders when outsiders question the importance the New Hampshire primary should have in the presidential electoral process. The idea that much of New England—and particularly northern New England—is still "small town," "traditional," and capable of conducting town-meeting democracy is still very much believed throughout much of the region. In other words, idealized symbols like the town hall meeting, the village common, the family farm, or even the industry that sustains an entire town may represent "The Way Life Should Be" (the Maine tourism motto, which greets visitors as they arrive by car in Maine) in the minds of both visitors to and natives of New England, even when native New Englanders are mindful that this is not necessarily "the way life *was*" or even "the way life *is*."

New England has long been a place suspicious of government, bureaucracy, and urbanization. This can be read in both classic and social histories of the region—in events like the Boston Tea Party, General John Stark's "Live Free or Die" (the New Hampshire state motto, which appears on its license plates), President Franklin Pierce's pro-Confederate sympathies (Pierce is the only U.S. president [1853–57] to have come from New Hampshire), accounts of the Sacco and Vanzetti trial, the stubborn refusal of northern New England textile and shoe factory laborers to unionize, the modern-day Vermont secessionist movement, the resistance of northern New England states to adopt helmet and seatbelt laws, and the ever-expanding Libertarian Party of New Hampshire. Themes of resistance to forces from outside of the community—particularly outside "values" as disseminated via national and international broadcast media—reverberate in the music and discussions of New England country and western musicians and audiences. The imaginary heart of self-reliant libertarian Yankee culture has steadily retreated northward—away from New England's most affluent and powerful urban centers in southern Connecticut and eastern Massachusetts—since the nineteenth century. In New England country and western folklore—and in the popular imagination—northern New England (and particularly Aroostook County, Maine) is imagined as the last frontier of self-reliance and self-direction. This does not just play out in country and western songs and spirited barroom banter: as recently as 2010, Maine elected officials drafted legislation to divide Maine into two states—the State of Maine (the northern, rural half of the state) and the State of Northern Massachusetts (the southern, coastal, more affluent half of Maine) ("State Lawmaker" 2010).

Though often ambiguous, the imagined geographic orientation of many New England country and western songs points toward northern New England, where cowboys (and cowgirls) and farmers actively resist changing times and serve as regional arbiters and protectors of threatened traditions. And New Englanders who are aware of, and embrace, their region's country music heritage enact a regionally specific working-class variation of "alternative country," which places a high premium on what Aaron Fox (2005) calls "emplacement," or the valuing of commodities that can be tied to a specific geographic place.

If outsiders perceive the sentimental nostalgia that pervades country and western music to be a trite indication of rural or small-town simplicity and naïveté, then they are mistaken and missing the point. These songs mask—or are the product of—an often deep and dark frustration with the current state of things. In New England country and western, nostalgia is produced by a bewildering historical cycle of industrial and national disenfranchisement. Maine country and western singer Jimmy Barnes's belief that the cultural values and country music heritage of New England working people have been extracted and repackaged by Nashville as a cultural import echoes a familiar plight for the New England working class: the departure of the agricultural industry to the Midwest in the nineteenth century, the departure of the textile industry to the South after the close of World War II, and the decimation of local fisheries by domestic and foreign factory ships in the late twentieth century. The rise of Nashville as the center of industrial country music production and the subsequent emergence of the southern thesis occurred during a painful and intense period of deindustrialization in New England, affecting virtually the same communities. Such a phenomenon gives credence to Barnes's belief that "we, the public, have been robbed of our local music heritage and independence, in part, by being told that if you're not from a certain geographic location or sing with a certain accent, you're not country."

Losing Our Roots: How the Displacement of Local Music from Local Country Radio Impacts Working Musicians

Many New England country and western musicians no longer feel that either a Nashville recording contract or access to satellite broadcasts is a viable, realistic, or even desirable option for them. These same musicians view the current state of affairs in country radio as tantamount to a corporate takeover of what should be—in their opinion—a more populist format inclusive of local and regional content. Maine country and western singer and part-time radio DJ Bob Elston has expressed deep frustration, resentment, and anger over the state of country radio in Maine and throughout the United States:

> All radio is controlled by two or three companies . . . all interested in making some money, not in the quality of the music, nor in the quality of the announcer. . . . I don't let them shove the crap down my throat. With 10,000 albums, 4,000 45's, 2500 78's, 1200 cassettes, and 4–500 CDs, I don't need the garbage out there and I am certainly not going to listen to it. I probably wouldn't be this

> bitter if I hadn't spent the last 20–25 years involved with radio and seeing how much music has deteriorated and how the listening public out there is being treated, and it's not a pretty sight. I can only hope something will come along to reverse that situation but I don't know how that could happen at the moment.
>
> We're not only losing our roots in country music here in Maine, but across the country. . . . I have probably been on a soapbox a little bit and got carried away, but these are my thoughts and I don't think I am far from wrong, and I don't think most people, a listening audience, would dispute that.
>
> Some folks are in the business for the money. Many are not. Some I call, "rapist of the industry": where they come in and make a dollar, and then they are gone. Lots of groups in early fifties came up here because it was virgin territory. They found there was a lot of country music in Maine. Got themselves TV shows and proceeded to rape the folks and leave. When I say, "Rape the folks," I mean not give an honest show for an honest dollar. Always looking for a scam or a quick way to make a buck. A lot of such outfits, carpetbaggers, if you will, came and did that. It soured some folks I think on country music. (Wincapaw interview 2002)

Elston's language here is certainly provocative and conjures the specter of regional divisions that stretch back nearly 150 years: an inversion of the northern carpetbaggers who attempted to reconstruct the South in their own image following the Civil War. It also signifies a remarkable reversal of fortunes: southern working people are enriched by developing industry, while Yankees (in Jimmy Barnes's and Bob Elston's opinions) produce the "virgin territory" and raw goods used by southern country music manufacturers that are then resold to Yankees as a cultural import. Ironically, while the CMA created country format radio partly in an effort to maintain a respectable foothold for working-class music and culture in commercial broadcasting, the Nashville industry's specifically southern brand has left working-class New Englanders resentful and without access to the very broadcast mediums that had so powerfully amplified their homegrown traditions. In New England country and western circles, the Nashville-based country music industry has come to represent the face of all that is wrong with country music, the media, and the multinational corporations that manage local affairs remotely. This resentment toward Nashville's corporate indifference is particularly strong in the postindustrial regions of New England that have yet to witness the growing middle-class life triumphantly chronicled in Nashville's contemporary country music.

This is a familiar theme in New England working-class heritage. The financial condition of New England's laboring people has hinged on urban politics, markets, and a few powerful industrialists for over two hundred years. This is not to say that laboring people in New England have been powerless historically—they have not been. Many have voted with their feet (Mayer 1993), and certainly countless have raised issue with local, regional, national, and industrial politics since at least the time of Shay's Rebellion in western Massachusetts and most famously during the Bread and Roses strikes at the textile mills in Lawrence, Massachusetts (Zinn 2003). Yet New England working folk have been caught up in a "great story" in which working people are brought to a region to develop the financial interests of a powerful network of outsiders (aristocrats, absentee landowners, governments, armies, and merchants) only to be abandoned without jobs. This has been the case in the northeastern sector of North America since the first European colony took root in Newfoundland. Corporate and government interests have repeated a pattern of land and industrial development and abandonment in the region over the centuries, stranding working-class, maritime, and agricultural New Englanders in a jobless state. This cycle—the "great story" New England's working-class people embody—has served to embitter working people in northern New England toward distant big-city outsiders, has come to frustrate the self-reliant character of New England, and has generated a nostalgic longing for an imaginary time of agrarian self-sufficiency. This frustration bears fruit in the songs of New England country and western music and in the adherence to older western cowboy styles by so many New England country and western musicians.

The story of New England country and western music is ultimately about how working-class New Englanders living in this region's first multiethnic age chose to understand themselves as Americans *together* through the frontier symbolism of western music. When the CMA coalesced in Nashville and rebranded the music as "country music," a fundamental change took place in how country music functioned within working-class New England. The radio industry that had been built on the backs of New England musicians no longer had room for them or any regional variations of country music. The courting and subsequent takeover and abandonment of New England country and western music by national or corporate entities is, quite simply, another in a long line of such losing battles for New England's working people and a cycle that leads many to believe that the interests of working-class New Englanders are not the interests of the nation.

While this "great story" of the abandonment of working-class people by powerful agents of industry and government is not unique to New England, this tale of industrial development and decay began in New England before arriving in other regions of the United States. Where it is pertinent to the music being discussed here is in the fact that urban corporations and governments have consistently extended a hand to New England working people, asking them to participate in what appears to be a mutually beneficial process, only to then ignore working-class people in favor of higher profit margins. This story can be located in the tale of country format radio in New England and the subsequent displacement of local music programming.

New England country and western musicians and fans have learned to live with the frustration voiced by men like Jimmie Barnes. They have done so because their deep engagement with the local community compels them to. This is, after all, a social music, a vehicle for community entertainment, dance, and identity. In the midst of the New England country and western event as experienced at the Legion Post 15 in Greenwich, Rhode Island, the Thompson Community Center in Union, Maine, or the Canadian-American Club in Watertown, Massachusetts, questions of authenticity or access to broadcast media are not invited guests. If their presence is at all felt, it is in the absence of young people. The sustainability of local and regional cultural heritage and identity—indeed, the very awareness that either ever existed with regard to country and western music—is certainly threatened by country format radio and the myth of southern authenticity, but it is by no means dead.

2

A HISTORY OF NEW ENGLAND COUNTRY AND WESTERN MUSIC, 1925–1975

Beginnings: Mellie Dunham and the Pageant of Progress

Between the time just prior to the American Civil War and 1925, the development of the textile industry and a shift in industrial agricultural production from the Northeast to the Midwest conspired to transform New England from a mostly rural, agricultural region to a mostly urban region. Outmigration from New England to the West and upper Midwest and the departure of young women from the countryside to work in urban textile mills depleted rural New England of many of its inhabitants. New England farmsteads were in such a state of abandonment by 1897 that New Hampshire instituted an annual Old Home Week and urged New England urbanites to reclaim their ancestral homes as annual vacation destinations (Conforti 2001, 213). New England's booming textile industry also drew massive numbers of immigrant laborers from Europe and eastern Canada (Hareven and Langenbach 1995; Temin 2000). A cacophony of languages pervaded industrial centers (Hareven and Langenbach 1995), and New England underwent an ethnic transformation from a mostly white, Anglo-Saxon, Protestant (WASP) population to a mostly Irish, Franco, Italian, and Roman Catholic one. Emerging technologies such as the phonograph, motion pictures, and radio accelerated the spread into New England of African American jazz, which was heartily embraced by many in a region where blackface minstrelsy was enormously popular. As early as 1925, reporters in Lewiston, Maine, were lamenting the passing of fiddle-based dance music in favor of jazz (Sanderson 2003). There was a palpable tension throughout the region as newcomers and old Yankees alike struggled to retain traditional customs and languages. Additionally, Americans had only recently emerged from the trauma of the Spanish influenza and World War I. During this same period of international conflict and pandemic crisis, New England was wracked by the stresses of interethnic and political conflict, as represented in the trial of anarchists Nicola Sacco and Bartolomeo Vanzetti in 1921. New Englanders—both new and old—were experiencing an identity crisis of unparalleled proportions (Post 2004; Thorson 2002; Conforti 2001; Hubka 2004; Nissenbaum 1996; Cronon 2003; Ryden 2001; Temin 2000; Hareven and Langenbach 1995; Feintuch and Watters 2005).

Against this backdrop of unrest in 1925 emerged a seventy-two-year-old fiddler from Norway, Maine, named Alanson Mellen "Mellie" Dunham. Prior to 1925, Dunham's claim to fame was that he had equipped Robert Peary's successful 1909 North Pole expedition with snowshoes that he had handcrafted himself. Standing all of five feet two inches, with a white walrus moustache and a full head of white hair, Dunham was well known around Norway for his fiddle playing at local dances. When a competition to establish Maine's champion fiddler was announced in the nearby mill city of Lewiston, Maine, Mellie entered on a dare by a friend. Reputed to be a fiddler of average ability, Dunham's old-time fiddle style and matching appearance won him the crowd's approval at the Lewiston Armory. He trounced the competition—men, women, old, young, Anglo-Saxon, Irish, and French alike—and the crown of Maine's champion fiddler was his (Sanderson 2003; Wells 1976).

Looking at photos of Dunham from 1925, listening to his Victor recordings from 1926, and learning about his handcrafted snowshoe business, one might develop the mistaken impression that Maine was a cultural backwater in 1925, untouched by the outside world and unaware of the complicated innovations of modernity. An analysis of the context of the fiddle competition that launched Dunham to national fame helps to rectify that impression. At the time of the competition, Dunham had owned a Ford automobile for six years, and he likely drove it the forty-one miles from his home in Norway to the fiddle competition in Lewiston. The competition was a ninety-minute portion of a five-day event called the Pageant of Progress, designed by a Lewiston entrepreneur to showcase innovations in agricultural, industrial, and electrical engineering (Sanderson 2003; Wells 1976). The emergence and sudden popularity of old-time fiddle competitions throughout New England and elsewhere was driven specifically by the fact that local towns and cities had modernized so rapidly. Folklorist Simon Bronner characterizes it this way: "It was 'old-time' because it symbolized old-time rural values for an era after World War One when everything seemed modern" (1987, xiii).

Lewiston, Maine's Pageant of Progress was no small-town or small-time affair. According to the 1920 U.S. census, the twin cities of Lewiston and

Auburn held over forty-eight thousand people. Seven thousand people jammed the Lewiston Armory to watch Mellie Dunham and the other fiddlers compete, and one lucky audience member was awarded a 1926 Ford (Sanderson 2003; Wells 1976). Mellie Dunham was not cowed by the size of the crowd, telling one reporter, "Was the old man scared? No he was NOT" (Sanderson 2003).

Maine was not the only place where throngs of spectators were turning out to see men and women sawing away in fiddle competitions. Between 1924 and 1926 the eastern United States witnessed an old-time fiddle revival whose competitions were newsworthy enough to be covered on the front pages of most major urban newspapers. Crowds reveled in the spectacle of cocky young fiddlers humbled by curmudgeonly old-timers. For most involved, the fiddle contest was a nostalgic distraction from difficult times and was attended and promoted in the name of entertainment. Old-time fiddle competitions were utilized by industrialist Henry Ford, however, as a platform for his ideology of racial and cultural segregation; Ford despised what he perceived to be elements of African and Jewish music that had "corrupted" traditional American (read, Anglo-Saxon) social dance music. His company frequently sponsored events in New England and elsewhere such as Lewiston's Pageant of Progress when they were produced in concert with old-time fiddle competitions. Ford hoped to revitalize old-time music and square dancing by spearheading a campaign to standardize and revive traditional Anglo square dancing (which, ironically, is an English adaptation of the French quadrille), and he made a practice of welcoming various winners of old-time fiddle competitions to his well-publicized square dance revival's headquarters in Dearborn, Michigan (Malone 2002a; Peterson 1997; Sanderson 2003; Wells 1976).

The state of Maine was on the front line of northern New England's burgeoning tourism industry, and the town officials and local press in Norway, Maine, recognized Dunham's crowning as Maine's champion fiddler as an opportunity for publicity. A letter was written—by Dunham himself, but possibly at the behest of town officials hoping to attract business interests to the town of Norway—to Henry Ford asking for an invitation to Dearborn (Sanderson 2003). It is possible that Ford was aware of Dunham's victory already. Ford's connections to New England included ownership of the Wayside Inn in Sudbury, Massachusetts (where the industrialist relocated a grist mill and the schoolhouse, which was considered the origin of the song "Mary Had a Little Lamb"), and annual vacations on Mount Desert Island in Maine. Ford's Maine connection and his company's affiliation with the Pageant of Progress doubtlessly inclined him toward extending an invitation to Mellie to visit Michigan. Ford obliged Dunham's request, and a fiddle-incited media storm of unprecedented proportions (and not repeated since) ensued. Dunham traveled by train through Canada to Michigan with his wife, Emma (or "Gram" in the newspaper accounts), and was trailed by an entourage of reporters and photographers who sent dispatches to newspapers throughout the nation about the journey (Wells 1976). By the time Dunham was received by Ford and had played for square dances at the Ford Dance Pavilion, he had attracted the attention of Keith's Vaudeville Circuit agents, who had, in turn, alerted Victor Talking Machine Company executives (Sanderson 2003; Wells 1976). Within a few months, Dunham was in New York recording a series of 78 rpm discs and preparing for his first and only vaudeville tour (Russell and Pinson 2004, 326; Sanderson 2003).

The music Mellie Dunham's Orchestra recorded for Victor in January 1926 amounts to a few original songs and social dance standards that Dunham used to accompany the Lady of the Lake dances traditional in Maine. Dunham's sound recordings featured the same arrangements (only shorter), instrumentation (piano, cello, sometimes a second fiddle), and personnel as his live performances in Maine (Sanderson 2003). A songbook issued at the same time as the 78s contains Dunham's signature original song "Rippling Waves Waltz" plus five original arrangements of traditional tunes and forty-four traditional standards inserted by the publisher and purported to be played by Dunham (Dunham 1926). The traditional songs include "The Irish Washerwoman," "Money Musk," "Devil's Dream," "Haste to the Wedding," "Sailor's Hornpipe," and other staples of the New England fiddle repertoire that migrated westward through New York and into the upper Midwest. It was this fiddle repertoire and style, more than its southern counterpart, that Ford's revival celebrated (Bronner 1987, 37).

Mellie Dunham's traditionalism was made the centerpiece of his press, his songbook, and his sound recordings. The brief time Dunham spent on the vaudeville stage was anything but traditional by rural Maine standards, however. Dunham's fiddling was augmented by an orchestra and a stage full of "traditional" square dancers culled from dance academies in the cities where Dunham appeared (New York, Providence, Boston, Portland, etc.). The sound of Dunham himself was entirely drowned out by the accompaniment, but his visual presence—often accompanied by Gram onstage beside him in a rocking chair—was an entrancing act of performed pastoral simplicity. What the audience witnessed was a dramatic urban approximation of rural old-time music that incorporated the genuine article. Audiences loved it, and the vaudeville version of Dunham's rural Maine social dance proved far more popular than Dunham's traditional sound recordings (Sanderson 2003; Wells 1976). What Mellie Dunham's vaudeville producers had stumbled upon was the same formula for success used by country and western performers in the coming decades: audiences appeared to gravitate toward an urban *approximation* of old-time music rather than the genuine article.

Following his successful 1926 vaudeville tour, Dunham retired quietly to the Maine woods. But there was resentment among New England fiddlers who deemed Dunham to be only an average (and overexposed) fiddler. The interest—and ire among New England old-time fiddlers—generated by Dunham's celebration in the national press as New England's champion fiddler (even well before his vaudeville tour) had prompted the organization of the All New England Fiddle Contest, held in Providence, Rhode Island, over three days in January 1926. Providence had been the home of an old-time fiddle club—the Rhode Island Fiddlers Club—since 1901. Highlights of the proceedings—along with square dance calling—were broadcast on radio station WJAR in Providence (Green 1998). The three-day event proved too well attended, and police had to clear the streets in front of the Albee vaudeville house when some five thousand people showed up to occupy twenty-three hundred seats (Green 1998, 20). Two of Dunham's heirs to the title of New England old-time fiddle champion—Uncle John Wilder of Plymouth, Vermont (uncle by marriage to President Calvin Coolidge), and Uncle Joe Shippee of Plainfield, Connecticut—followed Dunham into the recording studios in 1926 and cut several 78s for Perfect (Shippee in January 1926) and Okeh (Plymouth Vermont Old Time Barn Dance Orchestra with Uncle John Wilder in October 1926) that produced equally underwhelming sales figures. The same was true for other northern fiddlers like Jasper Bisbee who recorded in the wake of Ford's revival. What these sales figures were is unknown: Dunham claimed to have earned upward of $1,000 from sales of his records. Nonetheless, Dunham, Shippee, and Wilder were only booked for one recording session each. The standard practice of the hillbilly/race record industry at the time was that performers would be booked for follow-up sessions if any of their recordings sold over a thousand copies. So despite the efforts of Victor, Paramount, and other hillbilly/race record companies of the mid-1920s that encouraged dancing to records in their advertisements for portable phonograph players (Titon 1994, 284–85), the general public appeared not terribly interested in taking *actual* old-time music home with them to play on phonographs (Peterson 1997, 62).

Dunham's media blitz also drew the ire of fiddlers as far away as Texas (Malone 2002a; Mark 1930; Peterson 1997). Uncle Jimmie Stephens, an old Confederate soldier and house fiddle player on the WSM program that would become the *Grand Ole Opry* (Wolfe 1999), publicly challenged Dunham to a competition (Sanderson 2003; Wells 1976). "If Mellie Dunham will come down here to this WSM station, I'll lay with him like a bulldog," Stephens said (Wolfe 1997, 40). Despite the brief span of a year in which three prominent New England fiddlers made commercial recordings, Dunham's fame was fleeting. His fade to obscurity—along with Uncle John Wilder and Uncle Joe Shippee—was the high-water mark of a time when the national press considered New England a region likely to contain "authentic" country musicians. According to popular and commercial legend and history, Uncle Jimmie Stephens and the WSM's *Grand Ole Opry* quickly—and without resistance (Dunham agreed to a fiddle duel with Stephens, but it never materialized) (Sanderson 2003; Wells 1976)—overwhelmed Dunham and took on the mantle of country authenticity that has been generally conceded rightfully theirs ever since. No New England country—or western—performer would record commercially for another five years.

The Hillbilly Orchestra Era, 1925–1934

When Mellie Dunham's Orchestra recorded in 1926, they represented a diminishing breed of informal social dance bands. Dunham's orchestra was typical of the groups that played at the small-town barn dances and community hall dances that were prevalent in small communities through about 1900 and the small, mobile ensembles that facilitated "kitchen breakdowns" in private homes. Kitchen dances—whether they were Anglo-Saxon, Irish, Quebecois, Portuguese, Italian, urban, or rural—were multigenerational affairs where virtuosic dancing and heartfelt singing were highly prized. Music at kitchen breakdowns tended to consist of piano, fiddle, and/or accordion instrumental dance numbers, interspersed with ballad or novelty song singing (to give the dancers a rest). In time, the fiddles, pianos, cellos, and accordions that predominated in early kitchen dances were augmented by whatever was handy—guitars, banjos, basses, mandolins, uilleann pipes, clarinets, trumpets, trombones, spoons, drums, and saxophones (Devine and Devine 2005; Greenberg 2004; Hooper and Hooper interview 2005; Lane 1990; Makem 2005; Mark 1930; Post 2004).

As communities grew and revolutions in transportation occurred, dance ensembles grew in proportion to the distance locals were willing or able to travel for a dance. By the late 1800s, dances were being held in public spaces like town halls, churches, Grange halls, and schools (Post 2004, 83–86; Hubka 2004, 19). These dances were facilitated by large ensembles known as community dance orchestras (Post 2004, 83–85).

Whereas the Mellie Dunham–type groups played "head" arrangements (from memory) at private events, community dance orchestra musicians read from sheet music, and orchestras performed mostly instrumental music at dance pavilions or other fixed locations in larger towns and urban centers (Hand interview 1975; Littlefield interview 1975; Northeast Archives 1988; Post 2004; Wells 1976). These large ensembles had grown out of town bands—the same groups that had facilitated art music events for affluent society, and the same ones that had affixed themselves to Union regiments during the Civil War (Hamm 1983, 279–306, 373–409; Post 2004, 83–85).

Because community dance orchestras performed strict arrangements from notated music, it was hard for them to play audience requests, particularly regional traditional material and commercial hillbilly songs popularized on radio. Some seasoned orchestra musicians recognized an opportunity in this shortcoming. In the mid-1920s musicians like Seth Littlefield of Orono, Maine, began leaving their community orchestras to form "hillbilly" orchestras, ensembles that performed old traditional dances, newer "hillbilly" music, and popular requests because, according to Littlefield, "the people wanted it" (Littlefield interview 1975; see also Hand interview 1975; Porterfield 1979).

Hillbilly orchestras were smaller and therefore more mobile than community orchestras. And whereas community orchestras performed music solely for dancing, hillbilly orchestras provided two kinds of music to suit the needs of the community—social dance music, and songs for "show." Flexibility—of sound, style, repertoire, arrangement, and presentation—was the hallmark of the hillbilly orchestra, for example, Doc Converse and the Hillbilly Band of Colebrook, New Hampshire (Post 2004, 203–4). Hillbilly orchestras affected down-home dress (overalls, bandanas, straw hats, blackened teeth) and a "pioneer" or "mountaineer" persona, as can be read into the names of some of New England's first prominent hillbilly orchestras, for example, the Katahdin Mountaineers of Portland, Maine, and the Crockerville Mountaineers, who broadcast on WNAC in Boston, Massachusetts, in 1930 (Maine Hall of Fame 1998). Hillbilly orchestras doubled as blackface minstrels in local minstrel shows (Littlefield interview 1975), and the instrumentation of the hillbilly orchestra varied widely.

The term "hillbilly" is generally given a southern provenance (Green 1965), and its use in New England indicates the influence of commercial sound recordings in the region. Northern performers used the hillbilly image as a tool, "a kind of dialect joke made visual," writes folklorist Simon Bronner. On hillbilly musicians in upstate New York, Bronner writes that the hillbilly image "satirized a previous generation but also allied them to it" (1987, 51, 55). For New Englanders of the 1920s, it was used with the same intent, and, like their cultural cousins in upstate New York, it was intended to imply the rustic and rural Yankee, not the southern moonshiner. In New England the term appears as early as 1926 near Bangor, Maine, in the name of a group called Uncle Seth's Hillbillies (Littlefield interview 1975). "Uncle" names predominate in New England hillbilly orchestras and old-time groups from 1925 to 1934: Uncle Lem of Portland, Maine, Uncle John Wilder of Plymouth, Vermont, Uncle Ezra Jones of Bangor, Maine, Uncle Joe Shippee of Plainfield, Connecticut, and Uncle Bill's New Hampshire Corn Huskers (Senter and Senter interview 2004, 8).

The nickname "uncle" has a New England Yankee provenance. Country music historian Bill C. Malone attributes the prevalence of "uncle" names in early hillbilly groups to the popularity of cylinder recording artist "Uncle Josh" Weathersby, the fictive creation of a Virginia-born regional humorist named Cal Stewart. Stewart's Uncle Josh character was a New England Yankee farmer from the fictitious New England town of "Punkin' Corner." The recordings of Uncle Josh for Victor are filled with hayseed tales of Yankee horse trading and bumbling small-town New England arrogance. Significantly, several of the Uncle Josh recordings were paired with New Englander Charles Ross Taggert's "Old Country Fiddler" routines. Taggert—a Vermonter whose "Old Country Fiddler" and "Man from Vermont" stage routines were popular staples of Chautauquas from New England to Texas from 1904 until the teens—was likely the first vernacular artist from New England to record in a country idiom. Taggert occasionally was identified as "Uncle Zed" and made records for Victor as early as 1916 and cylinders for Edison even earlier. His 1916 Victor release "Old Country Fiddler on Woman Suffrage / Old Country Fiddler at the Party" was described in the Victor catalog as "rural classics, which have the flavor of the pine-covered hills of New Hampshire. The Old Fiddler's views on a burning question of the time, and his adventures at a swell function 'down to th' city' are most amusing" (Victor Record Company 1916). Here we find the Yankee dialect joke in action and also the spirit of the hillbilly paean to bygone rural heritage: the rustic New England rube whose routine eschews the effete nature of the city while donning a perfectly white starched collar and spectacles in the accompanying photograph.

The influence of both Uncle Josh and Uncle Zed and their famous New England rube routines seems a plausible explanation of the prevalence of uncles in New England hillbilly orchestras and old-time groups. By the time Cal Stewart and Charles Ross Taggart popularized Uncle Josh Weathersby and Uncle Zed on Edison cylinders and Victor Records and in early films (both Taggart and Stewart made early films, Taggart with sound, Weathersby without), the archetypal character they portrayed—the rustic Yankee—had already been a popular fixture on American stages since at least the 1830s (Dorson 1940). Uncle Josh is an amalgam of figures Stewart culled from American stage and literature—the homely, honest, and humble Yankee farmer found in nineteenth-century stage characters like Jonathan Ploughboy and the stingy, arrogant, and comical "codfish aristocrat" whose bloated sense of self-importance became the blueprint for nineteenth-century stage characters like Solon Shingle (Dorson 1940; Mercer 1967) and the interlocutor of blackface minstrelsy. Analyses of early American theater show that the Yankee Jonathan Ploughboy character eventually evolved into the archetypical figure of Uncle Sam (Johns 1986, 272). Dark or sinister variations of these Yankee characters also found their way into American literature, particularly the character of Adam Verver in Henry James's *The Golden Bowl* (Mercer 1967, 255) and the particularly twisted Simon Legree of Harriet Beecher Stowe's *Uncle Tom's Cabin*. Significantly—and likely related to the naming of Uncle Josh—is the name of the slave hero of Stowe's book, Uncle Tom. According to Frederick Douglass, young plantation slaves used the term "uncle" as a sign of respect for their elders involved in mechanical trades (cartwright, blacksmith, shoemaker, etc.) (Douglass 2005, 64). Southern whites used the term "uncle" as a sign of qualified respect in addressing older male slaves (Doyle 1936), though in the Jim Crow era—the same era as the old-time fiddle revival—whites used terms like "doctor" or "uncle" as a term of mock respect in addressing older African American men. Since the era of black and African nationalism, "Uncle Tom" has become a derogatory term used by African Americans to describe perceived accommodation of white commercial and political agendas by fellow blacks. Uncle Josh, then, both implies mock respect for an old-timer and suggests that the old-timer is but a lighter shade of his denigrated African American counterpart. The overlapping connotations of the rustic Yankee "uncle," the patronizing "uncle" aimed at African Americans, and the prevalence of the "uncle" in hillbilly orchestras lends credence to literary critic Constance Rourke's (2004) belief that America's three indigenous comic archetypes (the rustic Yankee, the backwoodsman, and the blackface minstrel) blended into a singular figure in early twentieth-century vernacular usage (see also Rourke and Brooks 1980).

In examining the cases of three musical New England Yankee "uncles"—Uncle John Wilder, Uncle Joe Shippee, and Uncle Seth Littlefield—we can deduce separate reasons for each dubious title. Uncle John Wilder was the uncle of Calvin Coolidge, who was president of the United States when Wilder won his fiddle championship and made commercial recordings in 1926, so the use of "uncle" was a dual reminder of his Yankee rusticity and of the fiddler's relation to the Yankee president. Joe Shippee was only "uncle" by way of his commercial recordings (he did not perform under the name "uncle"), making it likely that record executives at Perfect sought to affiliate him with old-time Yankee rustics Uncle Josh and Uncle Zed. Uncle Seth Littlefield's group doubled as a local blackface minstrel troupe, and as such his "uncle" persona would have easily served a dual, racial purpose, evoking the rustic Yankee during hillbilly orchestra shows and evoking the Uncle Tom/Uncle Remus figure during the blackface shows.

There were no "uncles" in the first New England hillbilly orchestra to make significant commercial recordings, however. In February 1931, Hank Keene and His Connecticut Hill Billies—a group from South Coventry, Connecticut—recorded two sides for the Brunswick label, including Keene's signature composition "The Run-a-way Boy." Keene recorded fifteen more sides between 1933 and 1935 for the Bluebird and Banner labels (Russell and Pinson 2004, 474), and he was New England's most prominent hillbilly artist of the early 1930s.

Keene's radio career had begun at WTIC in Hartford, Connecticut, in 1930, and over the next twenty years he moved to radio stations in Schenectady, New York, Cleveland, Ohio, Wheeling, West Virginia, and Louisville, Kentucky. Most of his musical activity, however, was based out of his home area of South Coventry, where he lived with his wife, the former "Miss Ohio," Jean Fadden, who played a scantily clad role in his traveling tent show. Though Hank Keene performed many "straight" songs—devotional hymns, tragic ballads, and love songs—projecting sincerity was not his forte. His periodic use of slide whistles, glass bottles, organ, and kazoos generated a sound akin to that of the Hoosier Hot Shots. Keene's music combined elements of the community orchestra, old-time, hillbilly, minstrel, Hawaiian, yodeling (Swiss, hillbilly, cowboy, and blackface styles), gospel, and cowboy musical styles. His music is typical of the hillbilly orchestra and is a precursor to the country and western sound and personas that would dominate in New England from the mid-1930s onward.

Keene's commercial success was indicative of broader trends in New England, but his work as a recording artist was anomalous. While record companies such as Okeh, Victor, and Columbia sent talent scouts throughout the South and parts of the Southwest in search of hillbilly recording talent in the 1920s and 1930s, scouts were not sent to New England. There is no evidence that New Englanders sought out recording sessions prior to the close of World War II. Old-time fiddlers Mellie Dunham, Uncle Joe Shippee, and Uncle John Wilder were invited to New York to make recordings only after their victories in fiddle competitions were highly publicized in the national press. Hank Keene's close association with vaudeville minstrel singer and prolific early recording artist Frank Kamplain is likely the origin of his work as a recording artist.

Commercial recordings of the 1920s and early 1930s did impact music in New England, however. Cowboy singers like Powder River Jack and John White had a powerful influence throughout the region, but none were more influential than Wilf Carter. Carter—known to most as "Montana Slim"—was born in Nova Scotia in 1904, and by 1931 his accent, cowboy regalia, and yodeling style had become the blueprint for all aspiring cowboy singers in New England. Wilf Carter's prodigious output of recorded material, coupled with his broadcasts on network radio, reinforced his influence on New England (despite the fact that he rarely made personal appearances in the region). By the middle 1930s, cowboy singers—from New England and "from away"—had begun working professionally in New England. The most notable of these early singers was Baron West of Beverly, Massachusetts (Little and Little interview 1975).

Blackface minstrelsy also played an important role in the development of country and western music in New England during this time. Broadcasts of Al Bernard's and Frank Kamplain's minstrel music influenced New Englanders like Yodelin' Slim Clark and Hank Keene. Kamplain recorded several sides (some with Al Bernard), including yodeling numbers like "Roll Along Silvery Moon" and "Sleep, Baby, Sleep." These songs were staples of blackface minstrelsy and had been yodeled by popular blackface performers like Matt Keefe as early as 1904 (Tosches 2001, 64).

"Sleep, Baby, Sleep" and other parlor ballads—with their themes of romance, tragic loss, and pastoral nostalgia—were heartily embraced by New England working people. By the early 1920s, sentimental songs such as "Just Plain Folks," "Way Down East among the Shady Maple Trees," "In the Baggage Coach Ahead," "Little Blossom," "Hills of Old New Hampshire," and "Bright Eyed Laughing Little Nell of Narragansett Bay" were staples of household repertoires and were duly represented in the developing New England country and western repertoire.

Like most New England hillbilly orchestra leaders, Hank Keene included old parlor ballads in his repertoire, as well as the songs of newer professional songwriters such as Billy Hill. Hill's seemingly fictitious name was indeed his own: born in Boston, Massachusetts, in 1899 to a sea captain father and a Latvian Jewish mother, William Hill grew up in Boston and Weymouth, Massachusetts, and studied violin under conductor Charles Muck at the New England Conservatory. By age seventeen, Hill was playing violin in the Boston Symphony Orchestra. That year, he quit the BSO and moved west for five years. Hill worked as a cowboy in Montana, worked for a mining company in Death Valley, and settled in Salt Lake City, Utah, where he led a jazz band in a Chinese restaurant. In 1921 Hill moved back east with his wife and occasional songwriting partner, Dedette, and the couple settled in New York City to try to make a living as professional songwriters. Sensitive about the likeness of his name to "hillbilly," Hill wrote under the assumed name of George Brown. As George Brown, Billy Hill met Jimmie "The Singing Brakeman" Rodgers in 1932 in the office of song publisher Ralph Peer, where Hill taught Rodgers and Slim Bryant (his sideman) the song "Prairie Lullaby." Rodgers recorded the song, which is credited to both Rodgers and George Brown. Hill kept his assumed name until shortly before his first major hit song—"The Last Round-Up"—was published in 1933 (Hall 2007). Hank Keene's rendition, titled "The Last Roundup," was recorded some three weeks after Gene Autry's in October 1933 (Russell and Pinson 2004, 79, 474).

Hank Keene did not perform in cowboy garb, and his vocal delivery is rooted in a different era. Still, he was the most prominent New Englander (locally and nationally) of the hillbilly era and was one of the first New England–based musical entrepreneurs to harness the commercial power of the phonograph, songbook publishing, and radio industries. He also ran a large and lucrative traveling tent show that worked extensively in western New England. The music and business acumen of Hank Keene and similar performers from his era provided a springboard for the so-called pioneer generation of New England country and western musicians that arose during the barnstorming era (1935–55).

Country and Western Music Arrives: The Barnstorming Era, Part 1, 1935–1946

Were you to add up all the minutes in the professional life of a New England country and western musician from the 1930s, you would find that most of them were spent in a car, traveling to or from a show. Shows were called "personal appearances," and touring was called "barnstorming." Radio enabled groups to develop lucrative, if hectic, careers as itinerant musicians. Limitations in broadcast technology in much of New England favored small ensembles over large ones. As a result, the large hillbilly orchestra gradually gave way to the smaller country and western ensemble. The change in moniker—from hillbilly to country and western—reflects the fact that by the mid- to late 1930s, the cowboy singer had become fully integrated into hillbilly groups and that these groups also combined the "show" function of the cowboy and pioneer singers and the "dance" function of the hillbilly orchestra into one event. Most groups wore full cowboy regalia and adopted "western" names and stage personas.

The barnstorming era ran from roughly 1935 until 1955. The first half of this era—ending shortly after World War II—was an era of live entertainment: live on the radio, and live at personal appearances. New Englanders exhibited little interest in engaging with the national country and western scene prior to World War II primarily because making records was understood as a prestigious novelty but not a money maker. The real money was in securing a regular radio spot, soliciting fan mail through radio, booking live performances in towns where fan mail originated, and promoting those appearances on the radio broadcast.

If one descriptive term had to be applied to the country and western ensemble, it would be "flexible." Playing from "head" arrangements and exhibiting an eagerness to play what the audience wanted, country and western groups could appease the requests of far more audience members—notably, newer immigrant ones—than the community orchestra. They also had an easier time fitting into sonically calibrated radio broadcast booths than their orchestra brethren: large community and hillbilly orchestras were occasionally broadcast live via "remote" from dance pavilions, but the sound—relayed via telephone and then broadcast over the air—was tinny and unpleasant. And country and western groups could easily fit into one vehicle, enabling them to take full advantage of their new far-reaching radio performances (Dinsmore interview 1975; Hand interview 1975; Littlefield interview 1975).

The result of these factors—access to radio, flexibility of repertoire—was that country and western audiences were far more diverse in every respect than those of the hillbilly orchestra. Country and western groups exhibited a willingness to play anywhere so long as they could get back to the radio station in time for their next broadcast the following day. This practice endeared them to their host communities. And broadcasts could reach into every home with a radio, drawing diverse, multigenerational crowds to personal appearances. The ensuing dance was a significant site of multiethnic socializing. Regionally important groups that coalesced during this time were Bud Bailey and His Downeasters, who worked between Portland, Maine, and Portsmouth, New Hampshire; Don Fields and His Pony Boys in Waterbury, Vermont; the Down Homers in Hartford, Connecticut; the Ken Mackenzie Tent Show in Manchester, New Hampshire; Al Rawley and His Wild Azaleas in Shirley, Massachusetts; Eddie Zack and His Dude Ranchers in Providence, Rhode Island; Pappy Howard and His Connecticut Kernels, who worked between Hartford, Connecticut, and Worcester,

Massachusetts; Gene LaVergne in Manchester, New Hampshire; the Red River Rangers in Athol, Massachusetts; and Lone Pine Mountaineer and Betty Cody in Lewiston, Maine.

Showtime: Cowboys and Mountaineers

Hillbilly orchestras were transformed by the popularity of several mountaineer and cowboy performers who worked as solo acts or who worked in small combos that performed only shows (no dancing). Early cowboy singers in New England like Yodelin' Slim Clark, Buck Nation, Tony and Juanita, George and Dixie, and Georgia Mae generally performed with one or two accompanying musicians or solo in the rugged yodeling style of Wilf Carter. Yodelin' Slim Clark was active as early as 1930 performing songs about cowboys and hoboes as well as folk ballads like "Tragic Romance" and old minstrel songs like "The Cat Came Back." Clark called the circuit of town halls and Grange halls he played in the early 1930s in western Massachusetts the "Kerosene Circuit," as most halls lacked electricity, and lighting was provided by lanterns. Most performances on the Kerosene Circuit were done "barefoot"—a term Clark and others used to describe stage performances done entirely acoustically without any form of electrical amplification (Cohen 1977).

Cowgirl singer Georgia Mae was typical of cowboy/cowgirl singers of the early barnstorming era in New England. Born in Dedham, Massachusetts, in 1926, Georgia Mae Kingsbury was raised in a singing family: her father and brother sang barbershop, and she and a female cousin from Connecticut were inspired by the music of Patsy Montana to become yodeling cowgirls (Harp interview 2004). By 1938 Georgia Mae had secured a sponsored daily morning broadcast on the powerful WBZ radio station in Boston. Georgia Mae was famous for her "triple yodel"—a Wilf Carter–inspired technique of "breaking" one's yodel in triplets. Georgia Mae performed extensively throughout all six New England states, returning each morning to Boston for her daily broadcast on *The New England Radio Farm Hour*.

Reports published by WBZ tracking Georgia Mae's fan mail show that her fan base stretched as far west as Kansas, well up into the Canadian Maritimes (Nova Scotia, New Brunswick, Prince Edward Island, and Newfoundland), and as far southeast as Puerto Rico (Westinghouse 1943; "Radio's Sweetest Personality" 1945). Though she was accompanied on accordion and fiddle in the studio, Georgia Mae always appeared solo at live performances, and she never performed for dancing. Her performances were for show: the regalia of the singing cowboy/cowgirl and the demonstration of virtuosic yodeling technique. Georgia Mae claimed to have spent most of her income on elaborately tailored cowboy clothes made by Ben the Rodeo Tailor in Philadelphia. She was known to her fans as "the girl with the white guitar," a nickname developed after Georgia Mae took the innovative step of commissioning the Vega company to make her a guitar with a white lacquer finish designed to match her all-white outfits (Harp interview 2004; Georgia Mae Harp, e-mail message to author, February 6, 2007).

Whereas most radio cowboy singers in New England appear to have been homegrown, most radio mountaineer or folk singers from the early barnstorming era in New England appear to have been imported to the region. Bradley Kincaid and Bluegrass Roy, both from Kentucky, sang old-time folk songs and parlor songs, interspersed with hillbilly and phonograph tunes, on the radio in Connecticut and Massachusetts in the early to mid-1930s. Kincaid collected folk tunes in New England and folded them into his repertoire of "Kentucky Mountain Songs & Ballads" (Jones 1980; Kincaid interview 1974). Hillbilly groups like Kincaid's did not play for dancing.

Bradley "The Kentucky Mountain Boy" Kincaid—star of the WLS *Barn Dance* out of Chicago—moved to Boston in 1935, taking two musicians from Kentucky with him: a guitarist and banjo player named Marshall Jones and "Harmonica Joe" Troyan. The trio broadcast out of WBZ radio in Boston—New England's only fifty-thousand-watt radio station—and barnstormed in all six New England states. WBZ was owned by the Westinghouse company, and Kincaid's group also broadcast out of Westinghouse stations in Springfield, Massachusetts (WBZA), and Schenectady, New York (WGY) (Jones 1980). They were unprepared to find just how popular the old-time folk and hillbilly songs were with New Englanders (Jones 1980; Jones and Wolfe 1984). Following an intense two-year period of barnstorming activity in all six New England states, the group disbanded and returned to Kentucky (Jones and Wolfe 1984). Kincaid moved to WTIC in Hartford, Connecticut, in 1938 before leaving New England to work at WSM in Nashville (Jones 1980).

Kincaid's broadcasts are well remembered as far north as Machias, Maine (Hooper and Hooper interview 2005), and native country music historians in New England take great pride in Boston being the birthplace of Marshall Jones's "Grandpa Jones" persona (Jones 1980; Jones and Wolfe 1984; Jones and Jones interview 1975; Brown interview 2004). Kincaid's songbooks and recordings include some folk songs he collected while barnstorming in New England, such as "The Frozen Girl," which he learned from an audience member at a personal appearance in Vermont (Kincaid interview 1974), but his biggest legacy in this area was the impact his business acumen had on fellow barnstorming musicians. Kincaid appears most responsible for inspiring other hillbilly or western performers in New England to sell merchandise at their shows, selling photos, postcards, and self-published songbooks to the audience. Commercial recording was not a lucrative endeavor, even for a prolific recording artist like Kincaid, and an effective management of barnstorming activity and merchandising was key to financial success in country and western show business.

How the Hillbilly Orchestra Became Country and Western

Transitional hillbilly orchestras like Hank Keene's or Bud Bailey's favored a variety show / dance format where groups were consciously formed to include different "specialists": ballad crooners, "girl" singers, comics, and so forth. Cowboy and mountaineer singers were folded into the specialist role, and their popularity subsequently transformed the group in their own image. Bud Bailey's accordionist was typical of the era: Jimmy Cal (born Vincent Calderone) could croon popular ballads, play Italian folk tunes, belt out Neapolitan pop songs, yodel cowboy songs, or perform some combination, like yodeling his way through "Volare" (Calderone interview 2004). The country and western ensemble—or the hillbilly orchestra transformed—synthesized several different strains of vernacular music: the combination of stage cowboy and mountaineer singers, the minstrel troupe, the parlor balladeer, the popular songs of the community orchestra, and the old-time dance traditions of the Mellie Dunham–style orchestra.

Calderone's role in Bud Bailey's group marks a major shift from the hillbilly orchestra to the country and western ensemble: groups and audiences became highly multiethnic. This is in contrast to hillbilly orchestras, whose members and audiences tended to consist of persons close in ethnicity: Anglo, Irish, and Scots-Irish descent. By the late 1930s the repertoires of country and western groups encompassed an even wider range of songs than the hillbilly and community orchestras. Country and western ensembles augmented the base repertoire of these earlier ensembles with cowboy songs and folk and popular musics of newer immigrant traditions of French, Italian, Polish, Greek, German, Armenian, and Portuguese origin. This process of inclusiveness made country and western groups better able to play to a wide range of tastes and helped facilitate multiethnic New England's shift toward a (new) shared working-class musical tradition.

Significantly absent from the country and western ensemble was the blackface minstrel. Though hillbilly orchestras sometimes doubled as blackface minstrels, country and western groups throughout New England made a conscious effort to purge their events of blackface performance (Gribben interview 2007). Though groups continued to play songs like "Oh Dem

Golden Slippers," performers never used greasepaint or burnt cork, nor did they allow performers in blackface to join them onstage. Country and western performers like "Windy" Betty Gribben, Gene Hooper, Yodelin' Slim Clark, and Dick and Phil Curless recall that they learned performance practices (stage dress, makeup, comic timing, microphone technique) from blackface performers but that they adamantly refused to incorporate burnt cork minstrelsy into their stage shows. Country and western acts incorporated minstrel interlocutors—sans blackface—into their shows, performing the roles of emcee, rube/hobo comic, and square dance caller.

Blackface minstrelsy was purged from New England country and western shows for the sole reason that—by the mid-1930s—the purpose of such performances in New England was to denigrate ethnic/immigrant groups as well as African Americans. Amateur blackface minstrel shows were held in much of New England until the rise of the civil rights movement in the 1950s, tailing off dramatically over the course of the 1960s. A study of one minstrel show that persisted in a Vermont community until the 1980s shows that blackface was used as a vehicle to criticize or ridicule multiculturalism (perceived as an actual threat to ethnically homogeneous communities) more than African Americans (perceived as a distant threat) (Hamm 1995; Majarian 2004). Such commentary was at odds with the multicultural makeup of New England country and western ensembles from the mid-1930s onward, so while blackface performance persisted in New England until the late twentieth century, country and western musicians had divorced themselves from greasepaint by the late 1930s. That blackface minstrelsy was a part of country and western performance elsewhere in the United States, continuing on the *Grand Ole Opry* until 1953 (Alden 1996), illustrates a significant difference between country and western in New England and elsewhere.

Regionally known minstrel performers appeared onstage with New England country and western groups only when performing caricatures of rustic Yankees, white hillbillies, or hoboes and never in blackface. Stage tutelage of "ethnic" musicians by blackface minstrels—like the French Canadian Hal Lone Pine by blackface interlocutor Uncle Ezra Jones (who performed as "Bozo the Tramp" with Lone Pine's group)—appears to have been limited to communities whose demographics had recently been transformed by immigration or by the migration of persons from homogeneous communities (such as Dick Curless, who participated as a child in minstrel shows near Athol, Massachusetts) into multiethnic communities. Some photos do exist of transitional groups—like Bud Bailey's—appearing onstage with blackface minstrels as late as 1938, but no evidence has come forward of blackface performers onstage with country and western groups with origins after 1935. Rather, the development of stage characters such as the French Canadian woodcutter comic Joe LaFlip enabled newer communities to poke fun at themselves. The inclusion of blackface minstrels simply ran counter to the multicultural/multiethnic sociability of the New England country and western group and event.

By 1940 the barnstorming era was in full swing, with multiple country and western groups working out of each major radio station in most major cities in New England (Boston, Lawrence, and Springfield, Massachusetts; Hartford, Connecticut; Manchester and Portsmouth, New Hampshire; Waterbury, Vermont; Providence, Rhode Island; Bangor, Portland, and Lewiston, Maine). Performers like Jerry and Sky worked on multiple radio stations simultaneously. Barnstorming groups generally worked six nights per week at personal appearances and six days per week on live radio broadcasts. The Ken Mackenzie Tent Show claimed to have played thirty-six straight nights out of Portland, Maine, just prior to the start of World War II (Gribben interview 2007). By the 1940s, most country and western events in New England featured bands and audiences fully garbed in "western," "pioneer," or "frontier" dress. Country and western events in New England's rural areas, small mill towns, and larger cities were vibrant multigenerational affairs that attracted large multiethnic audiences.

New England's Ranch Circuit

A circuit of outdoor music parks catering to the country and western crowd developed across New England in the late 1930s and early 1940s. This became known as the ranch circuit. These so-called ranches existed in a corridor running from the western border of northern Rhode Island as far north as Bangor, Maine. The first of the ranches was the Indian Ranch in Webster, Massachusetts, owned and operated by George Mahoney of the group George and Dixie. Mahoney also founded a ranch in North Smithfield, Rhode Island, called the Pine Crest Ranch. Other ranches included the M-Bar-C Ranch in Shirley, Massachusetts; the Lone Star Ranch in Reeds Ferry, New Hampshire; the Allan A Ranch in Wolfeboro, New Hampshire; the C-Bar-C Ranch in Bangor, Maine; and the Auto Rest Park in Carmel, Maine.

Ranches provided family-style entertainment for working-class families every Sunday and every holiday weekend in warmer weather, land for camping, nonalcoholic concessions, and ample opportunities for country and western musicians to interact with their audience in a personal, nonmusical way. The family experience of the ranch circuit encompassed the performers themselves; families would pack food for the performers, and the families "would actually be offended if you didn't sit down to eat with them," remembered one regional star from the early 1940s (Rego interview 2004, 1).

Ranch managers expected good manners onstage from the performers and dictated the stage rules to musicians: they were to be polite, mindful of improprieties, and professional in their stage demeanor and performance. And the music provided was "strictly country," according to Frank "Slim" Rego: "[The ranch manager] wouldn't even allow you to chew gum on stage, never mind getting up there with drinks like they do today. And no profanity whatsoever, so it was all strictly country music. And he didn't like you to swing it, either. At all. He wanted to stay with strictly the country sound" (interview 2004, 4–5). Up to six acts would perform on a given Sunday, and admission was generally between seventy-five cents and a dollar. Audiences typically amounted to some two thousand people who would sit on rough-hewn benches out in the open. "Yeah, they were outdoor," recalled cowgirl yodeler Georgia Mae, "and people would sit there. They would sit there in the rain, with papers over their heads, and I'd be up there on the stage singing, and I'm thinking to myself, 'why are they sitting out in the rain?' You know? But, they were sitting. They'd put newspaper up. They'd stay to the end. . . . Hundreds of people. Hundreds. It was amazing. And I have to say that the country music fans are the most faithful fans in the world. They really are" (interview 2004, 12).

World War II

Most male musicians between ages eighteen and thirty-five served in the U.S. military during World War II. Some, like Paul Roberts (born Paul Metivier) of Dorchester, Massachusetts, were stationed locally and continued to perform during their enlistments. Roberts wrote the seminal country song "There's a Star Spangled Banner Waving Somewhere" while stationed at Fort Devens near Worcester, Massachusetts (Metivier interview 2005). Those who remained home had their barnstorming activities severely restricted by gas rationing to the degree that some performers in the Bangor, Maine, area resorted to digging potatoes for area farmers in order to buy gas with "agricultural" gas stamps. Several groups, including the Circle C Ranch Boys and an all-female country and western group from Portland, Maine, called the Bombshells (consisting of the women from the Ken Mackenzie Tent Show), earned their living during the war through the USO by performing for wounded soldiers on national tours of rehabilitation hospitals (Boncore interview 2005; Calderone interview 2004). Upon the close of the war, many of the professional musicians who worked in barnstorming groups did not return to the profession (Gribben interview 2007). According to firsthand accounts, only the top-tier musicians and beginners continued to play after the war, and many of them had trouble readjusting to civilian life.

The Barnstorming Era, Part 2, 1946–1955

Several regional stars emerged between 1944 and the start of the Korean War in 1950, and they secured recording contracts with national recording companies. In 1944 Jerry and Sky, a yodeling hillbilly–style group originally from Nashua, New Hampshire, recorded with only regional fanfare for the Sonora label in New York. In 1946 a Massachusetts cowboy yodeler in the Wilf Carter style named Yodelin' Slim Clark was approached by Elton Britt about recording for his Continental label in New York City (Cohen 1977). Clark obliged and made commercial recordings in each of the next six decades. Also in 1946 the Down Homers, who worked extensively out of WTIC in Hartford, Connecticut, and WKNE in Keene, New Hampshire, recorded a series of 78 rpm records for the Vogue picture disc company. ("Picture discs" were records with vibrant full-color paintings of cowboy scenes embedded in the vinyl—a complete novelty both then and now.) Yodeling Kenny Roberts, who had been a member of the Down Homers until the Vogue sessions, also recorded for Vogue (with the Down Homers but under his own name) that same year (Roberts interview 2004, 1987; Awalt 2002). In 1947 an Armenian American country and western group from Providence, Rhode Island, named Eddy Zack and His Dude Ranchers (with Cousin Richie) made a local recording on their Dude Ranch label of a song called "The Rhode Island Polka." The song proved so popular in Rhode Island jukeboxes that the group was signed by Decca Records (White and Albro interview 2004). The following year, Jerry and Sky made a series of recordings for the MGM label (Snow interview 2006). Kenny Roberts and the Down Homers also recorded for the King record label in 1949 and 1950, respectively, and each had significant national chart hits, most notably, Kenny Roberts's 1949 recording of an old British music hall song "I Never See Maggie Alone," which went to number 4 on the *Billboard* pop chart.

The years between World War II and Korea also witnessed a period in which many of the top country and western groups in New England left the region for extensive residencies on large radio stations in the Midwest and Canada. In the case of the midwestern departures, powerful radio stations in Indiana, Ohio, Iowa, and Missouri actively courted several groups via telegraph to leave New England and take up residency at their stations (Roberts interview 2004; Rogers and Kempton interview 2005; Calderone interview 2004). This process saw the Down Homers leave for Iowa, Missouri, and Indiana. Kenny Roberts moved with the Down Homers and eventually settled as a solo act in Cincinnati, Ohio; Bud Bailey and His Downeasters left for Iowa; and both Hank Keene and His Radio Gang and Pappy Howard and His Connecticut Kernels left for stints in Cleveland, Ohio. Each of these groups would eventually return to New England, with the notable exception of Bud Bailey, whose performing career was effectively ended when he was incarcerated for statutory rape in Iowa (Rogers and Kempton interview 2005; Dennett 1991; Calderone interview 2004).

Departures from New England for Canada were a different story. Though two giants in North American country and western music history—Wilf Carter and Hank Snow—came from Nova Scotia, Canada, the region was largely ignored by barnstorming American musicians until shortly after World War II. Beginning in the 1930s, New England country and western performers—particularly those working in northern New England and Massachusetts—received a steady stream of fan mail from Quebec and Atlantic Canada (Nova Scotia, Prince Edward Island, New Brunswick, and Newfoundland) (Westinghouse 1943). According to the formula of the barnstorming business, musicians would "work" a certain broadcast region for two to four years before moving on to develop their interest in a different area. Eastern Canada represented an area that had, in actuality, already been "developed" with regard to radio exposure, but no personal appearances had been made. Broadcasts of New England country and western musicians traveled well into eastern Canada and even up to Newfoundland. New England country and western groups began actively touring in Atlantic Canada and working on radio there in 1946 (Little and Little interview 1975).

The credit for the "opening" of the Canadian Maritimes in 1946 goes to Ray and Ann Little. Ray Little (born Raymond Petit) was born in 1913 in Henniker, New Hampshire, and was a tenor banjo player in the Crockerville Mountaineers—the first known hillbilly orchestra in Boston—on WNAC in Boston in 1930. In 1935 he formed a group out of Fitchburg, Massachusetts, called the Musical Cowboys and by 1941 had married his singing partner, Ann, and opened the M-Bar-C Ranch in Carmel, Maine (Little and Little interview 1975; Maine Hall of Fame 1998). Ray Little felt that the allure of cowboy music began to wane in the greater Bangor, Maine, area during World War II, and, following Ray's discharge from active duty, he and Ann left Maine to begin barnstorming in Atlantic Canada. They worked out of radio stations in Moncton, New Brunswick, and Yarmouth, Nova Scotia, as well as in Prince Edward Island. Ray Little claimed that he and Ann and their group were the first American cowboy group to play in Newfoundland in 1948 (Little and Little interview 1975), and they are credited for bringing over other New England acts like Gene Hooper, Jerry and Sky, and Hal Lone Pine and Betty Cody (Hooper and Hooper interview 2005).

Accounts of the first tours by New England country and western groups in Atlantic Canada tell how New England performers were so immediately successful that they regularly had to play two or three separate shows in the same venue on the same night in order to satisfy the demand for tickets. Tales of tours to Newfoundland are particularly dramatic, relating how locals would run down to the train and carry the musicians' belongings wherever they needed to go (Little and Little interview 1975; Williams and Smik 2006). According to Gene Hooper, the popularity of New England country and western can be attributed mainly to a decade of broadcasts from Maine and Massachusetts radio stations with no personal appearances, but New Englanders were also perceived as being more "authentic" country and western musicians than local Canadians simply because they were American (Hooper 2005). Several New England country and western acts became so closely associated with the Canadian Maritimes—Gene Hooper, and Hal Lone Pine and Betty Cody—that some in New England considered them "herring chokers" (Bean and Bean interview 1980)—derogatory New England slang used to describe people from the Canadian Maritimes (a knock on their Catholicism and a suggestion that Maritimers were too poor to eat anything but fish).

Interest in New England country and western musicians in Atlantic Canada reached a high point with the arrival of Hal Lone Pine and Betty Cody in 1948. Hal Lone Pine and Betty Cody's guitarist, Ray Couture, wrote a song in 1950 called "Prince Edward Island Is Heaven to Me," which proved immensely popular on their radio broadcasts in Maritime Canada. The song extols the beauty of "Texas, Kentucky, and Maine" and likens the beauty and bountiful harvests of Prince Edward Island to those places along with the majesty of "London, Paris, and Spain." In February 1951 they traveled to an RCA Records studio in Montreal to make a test pressing of several of Couture's originals with the idea of pitching "Prince Edward Island Is Heaven to Me" to singer Hank Snow (Coté-Binette and Breau interview 2006). RCA executives found Lone Pine and Betty's recordings compelling and chose instead to sign Lone Pine and Betty to separate contracts in 1951. The success of their recording of "Prince Edward Island Is Heaven to Me" has come to symbolize the dynamic relationship between these two regions (Maine and the Canadian Maritimes) with regard to country and western music and culture.

Between 1951 and 1954 RCA would release some thirty sides by Hal Lone Pine and Betty Cody. With the exception of their first batch of recordings made in Montreal, all of their RCA sides were recorded in New York City and produced by Chet Atkins. Atkins took a liking to the guitar playing of Ray Couture, and the two men play harmonizing leads together on many of the sides. But Atkins chose to replace the other members of the group with studio musicians. The results are not fully representative of the group's live sound at the time—their performances tended to be less arranged than a Nashville session—yet are still compelling. Much of their recorded catalog consisted of songs written by Couture, and no attempt was made by RCA to curb the group's noticeable Maine (and in Betty's case, French Canadian) accents. The RCA sides—particularly those recorded as solos by Betty Cody—stand out from much of the recorded country material of its day, mostly on account of the guitar work, the vocal delivery, and the tendency of Betty Cody to use multitrack technology to harmonize with herself. According to Betty, part of the reason she recorded this way was that Lone Pine could sing the main melody line but was entirely unable to sing harmony, always drifting to the point where his vocal line would double hers (a problem he had little sense of humor about).

RCA was squarely behind promoting Hal Lone Pine and Betty Cody, booking them onto a package tour of the Deep South in 1954 with a multitude of *Grand Ole Opry* stars, including Chet Atkins, Hawkshaw Hawkins, and Minnie Pearl. A single by Betty Cody—an "answer" song to the Davis Sisters' hit "I Forgot More Than You'll Ever Know"—called "I Found Out More Than You Ever Knew" had reached number 10 on the *Billboard* country chart in December 1953. According to Betty Cody, the group received a cold reception from southern audiences on the package tour on account of their being from Maine, an observation she also made about Lone Pine and Betty's southern barnstorming activity in 1938 (Coté-Binette and Breau interview 2006).

Following the RCA tour, Lone Pine and Betty moved from New Brunswick, Canada, to Wheeling, West Virginia, to join WWVA's *Wheeling Jamboree* radio program. Colonel Tom Parker, then the manager of Hank Snow and Eddy Arnold and soon to be the manager of Elvis Presley, asked Betty Cody to leave Lone Pine and the *Wheeling Jamboree* and to move to Nashville to work exclusively as a solo act. In a series of gendered negotiations, Parker had his wife discuss these matters privately with Betty. Betty Cody refused the offer, in large part because Parker asked that she leave her children behind in Wheeling for at least the first six months of the deal (Coté-Binette and

Breau interview 2006). Betty Cody's chart success as a solo artist coincided with RCA's diminishing interest in Hal Lone Pine. During this same time, Lone Pine's marital indiscretions had strained the pair's relationship to the point that they became separated, and Betty quit playing music and moved the group home from Wheeling to Lewiston, Maine. At the time, she was one of the most popular female country singers in the nation, second only to Kitty Wells. Lone Pine's contract with RCA was not renewed. When Betty quit the group, Ray Couture also left, and Lone Pine moved from Wheeling to Winnipeg, Manitoba, with his son Lenny Breau to barnstorm in that region. It was a sudden and catastrophic end to what was New England's most influential—and nationally prominent—country and western group.

The WWVA Wheeling Jamboree

That Lone Pine and Betty had become regulars on the *Wheeling Jamboree* was an indication—more so than their RCA contract—that they had reached the highest level of success available to a New England country and western artist. WWVA's weekly *Barn Dance* program came in crystal clear every Saturday night throughout New England and Atlantic Canada. WWVA installed a new broadcast tower in 1948 and—according to the peculiarities of FCC regulations—had permission to boost their broadcast signal toward the North (they told listeners that they turned their towers north each evening) from the early evening until the early morning (Tribe 1996; Williams and Smik 2006). The *Wheeling Jamboree* was *the* professional aspiration for working country and western musicians in the Northeast.

The hosts of the *Wheeling Jamboree* were Doc and Chickie Williams and the Border Riders. Williams (born Andrew John Smik) was the son of Slovakian immigrants and grew up in Pittsburgh, where he and his brother Cy learned to play fiddle in their father's folk style (Williams and Smik 2006; Tribe 1996). Their father also enjoyed the same country and western tunes and "heart songs" that New Englanders like Gene Hooper did. With Doc Williams on guitar, Cy Williams on fiddle, Marion Martin on accordion, and Doc Williams's wife, Chickie, on vocals and bass, the Border Riders covered a broad spectrum of American song styles, from old chestnuts like "Abdul Abulbul Amir" and "Snow Deer" to original songs like "Roses Are Blooming," religious revival songs like "Beyond the Sunset," folk songs like "Mary of the Wild Moor," urban American polka like "When the Bees Go Buzzing Along," and cowboy songs like "Lullaby for Baby." The mixture of eastern European accordion and fiddle styles with Anglo-American folk and popular music could not have been tailored better for a New England country and western audience. In many ways, the music of Doc and Chickie

Williams does New England country and western music better than most New Englanders did.

The *Wheeling Jamboree* filled a niche market in New England, where there was no other country and western variety show with a strong, dependable signal. Based on oral testimony, only persons in the western portions of Vermont, Massachusetts, and Connecticut could hear WSM's *Grand Ole Opry* with any regularity. The WLS *National Barn Dance* out of Chicago had been extremely popular in New England prior to FCC regulations that limited reception of the WLS broadcast signal in New England. But what separated the *Wheeling Jamboree* from its better-known *Barn Dance* counterparts at WLS, WSM, and KWKH (the *Louisiana Hayride* in Shreveport, Louisiana) was its practice of including a broader demographic of country and western performers that extended well beyond the hillbilly South and the cowboy West, particularly country and western musicians from Maine, Connecticut, Pennsylvania, New Jersey, Maryland, West Virginia, Ohio, and Nova Scotia.

From 1948 until the early 1970s, the sound that emanated from the *Wheeling Jamboree* was an aural tapestry of North American country and western music that still maintained a diverse regional representation within it. New England and Canadian Maritime luminaries like Hank Keene, Hank Snow, the New England Country Gentlemen, Kenny Roberts, Hal Lone Pine and Betty Cody, Gene and Flo Hooper, Johnny White, and Dick Curless all worked at various points as regular members of the *Jamboree*. Not only could New Englanders listening back home hear sounds "from away" like the mountain music of West Virginia's Lilly Brothers and Don Stover and the cowboy music of Big Slim the Lone Cowboy, they could also hear New England country and western music represented in the voices of performers like Lone Pine and Betty Cody.

Wheeling Jamboree performers from New England recall being embraced by Doc Williams, Hawkshaw Hawkins, and other stars of the *Jamboree* as peers. This egalitarian spirit cut both ways, too—Gene and Flo Hooper were keenly aware of just how popular the *Wheeling Jamboree* broadcasts had become in New England, and they encouraged Doc Williams to come north for a winter tour of northern New England in 1950. The tour proved to be a smashing success, and subsequent years brought Doc and Chickie Williams into Quebec and Atlantic Canada. Hooper also brought other *Wheeling Jamboree* acts north, most notably Hawkshaw Hawkins, who was widely considered by New England country and western musicians to be *the* innovator of that time in country and western music. As they did when they appeared on the *Wheeling Jamboree*, the WWVA stars appeared as equals in New England alongside local performers like Gene Hooper on what they called a "package" show. The West Virginia–based stars would use New England bands to back them up on tour, and Hawkins and Williams recruited local musicians to come down to play on the *Jamboree*. In time, Ray Couture—Lone Pine's songwriter, lead guitarist, and arranger—left Pine's group to become Hawkshaw Hawkins's guitar player and served as the arranger for the house band on the *Wheeling Jamboree* from 1954 until the early 1970s.

Hawkshaw Hawkins was a national advocate for New England country and western artists. In 1954 he was invited to join WSM's *Grand Ole Opry*. After establishing himself there, he tried to recruit Maine musicians to join him on the *Opry*—particularly Maine singer/comedienne "Windy" Betty Gribben. Before Hawkins succeeded in landing any Maine artists on the *Opry*, he perished in the same plane crash that killed country star Patsy Cline in 1963. Hawkins's premature death also spelled the end for what was potentially New England's major ally in Nashville. National stardom eluded Hawkshaw Hawkins until his death, after which his recording of "Lonesome 7–7202" became a number 1 hit (Malone 2002a, 286). Hawkins was, however, a superstar in New England, and while the tragic death of Patsy Cline takes a prominent place in the national story of country music, the loss of Hawkins, whose *Wheeling Jamboree* performances had gripped the imagination of many New Englanders and whose personal appearances in the region alongside Lone Pine and Betty Cody, Gene and Flo Hooper, and Doc and Chickie Williams engendered many fond remembrances and personal relationships, resonated deeply in New England and is mourned today by the older generation of country and western performers and fans alike.

The Rise and Fall of the Hayloft Jamboree

Another promising development in New England country and western was the arrival of the WCOP *Hayloft Jamboree* radio show in Boston in 1952. The *Hayloft Jamboree* was founded around Eddy Zack and His Dude Ranchers, who hosted the show and worked as the house band for other guest acts from the New England region and visiting national stars like Hawkshaw Hawkins and Johnny Cash. For the first time, much of the region's major talent was drawn together into one space, illuminating the fact that New England held a substantial amount of homegrown country and western talent.

The early years of the *Hayloft Jamboree* were managed and emceed by a Boston radio personality named Nelson Bragg (aka the Merry Mayor of

Milo, Maine). Bragg infused the shows with Yankee humor; managed the cast of local and regional musicians; and brought in national acts, which tended to be from West Virginia and Texas. The *Hayloft Jamboree* proved an enormous success, selling out regularly in Boston's John Hancock Hall before moving to a weekly broadcast from Boston Symphony Hall. The *Hayloft Jamboree* claimed to have been the first non–Western art music performance ever held at Symphony Hall. The *Hayloft Jamboree*'s success at Symphony Hall remains a proud moment in the memories of many working-class New Englanders who attended—or performed in—shows there. For three years the New England country and western "scene" was becoming just that: it was building momentum that might generate real attention for New England–based musicians.

One national guest on the *Hayloft Jamboree* was Arkansas yodeler Elton Britt. Britt's high, clear, virtuosic, Wilf Carter–style yodel had made him enormously popular in New England. His 1942 recording of Massachusetts songwriter Paul Roberts's "There's a Star Spangled Banner Waving Somewhere" was the single most successful country and western single of all time to that point and had endeared him to the inner circles of the New England country and western scene. Britt helped secure a record contract for Yodelin' Slim Clark in 1946, which further established a great deal of goodwill among New England musicians. In 1954 a move was orchestrated—whether at the behest of WCOP executives or by Britt's manager Aubrey Mayhew—for Elton Britt and Aubrey Mayhew to take over the *Hayloft Jamboree*. The show's regulars, including host Nelson Bragg, arrived at the WCOP studios in 1954 and were greeted by the new manager/emcee (Mayhew) and the new star of the show (Britt) and an ultimatum: accept a pay cut, or lose your job. Most of the cast, including all of its established stars, like Eddy Zack and His Dude Ranchers and the Lilly Brothers and Don Stover, chose to quit (Senter and Senter interview 2004; White and Albro interview 2004). The success of the *Hayloft Jamboree* had shown music industry forces, whether in Boston, New York, or Nashville, that a weekly radio barn dance–type broadcast in Boston was capable of drawing significant attention to country and western acts and events. Executives decided that if *local* musicians could establish a lucrative model for success, then the same model could be exploited even further by a program centered on *national* acts. Performers were asked to take a pay cut so that the station could divert greater funds toward securing performance contracts with national stars. An all-new cast of young and unknown musicians—some locals like Jerry Devine or Jimmy and Ruth Senter, who went on to regional success, and some "from away," like Cowboy Jack Clement and Scotty Stoneman, who went on to national success—was hired at a lower wage to replace the older, more established musicians who had quit the program. Aubrey Mayhew emceed the show and attempted to book package tours of these new WCOP local "stars" and to launch a record label featuring recordings of those groups. The cost of hiring national stars, coupled with the wholesale departure of New England's most established homegrown groups, bankrupted the program, and by 1957 the *Hayloft Jamboree* was off the air for good.

The Shift toward Southern Country and Mountain Music

Shortly after the death of country star Hank Williams on New Year's Day, 1953, a Massachusetts singer named Charlie Carson recorded four sides for MGM Records in Nashville with Williams's former backing band, the Drifting Cowboys. Like the recordings of Ray Price from this same time period—also recorded with the Drifting Cowboys—Carson mimics the late Hank Williams's voice breaks and Williams's pronounced southern nasality. While Carson's recording is and was fairly obscure in New England and beyond, and while "nasality" and "nasal twang" can be murky terms for ethnomusicological discourse (Nettl 1970, 440), some explication is required here to fully understand the profound shift in vocal expression that is marked by Charlie Carson's recordings.

"Nasality" and "twang" are common descriptive terms used by musicians, fans, detractors, critics, and scholars to demarcate country musics from other styles of working-class vernacular music. Nasality and twang are heard by many as indicators of class, a lack of education, and even the sexual restrictiveness of the singer's society (Feld 1984, 404; Lomax 1962, 430). On account of the many linguists, educators, and speech therapists who have long sought to purge students of nasality and twang, the presence of these features in a person's voice indicates—or is used to imply or foreground—a working-class, ethnic, or regional background.

Early twentieth-century linguists and speech therapists were preoccupied with nasality, vehemently decrying it as a "defect" or "disorder" worthy of eradication (Bassett 1927; Davis 1944; Mulgrave 1937; Root 1926). In particular—and most pertinent to the subject at hand—linguists of the 1940s noted that "nasal pronunciation" was a "great acoustic horror" that plagued the rural American Northeast, the city of Philadelphia, the southern mountains, and the western plains (Davis 1944). As such, the appearance of nasal twang on a recording by a working-class New Englander should not come as a surprise. But it is the *type* of twang used—a southern twang, not a Yankee twang—that is noteworthy on the Charlie Carson MGM sides.

Using definitions typical of early twentieth-century speech therapists (Martin 1921, 26), the nasal twang incorporated in country and western singing style operates on a spectrum of increasing flexibility of the palate, moving from the South (at its least flexible) to the North and finally to the West (at its most flexible). The differences in this spectrum are readily apparent when imitating the vocal styles of "the three Hanks" of the 1950s: the nasal twang of the South (Hank Williams, Alabama), the Northeast (Hank Snow, Nova Scotia), and the West (Hank Thompson, Texas). Northeastern and western singers tend to accentuate flexibility of the palate when dropping to low notes, such as when Hank Snow sings the word "on" in the refrain of "Movin' On," when Dick Curless sings the word "off" in the line "count 'em off" in the refrain of "A Tombstone Every Mile," or when Texan Ernest Tubb sings the word "home" in the line "now I'm comin' home" in the song "It's Been So Long Darling."

Carson's MGM sides are noteworthy mainly because they mark the first time that a New Englander had recorded commercially while singing with an affected southern nasal twang. Carson's affected regional twang is indicative of a trend in New England that started sometime around 1950. This specifically *southern* vocal affectation was part of a larger trend, too, whereby the imagined geographic orientation of New England country and western musicians moved toward Nashville, coinciding (significantly) with the rise of bluegrass music and the founding of the Country Music Association.

The group singly most responsible for pushing New England toward an imaginary southern orientation is Jerry and Sky. Jerry and Sky were arguably the preeminent professional country and western group based in Boston in 1950. They had a regular broadcast slot on Boston's biggest radio station (WBZ), a recording deal, a lucrative barnstorming schedule, and an endorsement from the Packard automobile company. They aimed their imaginary compass to the south and recruited southern musicians to back them up in concert and on recordings. Jerry and Sky mentored several Boston groups and developed a circle of friends who had a deep, long-term impact on the way many New Englanders conceived of "country" music and their place in that tradition.

The story of the countrification (i.e., the emphasis on "country" music at the expense of "western" music) of New England can be traced to Jerry and Sky and to two Italian Americans born in Cambridge, Massachusetts, named Frank and Pete Loconto. The Loconto brothers grew up with a variety of musical influences but primarily emulated Jerry and Sky, from their style to their stage mannerisms. The brothers formed a band and adopted the stage names of Frank and Pete Lane, later becoming the Lane Brothers. The Lane Brothers began their professional career busking in the streets and pubs of

East Cambridge and in neighboring Boston, finally getting a coveted gig at the Mohawk Ranch in Boston's notorious, sailor-filled, red light district, the Combat Zone (Frank "Lane" Loconto, e-mail message to author, July 21, 2005).

The Lane Brothers became a major draw at the Mohawk Ranch. By 1950 the owners of a Combat Zone restaurant named San Remo approached the Lane Brothers about their interest in converting San Remo into a country music club. The owners (Frank Segalini and Ed Bernardi) wanted the Lane Brothers to leave the Mohawk to become the house band at their club. They asked Frank Lane to suggest a name. Lane considered that the usual fare at the cowboy-and-Indian-themed Mohawk Ranch to be in the western style and that the Lane Brothers played in a more hillbilly style. He proposed the Hillbilly Ranch as the name of the new club, and it stuck (Loconto e-mail 2005).

In 1947 Benjamin "Tex" Logan, a Texas-born fiddle player, moved to Cambridge, Massachusetts, to begin a position as a research assistant at MIT. Logan had learned fiddle while attending Texas Tech University in Lubbock. A mathematics professor of Logan's who had graduated from MIT encouraged him to pursue a position as a research assistant in mathematics there. Arriving in Boston, Logan befriended Jerry and Sky and the Melody Men and began performing (and recording) as a member of the group. Logan quit work at MIT to pursue a career as a full-time musician in 1950. After one year working on WWVA's *Wheeling Jamboree* with the bluegrass group the Lilly Brothers and Don Stover, Logan quit and returned to resume work at MIT on MIT's conditions that he no longer wear cowboy stage clothes to work (Wilson 1972; Snow interview 2006). Logan's experiences in New England with Jerry and Sky and the Melody Men had led him to observe that a vibrant country and western scene had coalesced around the country and western clubs of Boston's Combat Zone, along the New England ranch circuit, and in Boston's fledgling *Hayloft Jamboree* barn dance program on WCOP. Upon returning to MIT, Logan encouraged the Lilly Brothers and Don Stover to move to Boston to work at the Hillbilly Ranch. The Lillys moved from West Virginia to Boston in 1952. They would play every night of the week at the Hillbilly Ranch for the next twenty years, secure a regular broadcast spot on Boston's WCOP, and become featured members of that station's *Hayloft Jamboree* broadcast.

The Lilly Brothers changed country music in New England in ways that still remain obvious today. The arrival of the Lilly Brothers galvanized the shift away from western music and toward mountain and country music that had begun just prior to their arrival with Jerry and Sky and the Lane Brothers. The effect of the Lilly Brothers' music on a teenage country and western singer from outside of Boston named Jim Rooney had a far-reaching (and long-lasting) impact on the folk revival of the late 1950s and early 1960s, when Rooney attended Harvard and became the booking agent for Club 47 in Cambridge. Rooney's attendance at the Lilly Brothers' shows at the Hillbilly Ranch and his subsequent affinity for bluegrass and mountain music placed such music at the heart of music programming at Club 47 and are largely responsible for spawning the perception among folk revivalists that bluegrass was an "authentic" folk form of country music.

Ironically—in the face of preconceived notions of cultural authenticity and bluegrass music and in a twist that is typical of the history of New England country and western music—an Italian American mandolin player and typewriter repairman from Medford, Massachusetts, named Joseph Valenti (aka Joe Val) who sat in regularly with Jerry and Sky, the Lilly Brothers, and the folk revival bluegrass group the Charles River Valley Boys would have a particularly lasting impact in the region. Val would become the leading proponent of bluegrass music in New England, celebrated by no less a titan of bluegrass than Bill Monroe himself. Today he has an annual bluegrass festival in Framingham, Massachusetts, named in his honor.

Through the mid-1950s the interaction of the local country and western industry (musicians, agents, promoters, and broadcasters) with the Nashville country industry and its stars was a fairly fluid and positive one. In the programming of a *Grand Ole Opry* broadcast from the Boston Garden in the 1950s, local promoters worked successfully to get local country and western acts like Eddy Zack and His Dude Ranchers and Kenny Roberts prominent performance spots (Brown interview 2004). When sharing the same performance venue, country and western musicians, both national and local, appear to have intermingled freely, and New Englanders rarely recall being treated like second-class citizens by southern or western stars on account of their New England origins, nor do they recall any national stars finding anything unusual about finding home-grown country and western talent in New England. Likewise, rodeos toured through New England and incorporated national and local country and western performers into their shows, where local musicians like Rusty Rogers could perform alongside the Sons of the Pioneers and play music with them backstage (Rogers and Kempton interview 2005). The annual rodeo in Boston featured a national yodeling competition, which Kenny Roberts and Yodelin' Slim Clark both recall winning.

New England's outdoor ranch circuit fostered camaraderie between musicians backstage, occasionally prompting national performers to incorporate local talent into their stage shows, as happened with guitarist Merle Travis and teenager Lenny Breau at the Lone Star Ranch in Reeds Ferry, New Hampshire, in the early 1950s (Fournier 2005). After national country stars like Marty Robbins and Johnny Cash would play a show or a rodeo in Boston, they would inevitably wind up at either the Mohawk Ranch or the Hillbilly Ranch down in Boston's late-night Combat Zone district and interact with local musicians. Frank Lane's group (the Lane Brothers) was the house band at the Mohawk Ranch in Boston when, in either 1949 or 1950, Gene Autry stopped in. According to Lane:

> George Clarke, the entertainment writer for the *Boston Daily Record*, became interested in our style of both songs and attire and would write about the Lane Brothers in his column called, "Around Town." George also liked to drop by the Mohawk to see "Sagebrush Suzie" the club's cigarette girl. She was the Marilyn Monroe of her time. One night, while the rodeo was in town at the Boston Garden, it was announced that Gene Autry was going to drop by the Mohawk Ranch after the rodeo. None of us believed the rumor but we all kept an eye on the front door at around 11pm. All of a sudden, just like in the movies, the door opened and in walked George Clarke with a small entourage and sure enough, there he was with his cowboy hat and all, Gene Autry.
>
> All the musicians were up on stage and Pete and I were in the middle of a song which abruptly ended as Gene himself climbed onto the stage, said "Hi" to the audience, turned around and said to no one in particular, "What key do I sing 'Back In The Saddle Again'?" Brother Pete, without hesitation, said, "C," and Gene said, "Let's do it."
>
> And there we were playing for the Number One movie cowboy—and one of my idols of the day—Gene Autry. I was flyin' high, I'm sure. Unfortunately, there isn't a picture of that event.
>
> George may have kept Sagebrush busy while Gene was singing. (Loconto e-mail 2005)

Though interactions between national stars and locals rarely featured such brazen acts of arrogant—if funny and even welcome in this instance—upstaging, the event speaks of the familiarity local musicians had with national forms of country and western music and of the expectations of outsiders like Gene Autry that the local musicians would know their work (in this instance, better than Autry himself knew it). House bands along New England's ranch circuit would hire out to back up touring national acts like Elton Britt, Merle Travis, Hank Snow, and Ernest Tubb both at the ranch and at performance sites throughout New England while the performers were in the region. The rare act that brought its own backing band to town prior to the 1960s generally featured good-natured camaraderie between musicians. At one "package show" at the J and P Coates factory in Pawtucket, Rhode Island, Tony Poccia, steel guitarist for Eddy Zack and his Dude Ranchers, taught *Grand Ole Opry* star Carl Smith's steel guitarist, Johnny Siebert, to modify a steel guitar with chains that would enable him to bend certain strings. Poccia recalls learning this technique from his steel guitar teacher, whose last name was Petterutti, in Providence, Rhode Island. This technique was likely derived from those developed by pop and big band steel guitarist Alvin McBurney (aka Alvin Rey), who eventually modified and standardized the pedal steel guitar along with John Moore. Poccia said Petterutti learned the technique from his brother-in-law. Petterutti had connections to Ben Webster, who employed drummer Nick Fatool of Providence in his band. Fatool and Webster had played together in the Benny Goodman Orchestra during Charlie Christian's tenure (including the *Spirituals to Swing* concert and recording). Following a stint with Webster's band, Fatool played drums with Alvin Rey. Petterutti founded his music store in Providence in the 1930s, and it is likely that Fatool is the connection between Petterutti and Rey. Nevertheless, Poccia learned how to bend the strings on his steel guitar in Providence, a technique that amazed visiting musicians from Nashville: "And the steel player from Carl Smith was amazed. He couldn't understand what those chains were on my steel guitar. And I told him what it was all about. And, believe it or not, I'd say about a year later, Nashville came out with a pedal steel. I'm startin' to think that maybe this started here in Rhode Island" (2004).

Poccia's interactions with other steel guitarists also influenced his own playing. As a student at the Petterutti music store in Providence, Rhode Island, Poccia had learned to tune his steel guitar to an A6 but had seen that most western and western swing bands either had two steel players or had one steel player with a double steel (two steel guitars tuned differently). Poccia bought a second steel but never played it until he performed in a "package show" with Texan country and western star Hank Thompson, where Poccia sat with Thompson's two steel players and learned an E13 tuning, which he used alongside the A6 steel for the next fifty years (2004).

Trade-offs such as this were not entirely musical. Regional stars in Maine like Lone Pine and Gene Hooper made a practice of alerting national acts to their popularity in northern New England and Atlantic Canada, booking tours with them, loaning out their backing bands to decrease costs, and booking the engagements themselves. The local performers benefited locally from such "package shows" where Gene Hooper's reputation would be bolstered by appearing on an equal bill with a national star like Hawkshaw Hawkins. Up through the 1970s New Englanders would back up touring "name" artists "from away," including significant honky-tonk figures like Lefty Frizzell and Webb Pierce. Additionally, stars from Canada and Wheeling, West Virginia, would regularly return such favors, helping New England acts to develop fan bases in new regions and promoting their music to powerful regional radio outlets (particularly Doc Williams and the WWVA *Wheeling Jamboree*). From the first time Gene Hooper helped Doc Williams to tour through Maine and Atlantic Canada in 1950 (Hooper and Hooper interview 2005; Williams and Smik 2006), New Englanders were regularly seen on the stage of the *Wheeling Jamboree* (Gene and Flo Hooper, Hal Lone Pine and Betty Cody, Kenny Roberts, Dick Curless, and Johnny White, to name a few).

Nevertheless, by 1956 New England country and western music was at a crossroads. The areas around Boston, Portland, and Bangor in particular proved fertile ground for young country and western–inspired musicians like guitarist Dick Dale (Brockton, Massachusetts), Peter Rowan (Brockton, Massachusetts), Jim Rooney (Wayland, Massachusetts), Bill Keith (Dedham, Massachusetts), brothers Clarence and Roland White (Lewiston, Maine/Portsmouth, New Hampshire), and George Moody (Bangor, Maine), all of whom would become important figures in later decades and associated with regions outside of New England. Yet the rise of national network television, a radio industry shift from live musical performance to disc jockeys, a music industry shift away from cowboy music, and a deep economic depression brought on by the collapse of New England's textile and military industries helped to feed a growing resentment among local people over a seeming abandonment of locality on nationalized network programming. The raw sounds of bluegrass and the fiercely independent business acumen of its performers had an appeal to disenfranchised New Englanders of all classes that cannot be fully expressed in this work. Yet the region's most noteworthy performing group of the previous twenty years—Hal Lone Pine and Betty Cody—had disintegrated at the peak of their popularity and at a time when they seemed poised for national notoriety. Lone Pine, like several other popular performers in New England before him, left New England for western Canada. The Down Homers had all but disbanded, and their most noticeable singers—Rusty Rogers, Bill Haley, and Kenny Roberts—had scattered throughout the Midwest and the mid-Atlantic. New England's only major radio barn dance program—

Boston's WCOP *Hayloft Jamboree*—had been bankrupted. At this same time, the New England working class was in a period of crisis, whereby the region was rapidly deindustrializing, and most factory work was moving south. (The exception to this rule was that some shoe factory and tannery work moved north into Maine, where labor unions were weakest [Temin 2000].) Simultaneously, the heart of New England country and western activity and identity also moved into Maine.

The Rise of Rockabilly, Dick Curless, Bluegrass, and the State of Maine: The Beer Parlor Era, 1956–1965

Much had changed in New England country and western music by 1956. For starters, a profound shift had taken place in music-based community sociability. Whereas the country and western event of the barnstorming era had been defined as a multigenerational gathering in a community hall where alcohol played a background role, the end of the barnstorming era witnessed the development of youth culture and the drifting of country and western music away from community halls and into drinking establishments for adults—or what some New Englanders called "bottle clubs" and "beer parlors."

Country and western groups also migrated from the medium of radio and onto television. The music was also changing, particularly through the use of the electric guitar. Electric instruments had been present in New England country and western music since the 1940s with the steel guitar, and many groups used drums to some degree even as far back as the days of Mellie Dunham. But the music began to reflect the influences of rhythm and blues and swinging jazz to an unprecedented degree. With the arrival of Bill Haley and His Comets on radio in 1953 and Elvis Presley in 1954, many of the young people who turned out at country and western events wanted to hear rockabilly, and—regardless of their private feelings about the style itself—New England country and western groups tended to oblige. Typical of the evolving trends and roles in the country and western ensemble from the 1920s onward, a new specialist role was born to accommodate the wishes of the audience: most country and western groups working in New England in the mid- to late 1950s added a teenage rockabilly singer to their ensemble and featured that singer on a number of songs to placate the younger people in the crowd.

However, there are indications in the music of New England country and western that performers were already inclined to drift toward rockabilly in the early 1950s before such a genre had become crystallized in the national imagination in the music of Elvis Presley in 1954–55. Most notable of these older New England-based performers is Bill Haley, who worked in New Hampshire as a member of the Down Homers in the late 1940s and with his own group, the Range Drifters (later known as the Saddlemen and then the Comets), on WKNE in Keene, New Hampshire, in the early 1950s. Haley's recording of "Rocket 88" with the Saddlemen in 1951 is considered by many to be the prototypical white rhythm and blues recording, and his 1954 recording of "Rock around the Clock" with the Comets is a landmark recording in early commercial rock and roll history (Tucker 1989; Tallmadge 1983). The origins of New England country and western music's early inclinations toward an electrified sound can be traced backward from Haley, to the Down Homers, to the Downeasters, to the encounter of Uncle Lem and His Mountain Boys and Katahdin Mountaineers guitarist Johnny Smith and the great Oklahoma-born electric jazz guitarist Charlie Christian.

In January 1940 Charlie Christian made a weeklong stand at the Strand Theater in Portland, Maine, with the Benny Goodman Sextet. Johnny Smith, then the guitarist for Uncle Lem and His Mountain Boys (a hillbilly orchestra from Portland), went to see Christian play and met him while he was playing in a small Portland club after hours, and the event changed Smith's life. Though Smith considered his style chiefly influenced by Django Reinhardt and Les Paul, Smith dedicated himself to electric guitar after seeing and hearing Charlie Christian. Johnny Smith was affiliated with three important hillbilly orchestras and country and western groups from Maine at this time: Uncle Lem and His Mountain Boys, the Katahdin Mountaineers, and Bud Bailey and His Downeasters (Smith interview 2007). The electric guitar playing of Johnny Smith would come to impact the music of the Downeasters and other similar swinging cowboy and hillbilly bands of the day. Johnny Smith eventually left Portland for Boston to focus on jazz full-time with a group he called the Airport Boys in the early 1940s. The Airport Boys shared radio time on WHEB in Portsmouth, New Hampshire, with Bud Bailey and His Downeasters in 1942. By the mid-1940s, Smith was in New York City, where he developed his hit version of "Moonlight in Vermont" and would write and record the song "Walk, Don't Run," written by Smith in 1954 and made into an international hit by the Ventures in 1964 (Rogers and Kempton interview 2005; Smith interview 2007; Calderone interview 2004).

The Downeasters added an electric guitar, and they in turn influenced the music of the Down Homers, who would come to define a sound that some call "eastern swing." During World War II, the Down Homers' lead singer, Kenny Roberts, was drafted into the U.S. Navy. The group was playing at

WKNE in Keene, New Hampshire, at the time and advertised in *Billboard* magazine for a temporary replacement for Roberts. The Down Homers hired Bill Haley from Chester, Pennsylvania, as Roberts's substitute. Roberts taught Haley how to yodel, and Haley remained with the group for the duration of Roberts's tour of duty. Following Roberts's discharge from the navy, Haley left the Down Homers in 1948 and took several members with him to form his own group, the Saddlemen (originally called the Range Drifters), in Philadelphia. Not long afterward, Kenny Roberts left the Down Homers and was replaced by one of Roberts's chief influences, Rusty Rogers, the yodeler from Bud Bailey and His Downeasters (Roberts interview 2004; Rogers and Kempton interview 2005).

Based on the ample number of radio transcriptions made by the Down Homers during their time in New England, they sounded at times like a jump-blues version of the Sons of the Pioneers or a hillbilly version of Louis Jordan. In 1950 they recorded several sides for King Records in Cincinnati, including a song called "There's Nothin' Clickin' Chicken," which charted in the Top 10 of the folk/country charts. It bears the distinct stamp of the protorockabilly sounds of rhythm and blues performers from the late 1940s like Big Joe Turner, including an electric guitar solo. Rogers says that the group was given the song to record by King executives and that his vocals sound to him like "I'm screamin,' not singin'!" (Rogers and Kempton interview 2005). Yet as a protorockabilly song, it is highly unusual for its combination of rhythm and blues and Wilf Carter–style yodeling.

"There's Nothin' Clickin' Chicken" is representative of King Records executive Syd Nathan's practice of encouraging white artists signed to King to cover black artists also signed to King, and vice-versa (Malone 2002a, 209). "There's Nothin' Clickin' Chicken" was recorded for King by blues/jazz guitarist Lonnie Johnson in 1950 and shortly afterward by the Down Homers. A comparison of the two recordings shows the Down Homers' interpretation of Johnson's song to be more hard-driving, with Rusty Rogers hammering a strained and growling vocal on the downbeat, in marked contrast to Johnson's hard-swinging vocals in the original. Likewise, Rogers adds Wilf Carter–style yodeling breaks after each refrain and sings the song in his own dialect (e.g., making Johnson's "when I wants a date" into "when I'm on a date"), and the Down Homers convert Johnson's arrangement of the song with piano and electric guitar into a fiddle, electric guitar, and steel guitar version.

Though Shorty Cook's steel guitar breaks demonstrate a remarkable aptitude for this stylistic medium, "There's Nothin' Clickin' Chicken" is clearly singular in the catalog of the Down Homers' recordings as being the closest the band came to approaching rhythm and blues, rockabilly, or rock and roll. Nevertheless, the recording does not clash with their catalog either, comparing favorably to the group's various yodel-punctuated polkas that feature a heavy emphasis on the snare drum on the backbeat (most of which were recorded prior to their deal with King). The recording is suggestive of a direction the Down Homers might have been inclined to lean toward had they performed in regions with any dynamic interplay between whites and African Americans or if they had made more recordings for the King label. This was the kind of transformation of repertoire and style demonstrated by Bill Haley when Haley left New Hampshire for Philadelphia to form the Saddlemen in 1948. "There's Nothin' Clickin' Chicken" is a remarkable moment of integrationist (proto)rockabilly of the sort that would not arrive again in New England for nearly another thirty years with the relocation of Arkansas rockabilly singer Sleepy LaBeef to Amesbury, Massachusetts, in 1977.

Still, the changing sounds of New England country and western appear to have mirrored the changing cultural landscape of the day. Many New England country and western performers began to feel that the bottom had fallen out of the cowboy music market in New England: their ability to make a living had been seriously compromised by a recent shift away from live regional music on local radio stations (reflected in an inability by new performers to secure radio slots), the negative impact of television on turnouts at live performances, and the declining industrial and military base of the New England working-class economy (Temin 2000). Rusty Rogers quit the Down Homers in 1956 to become a professional wrestler (Murphy 2005; Rogers and Kempton interview 2005; Dennett 1991). The subsequent demise—or permanent departure from New England—of the Down Homers heralded the end of the barnstorming era in New England country and western. Most of the region's marquee barnstorming groups had split up by this point (Hal Lone Pine and Betty Cody, Hank Keene and His Radio Gang, Jerry and Sky, Bud Bailey and His Downeasters, the Down Homers), and most of those who remained moved off the road and onto television (Ken Mackenzie, Curley O'Brien, Georgia Mae, Yodelin' Slim Clark, Eddy Zack and His Dude Ranchers).

The New Order: Event Records

The interruptions of World War II and the Korean War had preceded the arrival of rockabilly music in New England and the demise of most of its marquee groups. This transitional moment in New England country and western music witnessed the rise of a new order of performers and styles. The establishment of Event Records in Westbrook, Maine, brought together the major players in this transitional period and marks the beginning of what can be considered the modern era of country and western music in New England—an era that continues to define the music as it is today.

The key figures in this transitional period were country and western singer Dick Curless and the bluegrass group the Lilly Brothers and Don Stover. Dick Curless was born in 1932 in Fort Fairfield, Maine, along the U.S.-Canadian border in Aroostook County. As a boy, he moved with his family to the small town of Gilbertsville in Massachusetts's Pioneer Valley, where he and his brother, Phil, were mentored by Yodelin' Slim Clark. By 1950 Curless was touring in support of Clark with a group called the Trail Riders and using the stage name the Tumbleweed Kid. That year, he recorded a song for the Standard label called "The Coast of Maine." He was drafted into the U.S. Army and served in Korea from 1952 until 1954. Curless's return to the state of Maine in 1954 heralded the arrival of someone who would become New England's signature country and western performer.

The Korean conflict had a direct impact on the lives of many New England servicemen and their families and profoundly shaped the life and career of Dick Curless. Curless had just been married and had recorded four sides for Standard when he got his draft notice. He left for Korea while his wife, Pauleen, was pregnant with their first child, Rickie. Legally blind in one eye, Curless was not assigned to combat duty, working instead in Korea as a truck driver and an entertainer on United States Armed Services Radio, where he performed as the Rice Paddy Ranger. In this latter role, Curless developed a significant following among servicemen on account of his adaptation of a Japanese pop song called "Shina No Yoru," or "China Nights." The song, which derives from a Japanese movie of the same name, was popular in Korea during the war. According to Korean War veterans, "Shina No Yoru" was sung by every Korean street performer and was played in every Korean bar at the time. Vets would often sing their own versions of the song, making up nonsensical English lyrics based on the sound of the Japanese words (Algeo 1960). Dick Curless took the unusual step of asking a local Korean man to translate the song for him into English, and he performed the song in English with alternating verses in Japanese. Curless's rendition of the song was heard regularly over the Armed Services Radio Network, and the song was so closely associated with veterans' memories of Korea that Curless kept it as a part of his live repertoire long into the 1980s and released singles of at least five different versions of the song (Curless 1996, 2000; Moody 2006).

Upon his return to Maine, Curless dropped his Korean War radio nickname, the Rice Paddy Ranger, and landed a spot on Lone Pine's weekly coast-to-coast broadcast on the ABC Radio Network out of Bangor, Maine. By 1956 he was eager to be making records again. Until that point, making records entailed going to either Boston, New York, Montreal, or Nashville. But innovations in recording technology during the Cold War had infused America with better, more accessible options for sound recording. Al Hawkes, a country and western musician from Westbrook, Maine, who had trained in sound technology in the armed services, decided to start an independent record label upon his return to Maine. He called the label Event Records (Hawkes interview 2006).

Westbrook borders Portland, the largest city in the state of Maine. Portland was home to television station WGAN, which broadcast the Ken Mackenzie variety show. Mackenzie's country and western variety show featured regional talent—known figures like Hal Lone Pine and Betty Cody, as well as up-and-coming talent like Dick Curless. Al Hawkes utilized this close proximity to Portland to invite Maine country and western artists to record demos at his studio. Lone Pine and Betty Cody, who, though separated, maintained an on-again-off-again professional relationship, and their oldest son, Lenny Breau, made a series of recordings for Hawkes in 1956. They brought with them Dick Curless, who impressed Hawkes with his vocal talent (although to Hawkes, Curless spent too much time trying to use his impressive baritone to imitate a rising rockabilly star named Johnny Cash). Curless hung around the studio for days rifling through Hawkes's extensive collection of blues, jazz, folk, and hillbilly 78s. The two men discovered a shared affinity for the music of blues and cabaret folk singer Josh White (Hawkes interview 2006).

Curless began recording at Event Records in July 1956 with Lenny Breau and Sleepy Willis (born Taso Golios) on electric guitars. The sessions utilized the two guitarists' progressive styles and some sound effect dramatics, particularly the use of multitrack vocal effects and echo manifolds. Curless recorded two interpretations of traditional material recorded by Josh White ("Foggy Foggy Dew" and "Streets of Laredo"), as well as Jimmie Rodgers songs ("Blue Yodel #6"), traditional songs ("Naponee"), the Korean War anthem he had translated ("China Nights [Shina No Yoru]"), some Merle Travis ("Nine Pound Hammer"), Mills Brothers ("You'll Never Miss Your Water 'til the Well Runs Dry" and "Just a Closer Walk with Thee"), and a number of compelling originals of a decidedly western orientation ("Cottage in the Pines" and "Rocky Mountain Queen"). Curless's Event recordings are singular in the annals of New England country and western music, as they encapsulate the propensity of singers from this region to incorporate folk, blues, and popular standards into their repertoire.

The standout tracks from the Event sessions were released as singles. Initially, Curless's versions of "Foggy Foggy Dew" and "Streets of Laredo" were a regional radio sensation; local folklore attributes this to the long duration (for that era—they are 4:03 and 4:15 long, respectively) of the singles, which enabled DJs to take much-needed bathroom breaks while working alone in the studio late at night (New England disc jockeys called it the "piss record"). Nationally, Curless's single of "Nine Pound Hammer" took off—likely owing to the pairing of Curless's striking baritone vocal with the electric guitar pyrotechnics of the fifteen-year-old Lenny Breau—and sold tens of thousands of copies nationwide (Hawkes interview 2006). Curless and Lenny Breau were booked on to *The Arthur Godfrey Show* in New York City, and it appeared that Curless's career was about to take off.

During this same time, the Lilly Brothers and Don Stover came north to Westbrook, Maine, and recorded a series of landmark bluegrass records for Event. Their sides captured the band in its youthful exuberance and its newfound world-weariness. Their recording of "John Henry" has been described by bluegrass historian Neil V. Rosenberg as being like both "a letter from home"—telling the broader New England audience about familiar places back in West Virginia—and a letter "*to* home," using the story of John Henry as a metaphor for the exhausting hard work of a working bluegrass band in Boston (1993, 158). Between the Lilly Brothers, Dick Curless, and a series of rockabilly singles by bands active in the Bangor, Portland, and Boston areas, Event Records' ability to turn out hit material seemingly out of nowhere was nothing short of sensational.

And yet, as is often the case for independent record labels, the seeds of Event's destruction were rooted in its very success. Event's attempts to keep inventory up in the face of high sales figures and national distribution placed an enormous stress on the small label's finances. A deal was cut between Event and Tiffany Records in Boston whereby Event gave the rights to Curless's materials (and his contract) to Tiffany in exchange for manufacturing, warehousing, and distribution privileges. The timing could not have been worse: months later, a fire of catastrophic proportions destroyed Tiffany's warehouse, complete with the entire stock of Event's singles, and Event Records was out of business by 1957 (Hawkes interview 2006).

Fortunately, the Event masters remained intact in the possession of engineer Al Hawkes. (Bear Family released the entirety of Curless's recordings for Event in 1996 in an extensive CD boxed set titled *A Tombstone Every Mile*.) The recordings made by Event Records took the bands in question and added some technical innovation, and they represent a sound that is distinctive for its *variation* on more national genres of country and western, bluegrass, and rockabilly. Generally speaking, the "name" artists on Event utilized their own backing musicians in the studio, and as such the records are a fair approximation of how these musicians actually sounded in concert when left to their own devices.

Most interesting is Curless's rendition of "China Nights (Shina No Yoru)" for its explicit inclusion of pentatonic scales, Japanese lyrics, and Asian lyrical themes. Other Korean War vets recorded versions of "China Nights," but they were tongue-in-cheek sendups of the Japanese tune (Algeo 1960). Curless's version is dead-serious, and its success in the region—in terms of both sales and its longevity in Curless's live repertoire—speaks to just how relevant the tune was to a working-class New England audience that had spent the better part of four decades roiled in military conflict on the Asian continent.

With the dissolution of Event came a crisis moment in the life of Dick Curless. First, his successful appearance on *The Arthur Godfrey Show* and the success of his Event recording of "Nine Pound Hammer" was followed by a physical breakdown instigated by stomach ulcers, which had begun to plague him in Korea and were exacerbated by a budding alcoholism. Curless retreated to his home in Maine to recuperate with his family and spend time at their hunting camp in the Maine woods. Until his conversion to evangelical Christianity some twenty years later, Curless suffered recurring breakdowns brought on by acute alcoholism, drug addiction, and stomach ulcers. Curless's return to music two years later (1959) was hindered by his remaining contract with the Tiffany label (what remained of his Event contract). The sides recorded for Tiffany were indicative of many of the musical (as opposed to personal) issues that would dog Curless later in his career—chiefly, that his producers did not allow him to be an interpreter of songs, arrangements, and repertoire in his own right. Curless recorded an album of cowboy songs and gospel songs for Tiffany that have polished and saccharine arrangements entirely out of step with what he sounded like as a live performer. When his contract with Tiffany ran out in 1960, Curless was back on his own.

What we can see in the examples of both Event Records and the *Hayloft Jamboree* is that New England country and western music was never able to generate enough momentum to make the transition to national awareness. Not only that, but its proudest and most successful interactions with the music industry also contained the seeds of its own destruction. This is a phenomenon that would once again reveal itself in the second rise of Dick Curless in the mid-1960s.

The Rise of Maine Authenticity

Curless's retreat to the Maine woods is symbolic of a larger phenomenon in New England at the time. The center of New England identity had, for many years, resided in southern New England, particularly in Massachusetts and Connecticut (Conforti 2001). The rapid urbanization of southern New England in the early twentieth century and the massive influx of immigrants during that time caused an identity crisis in the region. Agents of culture, tourism, and industry caused an imaginary shift in the center of New England identity from southern New England to northern New England. By the early 1950s, two key figures in Massachusetts's country and western music—Dick Curless and Yodelin' Slim Clark—had chosen to relocate to the Bangor, Maine, area. A new "scene" coalesced around them in the period following Curless's success on Event Records, and despite the failure of Event to stay afloat, Curless was able to make a comfortable living playing in the copious beer parlors of Bangor's Exchange Street.

Exchange Street was rowdy and occasionally violent. Curless took up residency at the Silver Dollar—owned and operated by his lead guitarist, Sleepy Willis—and by the early 1960s was holding his own on a nightly basis there. It was a shift not unlike that experienced by most working in country and western music in New England at the time. The country and western event of the community hall and the ranch circuit was now only a small part of the types of shows performers were involved in by the 1960s. Most were playing for adults in drinking establishments like the Silver Dollar.

In 1964 an acquaintance of Dick Curless named Dan Fulkerson, a copywriter at WLBZ-TV in Bangor, Maine, approached Dick with a song he had written called "A Tombstone Every Mile." The song chronicled a stretch of narrow, icy highway utilized by Maine truckers to ship goods from Aroostook County (Maine's northernmost county) to urban markets due south. The song was born of an impulse similar to that of working songsters Joe Scott, Larry Gorman, Larry Doyle, and others from the nineteenth-century lumber trade who chronicled the dangerous and oft-tragic lives of working men in the North Woods (Ives 1964, 1971, 1978). Fulkerson, who hitchhiked regularly from Bangor deep into Aroostook County's potato-growing region, heard truckers tell tales of wrecks along the Haynesville Road. The song is a compilation of those truckers' stories. Curless was moved by the relevance of the song's lyrics and its direct narrative style—no doubt in part because it resembles the "Come All Ye's" of the North Woods' songster tradition (in which so many of the old North Woods ballads begin with either "Come all ye" or "Come all you"), such as "The Jam on Gerry's Rock," which Curless learned as a boy in Aroostook County. Fulkerson took Curless's band to WLBZ's studio after hours, and they recorded the song. Fulkerson and Curless decided to release "A Tombstone Every Mile" on their own record label, Allagash, and to utilize a network of truck drivers along the eastern seaboard to get the record placed in jukeboxes along major truck routes. The plan worked, and the record pressing plant Allagash used noted that this small release was notching significant sales figures. The plant also pressed records for Capitol, and they alerted Capitol to the success of Curless's single. Capitol contacted Allagash and struck a deal to reissue the record on a Capitol subsidiary called Tower Records (Cohen 1977; Curless 1996). The Tower single peaked nationally at number 5 on the *Billboard* country charts in March 1965, about the same time as Roger Miller's "King of the Road." That both "A Tombstone Every Mile" and "King of the Road" were in the Top 10 at the same time is somewhat remarkable. This year, 1965, marked the first time since Jimmie Rodgers's 1928 recording of "Brakeman's Blues" that a hit country and western or hillbilly song mentioned the state of Maine—a span of some thirty-seven years. It appeared—however briefly—that New England might be capable of acceptance into an increasingly corporate-run, nationalized professional music market.

Off the Air: New England Pushed off the Radio by Nashville, 1966–1975

Dick Curless's success with "A Tombstone Every Mile" marked the beginning of a ten-year relationship with Capitol Records and its subsidiary label, Tower. Tower repackaged some of Curless's old Event, Tiffany, and Allagash recordings along with one recording session produced by Curless in Boston in 1965. However, with the exception of these repackaged recordings made in New England, a live recording ("Live from the Truck Drivers Jamboree") in 1973, and an instrumental track called "Mumble Boogie," none of the recordings Curless made for Tower/Capitol feature his distinctive guitar playing, and few feature musical backing from his working backup band (Curless 1996). Like most artists recording country music for major labels, Curless was plugged into a system of sound production geared toward time-efficient production of commercial recordings and toward achieving the artistic vision of the *producer* of the recording session and not of the recording *artist*. This was not a new system, and in fact it marks most recording sessions made by country and western performers recording in New York, Nashville, Los Angeles, Cincinnati, and other centers of major label country music production from the 1950s to the present (Jensen 1998; Malone 2002a; Peterson 1997).

Country and western record producers like Steve Shoals, Don Law, and Cowboy Jack Clement emphasized to New England country and western recording artists (Eddy Zack, Dick Curless, Jerry and Sky, and others) the practical elements of allowing production teams to take over the musical (arrangements and repertoire) aspects of making country music recordings. The careers of Nashville-based vocalists like Roy Acuff and Eddy Arnold had created a blueprint for success that granted the singer—not the band—primacy in the star system (Jensen 1998; Malone 2002a; Peterson 1997). Records were created by producers around vocalists, a decidedly different tack from the late 1920s and early 1930s, when performers like Mellie Dunham and Hank Keene utilized their own bands and their own repertoires to make major label recordings and were just as likely to feature instrumental numbers (or long instrumental passages) as they were vocal numbers. By the time Eddy Zack and His Dude Ranchers or Lone Pine and Betty Cody were picked up by Decca and RCA Victor in the early 1950s, the system used by large record companies like Decca and Columbia was to ask instrumentalists to stay home while singers traveled to their New York studios to record with session musicians. Dick Curless was no exception to this rule, and his producers asked him not to play guitar on his own records. In light of Curless's catalog as a whole, his most successful and compelling recordings incorporate his signature and unorthodox guitar style, an up-strumming technique down along the bridge of the guitar that Curless mistakenly thought was how guitarist Josh White played. On the Event sessions from 1956, as well as in sessions recorded independently in the 1970s through the 1990s, Curless's guitar acts as the hub for the rhythmic propulsion of the group as a whole, accentuating the backbeat on the bass strings of the acoustic guitar and played percussively down by the bridge.

On the heels of the success of "A Tombstone Every Mile," Dick Curless was invited to join the Buck Owens All-Stars—a touring revue featuring Owens and Merle Haggard—on a cross-country tour. Curless worked with Owens's show for three years, during which time he also recorded in Los Angeles under the production guidance of Owens. The sonic quality of these records is similar to that of Merle Haggard's recordings from the late 1960s like "Mama Tried," yet Curless's vocal delivery often sounds disembodied from the rest of the tightly arranged recording. Owens's high-profile assistance should have enabled Curless to develop significant momentum as a national country music performer, but instead their relationship fractured over jealousy—a problem aggravated by intense binge drinking on Curless's part and a clash of egos on the road. By all accounts, Curless was not always demure like a newcomer is expected to be, and the wild response he generated when opening for Buck Owens fueled a confident swagger that made the normally friendly Owens both angry and jealous. Though the experience of touring with the Buck Owens All-Stars produced one of Curless's fondest musical memories—sitting up all night with Bonnie Owens and Merle Haggard in an Alaskan motel room swapping Lefty Frizzell and Jimmie Rodgers songs—most of this three-year period was characterized by deep depression, pill addiction, and alcoholic blackouts. Curless was hospitalized on tour multiple times in 1968 because of stomach ulcers, and—by his account—he quit the Owens show after he "hit bottom" in a hospital in Georgia (Cohen 1977).

One noteworthy Curless recording from the late 1960s and early 1970s is "Memories, an Old Picture, and a Ring" (1966), a song about a soldier in Vietnam who longs for his new wife at home and to see a son he has never met. The song poignantly chronicles Curless's experiences as a new husband and father in Korea and adapts them to fit the contemporary audience grappling with the Vietnam War. Other New England artists were also beginning to address contemporary issues of the Vietnam era, particularly Wendell Austin. Austin was raised in Maine's Haynesville Woods but by the late 1960s was living in Connecticut doing work for the defense industry. Wendell Austin and the Country Swings recorded a series of singles—"Talk of the Town," "LSD," and "The Battle of Vietnam"—indicative of the times, addressing the stresses of the sexual revolution, psychedelic drugs, and Cold War conflict. Where Curless's Vietnam song makes separation from a loved one the centerpiece of the emotional content, the political theme of the expansion of democracy into Asia marks Austin's "The Battle of Vietnam" (1967).

Wendell Austin and the Country Swings' recordings for Wreck Records in Connecticut between 1966 and 1969 are emblematic of the quirky recordings released independently by New England country and western musicians in the 1960s and 1970s. Rhyme schemes, numbers of measures, and tempos could vary unpredictably in the manner of early hillbilly recordings by Jimmie Rodgers or in the elastic manner of the early commercial releases of bluesmen like Muddy Waters. What is clear in the recordings of regional, independent New England country and western musicians in the late 1960s like Wendell Austin and Johnny "The Yodelin' Yankee" White is that the singer and his or her acoustic guitar anchored the song's rhythmic and melodic structure in much the same way as the early recordings of Jimmie Rodgers or Muddy Waters, where the accompanying musicians took their musical cues from listening intently to the singer and his or her guitar for chord changes. In the case of Johnny White (born Jean LeBlanc, son of Nova Scotian immigrants in East Boston, Massachusetts), his first 45 rpm record—"Rose in the Garden"/"Cryin' Roses" (1966)—features a lead vocal audibly influenced by Yodelin' Slim Clark and Hank Snow. White's lilting vocal is laced with falsetto voice breaks that hint at his virtuosic Wilf Carter–style yodel and entrench the song firmly into a New England / Down East country and western tradition, while the loping rhythm of the electric guitar and drums played by the LeBlanc brothers (his backing band) is highly individualistic.

The Intersection of New England Country and Western and Country-Rock

As can be heard in the electrification of Johnny White's music and in the Byrds-influenced folk-rock backing vocals on several of Wendell Austin's recordings from the late 1960s, the emergence of independently produced New England country and western music coincides with another important event in New England country and western history: the rise of country rock from the counterculture and the emergence of John Lincoln Wright, New England country and western music's most prominent regional recording artist since Dick Curless.

> Too Old to Die Young Now
> Words and Music by John Lincoln Wright, Glen Shambroom
>
> In 1965, they said I'd never get out alive
> That I'd burn myself right out before my time
> Then the years went by so fast, I still ain't run out of gas
> But I'm too old to die young now

Born in Cambridge, Massachusetts, in 1947, singer John Lincoln Wright was the son of a truck dispatcher whose job moved the family back and forth between Cambridge and the small mill town of Sanford, Maine. A prolific country and western songwriter until his death in 2011, Wright was New England's most significant country and western performer since he founded his band, the Sour Mash Boys, in 1973 (later known as the Sour Mash Revue when Kathy Burkley became the group's drummer). But Wright's career as a professional singer predates that of his country and western career, going back to 1965, the year the British rock band the Who released their signature song "My Generation," featuring the anthemic line "I hope I die before I get old." The self-destructive theme of John Lincoln Wright's "Too Old to Die Young Now" identifies his musical origins squarely with the rock generation.

"Too Old to Die Young Now" also contains a direct reference to the song "Five to One" by the psychedelic blues-rock band the Doors, which contains the line, "Five to one, one in five, no one here gets out alive." The lyrics of Doors' lead singer Jim Morrison often focused on morbid and vaguely apocalyptic themes. Morrison died at age twenty-seven in 1971, allegedly from a heroin overdose, and his untimely death made him—along with Janis Joplin and Jimi Hendrix—a romantic icon of many musicians of John Lincoln Wright's generation. *No One Here Gets Out Alive* would become the title of a highly sensationalized (and best-selling) biography of Jim Morrison published in 1980.

Wright's autobiographical association with the Who and the Doors' Jim Morrison is important here, as Wright's origins as a stage performer began in 1965 at Boston College as the lead singer of a psychedelic blues-rock band cast in the mold of the Who and the Doors named the Beacon Street Union. The first in his family to attend college, Wright dropped out after one year. The Beacon Street Union was one of several Boston rock bands signed in 1967 by MGM Records, which sought to promote what they called the "Bosstown sound." Wright's group rubbed shoulders with some of the biggest names in rock of the 1960s, opening for Jimi Hendrix and Janis Joplin in 1968 and loading the Beatles' amplifiers for a 1966 concert at the Suffolk Downs racetrack in Revere, Massachusetts. Wright had gained access to the roadie gig for the Beatles by way of his friendship with singer Barry Tashian, whose Boston-based group the Remains toured as the opening act for the Beatles on their final tour as a live band (including the aforementioned Suffolk Downs show and the Beatles' famous concert at Shea Stadium). A native of Westport, Connecticut, Barry Tashian was a former student at Boston College who helped anchor the rock music scene in Boston. While living in Cambridge, Massachusetts, Tashian became a mentor to John Lincoln Wright and singer Peter Wolf of the J. Geils Band. While rooming in an apartment in Cambridge with Peter Wolf in 1966, Tashian introduced Wolf to a Harvard student named Gram Parsons.

Gram Parsons arrived in Cambridge from his native Florida for his first semester at Harvard University in 1966 saddled by family problems. His father had committed suicide when Gram was in high school, and his mother had died from alcohol poisoning the night of Gram's high school graduation. He was a dedicated fan of the Beatles and the Byrds and wanted to find stardom as a folk-rock musician. Within weeks of arriving in the Boston area, Parsons had ingratiated himself with several white rhythm and blues, rock, and folk-rock groups active in Boston and Cambridge, including the Remains and Peter Wolf's groups (the Hallucinations and the J. Geils Band). After one semester at Harvard, Parsons dropped out to form a folk-rock band with John Nuese called Gram Parsons and the Nice. A fellow Harvard student, Nuese had introduced Gram to the music of country and western artists like Merle Haggard and Buck Owens, and the group's repertoire gradually came to include more and more songs like those of Haggard and Owens.

Of the bands in question—the Remains, the Beacon Street Union, Gram Parsons and the Nice, and the J. Geils Band—only Peter Wolf's group (the J. Geils Band) achieved widespread and long-standing commercial success. As a marketing strategy, the Bosstown sound—which also included Earth Opera (featuring Peter Rowan and David Grisman)—never gained national commercial momentum. By the close of the 1960s the Beacon Street Union, Gram Parsons and the Nice, and Barry and the Remains had disbanded. Following the breakup of the Remains and the Nice, Barry Tashian was instrumental in the somewhat concurrent formation of Gram Parsons's next two bands, the International Submarine Band and the Flying Burrito Brothers, both widely considered the "first" country-rock groups and the inspiration for the alternative country movement of the 1990s. After recording one album with the International Submarine Band, *Safe at Home* (1967), Parsons was invited to join the Byrds for their *Sweetheart of the Rodeo* LP (1968), on which his signature song, "Hickory Wind," appears. Parsons is credited with transforming the Byrds into a country-rock group along with former Kentucky Colonels guitarist Clarence White (born Clarence LeBlanc in Madawaska, Maine, in 1954), who also joined the Byrds on the *Sweetheart of the Rodeo* sessions.

Gram Parsons left the Byrds after less than one year and turned his energies toward the Flying Burrito Brothers. Barry Tashian was an early member of this group (although he never recorded with them), and he recorded with Emmylou Harris on Gram Parsons's first solo recording ("GP") in 1973. By 1973 both Barry Tashian and John Lincoln Wright had become firmly entrenched in making neotraditional country and western music. Tashian formed a group called the Outskirts with his wife, Holly, which disbanded in 1980 when Barry was invited by Emmylou Harris to join her Hot Band after the departure of Ricky Skaggs. Tashian toured with Emmylou Harris until 1989, playing guitar and singing harmony vocals on ten of her albums. (In a rather strange twist documented in *The Gibson Guitar Book*, Emmylou Harris's signature black Gibson acoustic guitar with the red rose on it, which is the subject of a photo essay in Cecelia Tichi's book *High Lonesome*, originally belonged to Hal Lone Pine.) Following the breakup of the Beacon Street Union in 1968 and a short-lived spinoff group called the Eagle in 1970, John Lincoln Wright formed his own group in Boston, named the

Sour Mash Boys, in 1973, lending an electrified rock edge and swagger to a sound that was otherwise rooted firmly in the swinging honky-tonk music of Merle Haggard, Buck Owens, Bob Wills, and Dick Curless. The Sour Mash Boys included Dick Curless's son, Rick Curless, on drums for a time and notched what are likely the last singles by a New England country and western group to achieve "hit" status on local radio in the greater Boston area with the songs "Takin' Old Route One" (1977), "Living in Lowell (or It's So Lonely In Braintree with You In Metheun; It's Almost Like Living in Lowell)" (1977) sung by the band's bassist, Larry Flint, and "They Tore Down the Hillbilly Ranch" (1981), an ode to the newly demolished Combat Zone club launched by the Lane Brothers in the 1950s.

A new country and western scene began to form around John Lincoln Wright and the Sour Mash Boys in the mid-1970s. Boston became a destination point for new country and western groups of the same rock generation as Wright, including Chuck McDermott and Wheatstraw, the Estes Boys, and Tina Welch. This scene was bolstered by the arrival of Arkansas country and rockabilly singer Sleepy LaBeef. While touring through New England in 1977, LaBeef found a welcome audience at Trader Alan's 5th Wheel Truck Stop in Amesbury, Massachusetts, a performance venue and truck stop frequently played by Dick Curless. When LaBeef's tour bus broke down and caught fire on the Maine Turnpike, he made Trader Alan's his permanent home and developed a substantial following in New England, becoming the subject of a chapter of Peter Guralnick's *Lost Highway: Journeys and Arrivals of American Musicians* (1999) and signing with Rounder Records, based in Cambridge, in 1981.

The rock and roll orientation of New England country and western groups that formed in the 1970s was decidedly different from previous generations with regard to performance and function. Whereas generations of musicians before rock made a commitment—ideologically and rhetorically, if not always in practice—to playing "what the people want" and tailoring their repertoires to a wide range of popular and traditional styles, groups from the rock generation made a firm commitment to artistic vision and commerce, maintaining a firm grip on repertoire and favoring original material over the songs of others. Likewise, the function of the live musical event also changed, with couples dancing falling off considerably from previous generations. In addition, musicians like John Lincoln Wright who were deeply affected by the work of Jack Kerouac envisioned themselves as romantic artistic figures defined entirely by their musical role. By the time the Beach Boys released their *Pet Sounds* LP in 1966, followed by the release of the Beatles' *Sgt. Pepper's Lonely Hearts Club Band* LP in 1967, the guiding creative forces in rock music provided an artistic and professional example that art drove music commerce, to the degree that the Beatles and the Beach Boys' Brian Wilson no longer had to perform concerts in order to make a living through music. Unlike country and western musicians from previous generations, performers from the rock era like John Lincoln Wright viewed music as an all-or-nothing endeavor, opting to eat and pay rent (or not eat and not pay rent, as the case often was) solely through professional, artistic musical means. Working in the flooring department of Jordan Marsh, as local Boston star Frank "Slim" Rego had done some thirty years earlier to supplement his music income, was not considered a respectable option among the newer generation of musicians.

Such a philosophical transition or transformation could not have been more poorly timed. The rise of FM radio formats in the 1970s was accompanied by sweeping changes in musical programming. Though this occurrence is detailed elsewhere in this book, by the 1970s the music played on the radio throughout New England (and the rest of the nation) originated almost entirely from national and international markets. Some AM stations still allotted a small amount of broadcast time to local acts, but by and large the disappearance of local music from local and regional airwaves (radio and television) marked the end of country and western music as a viable profession for New England–based groups. Those groups like John Lincoln Wright and the Sour Mash Boys that managed to eke out a living into the 1980s (and perhaps even into the very early 1990s) were either truly exceptional (like Wright's group), had gotten their start in an earlier decade (like Dick Curless, Betty Cody, and Kenny Roberts), or survived by performing under multiple musical identities, including folk musician, rock musician, wedding band musician, and country musician (like Betty Cody's son, Denny Breau).

Ironically, this broadcasting shift away from local and regional coincided with a veritable explosion of small, independent record labels and releases. The age in which self-producing one's own commercial recordings became significantly easier was also the age in which getting those recordings into the hands of radio programmers became next to impossible. The confluence of these events brought about two divergent streams of country and western music in New England: those from the "rock" generation who aspired to an artistic countercultural philosophy, and a second stream of musicians who eschewed the counterculture and oriented their music, accents, and stage personas toward achieving acceptance in Nashville. The counterculture associated themselves with the developing "outlaw" movement (particularly with ex–rock and roller Waylon Jennings and the rock sounds of Hank Williams Jr.), and their performances tended to be located in rock-style clubs or heavy drinking establishments like the Hillbilly Ranch, although their music tended toward a more "traditionalist" country and western *sound* akin to Dick Curless or Merle Haggard. Their newfound ability to self-produce recordings, coupled with their embrace of a countercultural philosophy, witnessed a rise in local and regional content and references in their version of country and western music, in which performers set themselves apart from Nashville country groups by drawing attention to their newfound status as industrial outsiders. The Nashville-oriented musicians adopted a musical style reflective of what was played on Nashville-oriented country radio, with string-laden balladeers and self-styled "southern" outlaws alike. But while the Nashville crowd was not above playing rock-styled country now in vogue on country radio, they performed it largely for multigenerational family audiences at county fairs, fundraisers, and community halls.

Epilogue: *Stacey's Country Jamboree* and the Rise of the Local Country and Western Organization

In the early 1970s, WEMT-TV in Bangor, Maine, sold an hour of television time to a local general store / gas station named Frankenstein's. The store used the hour-long slot to host a live country and western broadcast called *Frankenstein's Country Jamboree* and to advertise its gasoline. Country and western musicians were welcome to stop in unannounced, and each was allotted a performance slot regardless of talent or, as was often the case, sobriety. The freewheeling show—which was as likely to feature a top-notch veteran like Bob Elston as it was a drunken crew of college students from the University of Maine, an eighty-year-old grandmother, or a nervous group of musicians from St. John, New Brunswick, who had driven down from Canada for a big break on American television—was spectacularly erratic in quality and talent, and Mainers and Canadians watched the show with a mixture of self-conscious embarrassment, rubbernecking anticipation, and genuine love of country and western music in the raw. Though the quality of the show is subject to debate even today among country and western musicians and fans in Maine, it remains a touchstone of Maine culture.

By the late 1970s Frankenstein's show had been renamed *Stacey's Country Jamboree* when it was purchased by Bangor entrepreneur Dick Stacey. Stacey installed a small gallery from which an audience could watch the show, and the viewing audience expanded deeper into Maritime Canada when Stacey moved the show onto local cable access. But despite these changes, Stacey maintained the informal nature of the program, welcoming all performers who showed up to play live on television. However, by the 1980s it had become too expensive for Dick Stacey to purchase airtime, and *Stacey's Country Jamboree* went off the air. In 2001 Dick Stacey organized former *Jamboree* regulars for a short tour of Nova Scotia. The old regulars played to sold-out theaters in Canada, and a DVD of highlights from the show was released in 2005. The show became a symbol within Nova Scotia of common, down-home values shared between Maritime Canadians and New Englanders. In a debate in the Nova Scotia parliament in 2001, *Stacey's Country Jamboree* was mentioned as representative of northern New England's interest in self-rule—which is to say that Nova Scotians perceived persons from New Hampshire and Maine as kindred souls who were averse to urban sophisticates from wealthy, powerful states and provinces coming in to run local and regional businesses.

By the mid-1970s Maine had secured its place as the heart of New England's country and western culture. A series of country music organizations grew up across New England as a means of counteracting the loss of access to local radio. Most notable is Gordon "Country Gordy" Brown's founding of the New England Country Music Historical Society (NECMHS) and its ongoing crusade to create a freestanding museum to house the New England Country Music Hall of Fame and Archives. To this date, New England country and western events are almost entirely driven by local country and western organizations like NECMHS. The social capital generated by these organizations sustains a music culture that has been denied access to the mass media outlets that once allowed it to flourish. Maine, in particular, has produced a plethora of country and western organizations since the mid-1970s, including the Downeast Country Music Association, the Maine Country Music Hall of Fame, the Maine Academy of Country Music, and the Pine Tree Country Music Association. These organizations—as well as similar organizations throughout New England—seek to promote local and regional practitioners of country and western music and to preserve the history of the music in this region. Thanks in part to these grass-roots organizations, awareness of New England country and western music's rich heritage persists. And despite the disappearance of local music making from New England broadcast media, New England country and western events still go on today in Grange halls, churches, high school gymnasiums, American Legion halls, and other community centers from Maine to Rhode Island.

Figure 1. Postcard of Mellie Dunham in front of his home in Norway, Maine, in 1926. (Courtesy of the University of Maine Folklife Center, P 0760.)

Figure 2. *"Mellie" Dunham's 50 Fiddlin' Dance Tunes, Composed, Selected, and Played by "Mellie" Dunham (Maine's Champion Fiddler)*. 1926.

Figure 3. *Hank Keene's Number Four Book of Original Mountain, Cowboy, Hill-Billy and Folk Songs with Guitar Chords.* 1935.

Figure 4. Uncle Lem and the Mountain Boys, with Johnny Smith on guitar (*front right*). 1940. (Photo courtesy of Patty Kempton, wife of Rusty Rogers.)

Figure 5. Reid Hand and group, Auto Rest Park, Carmel, Maine, circa 1930s or 1940s. Note the varied instrumentation of the group (including brass, vocal trio, drums, and strings), Hand's attire (which hints at Yankee minstrelsy), and the mixed attire of the audience (frontier outfits and formal clothes). Hand's performances at Auto Rest Park were broadcast on WABI radio via telephone. (Courtesy of the University of Maine Folklife Center, P 0583.)

Figure 6. Russell Kempton, aka Rusty Rogers, at age nineteen as a member of Bud Bailey's Downeasters, 1942. (Photo courtesy of Patty Kempton, wife of Rusty Rogers.)

Figure 7. Fiddlin' Harold Carter of Bud Bailey's Downeasters. 1941. Inscription reads, "To a Swell Yodeler Rusty. Thanks for appearing at Rainbow Ranch. From yours truly, Trick Fiddlin Harold." Note Carter's long hair and sideburns—Carter would sometimes cross-dress and walk in public holding hands with Rusty in order to start fights. (Photo courtesy of Patty Kempton, wife of Rusty Rogers.)

Figure 8. Sheet music for "My Soldier Boy Is Coming Home, as Introduced and Sung by Bud Bailey & His Downeasters." Note Rusty Rogers in the upper right and song's author, Vinny "Jimmy Cal" Calderone, at the lower right. 1941. Though the group traveled as far as Missouri, the Downeasters were based in Portland, Maine, and Portsmouth, New Hampshire. (Photo courtesy of Patty Kempton, wife of Rusty Rogers.)

Figure 9. WBZ radio (Boston) promotional photo of Georgia Mae donating half a ton of her fan mail (100,000 letters) to the Waste Paper Conservation Program during World War II. 1942. (Photo courtesy of Georgia Mae Harp.)

Figure 10. Jerry and Sky promo picture, circa 1944. Jerry Howarth (*left*) and Schuyler Snow (*right*) comprised the most prominent country and western group to come out of New Hampshire. Their popularity and repertoire marked a shift from western cowboy music to southern mountain music.

Figure 11. The Down Homers when Bill Haley was in the group (shortly after Kenny Roberts left and shortly before Rusty Rogers took his place). At this time, the group was based in Keene, New Hampshire. 1945. (Photo courtesy of Patty Kempton, wife of Rusty Rogers.)

Figure 12. Yodelin' Slim Clark on WHOB in Gardner, Massachusetts, circa 1946. (Photo courtesy of Jewel Clark.)

Figure 13. Eddie Zack and His Dude Ranchers, circa 1947. *Left to right, back row*: Tony Poccia, Jackie Menna, Maril and Babs Zack, Harold Allen; *front row*: Eddie Zack, Richie Zack. (Photo courtesy of Babs White.)

Figure 14. The Down Homers with Rusty Rogers (*squatting*). 1948. (Photo courtesy of Patty Kempton, wife of Rusty Rogers.)

Figure 15. Yodelin' Slim Clark performs with the Trail Riders at the Ford Farming Show in Athol, Massachusetts, circa 1948. A teenage Dick "The Tumbleweed Kid" Curless is third from the left. (Photo courtesy of Jewel Clark.)

Figure 16. The Cumberland Ridge Runners, Allerton and Alton, circa 1949. Allerton "Al" Hawkes and Alton Meyers of Westbrook and Portland, Maine, comprised the first known interracial country and western group in history. Hawkes went on to found Event Records and recorded Dick Curless and the Lilly Brothers, among others.

Figure 17. The Trail Riders onstage at the Bangor Drive-In in Bangor, Maine, on a Sunday in July 1950. Note the screen behind the musicians and how high the "stage" (platform) is off the ground. It was typical for fans to honk their horns between songs instead of clapping. *Back row, left to right*: Pete Petri, Dick Curless, Don Calvi, Doug Rich, Jim and Babe Sherwood; *front row, left to right*: The Fiddlin' Sisters and Little Brenda.

AUTO-REST-PARK
SHOW and DANCE TONITE
R. F. D. JAMBOREE
Starring Jimmie and Willie, with a Host of Fun Makers
NEW ENGLAND'S LARGEST JAMBOREE!
Extra Added Attraction — "THE TRAIL RIDERS"
Show and Broadcast, 8:30 to 9:30—Dancing 9:30 'til 12
Adm.: Adults 65c, Tax Inc. — Children 35c, Tax Inc.
FREE SUNDAY PROGRAM
• TWO WESTERN SHOWS — 3 to 4 P. M. and 6 to 7:30
Featuring Curley Glidden and The Haymakers
• BIG AMATEUR NITE
• FREE — MOVIES — FREE — 9:00 to 11:00
ROLLER SKATING Sunday Afternoon and Evening

Figure 18. Newspaper ad for the R.F.D. Jamboree at Auto Rest Park, featuring the Trail Riders, circa 1950. The ad demonstrates how New England country and western events were formally structured as a show and a dance. The content of the show was dictated by the musicians and consisted of ballads, novelty songs, folk songs, and skits. Dances were based on requests and heavily favored instrumentals. Musicians tended to be paid for the show and played the dance for free. In this case, the show was broadcast via radio, but the dance was not. The Sunday event at Auto Rest Park includes Amateur Night, an important stepping stone for aspiring professional musicians.

Figure 19. The Trail Riders perform on the R.F.D. Jamboree at Auto Rest Park, Carmel, Maine. July 1950. Curless (*second from right*) notes on the back of the photo: "Just like WWVA. Pete Petri (half Indian) at the mike." Native Americans played a visible role in the development of country and western music around Bangor, Maine. (Photo courtesy of Terry Chinnock.)

Figure 20. Hawkshaw Hawkins and the West Virginia Night Hawks (featuring the Kentucky Twins) at Auto Rest Park, Carmel, Maine. October 1950. Hawkshaw Hawkins was the most prominent member of the *Wheeling Jamboree* and the *Grand Ole Opry* to regularly tour through New England because of his close professional relationships with Hal Lone Pine and Betty Cody. He recruited New England performers to move to Wheeling and Nashville until his death in 1963 in the same plane crash that claimed the lives of Patsy Cline, Cowboy Copas, and Randy Hughes. *Left to right*: Billy Grammer, Mel Hankinson, Hawkshaw Hawkins, Stan Hankinson, Sammy Barnhart. (Photo courtesy of Terry Chinnock.)

Figure 21. Rusty Rogers and Shorty Cook of the Down Homers in casual dress stand in front of their limousine. At the time, the group was broadcasting daily on WTIC in Hartford, Connecticut. 1952. (Photo courtesy of Patty Kempton, wife of Rusty Rogers.)

Figure 22. Betty Cody and Hal "Lone Pine" Breau, May 4, 1954, during the RCA Victor Country & Western Caravan tour, location unknown. The tour included Hank Snow, Minnie Pearl, Chet Atkins, Hawkshaw Hawkins, Charline Arthur, and Skeeter and Georgie Davis. (Photograph by Bob Sandberg, *LOOK Magazine* Photograph Collection, Library of Congress, Prints & Photographs Division [reproduction number LC-L9-54-3081-L, figure 1].)

Figure 23. Promotional photo of a young Dick Curless before he began wearing his signature eye patch, circa 1957.

Figure 24. Eddie Zack and His Dude Ranchers on the set of their *Rhody Hoedown Show* at WJAR-TV studio in Providence, Rhode Island, circa 1960. *Left to right*: Richie Zack, Maril Zack Albro, Bill Zompa (on drums, behind Maril), Eddie Zack, Babs Zack White, Jack Thompson, and Tony Poccia. (Photo courtesy of Babs White.)

Figure 25. Hal Lone Pine, *Coast of Maine* LP (ARC-600), circa 1960.

Figure 26. Dick Curless promotional photo for Capitol Records, circa 1970. (Photo courtesy of Terry Chinnock.)

Figure 27. Dick Curless in full traditional garb of Maine woods workers and river drivers outside of Bangor, Maine. 1972. (Photo by Orlando Frati, courtesy of Terry Chinnock.)

Figure 28. John Lincoln Wright and the Sourmash Boys, *Takin' Old Route One* LP (Esca-Er1300), 1977.

Figure 29. Circle C Ranch Boys (*left to right*: Angelo Boncore, aka Al Blake, Joseph Calderone, aka Joey Cal, and Vincent Calderone, aka Jimmy Cal), Everett, Massachusetts, 2005. (Photo by the author.)

Figure 30. Jewel Clark performs while wearing her father's shirt (Yodelin' Slim Clark) on the Maine Country Music stage at the American Folk Festival in Bangor, Maine. 2006. (Photo by the author.)

3

FINDING COMMUNITY IN THE NEW ENGLAND COUNTRY AND WESTERN EVENT

That night, the couples twirled past the folding tables along the edge of the brightly buffed dance floor; smiling and pressed against one another, they each looked over at my wife and me as we sat and watched.

"It's so nice to see young people here."

We nodded and smiled and turned our attention back to the band. But the white-haired couples continued to twirl by us in their matching western outfits like we were in some kind of choreographed receiving line.

"Why don't you young people get up and dance?"

My wife, Monica, and I laughed and protested. I explained that while Monica could certainly cut a rug, dancing wasn't one of my talents. But the question kept on coming.

"Don't you young people dance?"

This had not been in the plan for that evening. This was my first night out as a budding ethnographer, and I had committed myself to making a low-key entrance at the Legion.

A few days before, I had come across a 1953 Columbia 78 rpm record of Eddie Zack and His Dude Ranchers' "You Knew Me When You Were Lonely / Little Donkey (La Burrita)" at a dusty record store in Allston, Massachusetts, and learned they were still playing every Saturday night—under the name the Hayloft Jamboree—at the Legion Post 15 in East Greenwich, Rhode Island. I tracked down singer/guitarist Richie Zack's phone number and called him up. (Richie was Eddie's brother and historically the lead singer of the band.) Richie told me that after sixty years in the business he was sick of talking about the band but that I could feel free to call his sister (and fellow band member), Babs.

Where Richie was dismissive and openly jaded about a life in country and western music, Babs was sprightly and proud. She welcomed me down to the show, encouraged me to bring my wife along, and instructed me to introduce myself at the door when I arrived.

We drove down from Cambridge, Massachusetts, that night and pulled into the nearly pitch-black parking lot of the Legion Post 15 along the sprawling side of U.S. Route 1 in East Greenwich, Rhode Island. A friendly man with a sandy-brown toupee looked up over his glasses, beyond his cashbox, over his red rolls of "Admit One" tickets, and asked: "Are you the gentleman from Brown University . . . and his wife?"

So much for a low-key entrance. And so much for country and western credibility. I blanched. What could be less country and western than a tweedy title like "the gentleman from Brown University . . . and his wife"? Monica and I slouched into the fluorescent-lit function hall and scanned the room.

So here we sat, placed prominently at the "band" table right up front where everyone could see us. We hadn't even been charged the cover, and Babs White had refused payment for a stack of CDs she'd given us. And not only were we sitting with the band's inner circle of friends and boosters, but a cake sat at our table, too. Unbeknownst to us, it was singer/guitarist Maril Albro's seventy-eighth birthday, and we hadn't even brought her a gift.

And the couples kept twirling by, asking over and over, "Why don't you dance?"

Finally, in desperation I laughed and said, "We only know how to polka."

Minutes later, a honky-tonk song came to a reverb-drenched halt. Babs White, a petite septuagenarian with jet-black hair that neatly matched her bejeweled cowboy shirt and piercing dark eyes, stepped to the microphone to introduce the next number.

"This next song is for the gentleman from Brown University and his wife. They only know how to polka."

With that, the Hayloft Jamboree kicked into "Beer Barrel Polka." The crowd of some one hundred people clapped in unison and waited for us to take our place on the empty dance floor. It was a good thing I hadn't told a lie when I said we could polka.

"Roll out the barrel. We'll have a barrel of fun . . ."

A barrel of fun, indeed; the crowd of some one hundred people cheered when they saw they had rousted us out. We took a few laughing spins around the dance floor to the glee of the crowd, and the couples filled in around us (Murphy 2004a).

Upon sitting down, our self-consciousness lingered, yet the resulting goodwill of our active participation was more than either one of us could have anticipated. After all, we were outsiders to this community dance, and that was acknowledged in—or was the message behind—the collective "outing" of us onto the dance floor. It was also a mostly successful attempt by the band and the audience to forcibly disperse our feelings of social discomfort or awkwardness by making our unusual presence there the focal point of the moment—an act made manifest in our solo turn on the dance floor before being joined by the rest of the couples. The audience and the band worked in concert to make us participants, and not at all on our terms either: we had hoped to be allowed to attend in order to watch, without being noticed, without participating, and without disrupting the normal events. And it was a message to us that attending this kind of event and not participating was not acceptable behavior. (Our wearing of pearl-snap western shirts and our rapt attention had been deemed insufficient to constitute "participation.") Based on my observations of this event and numerous others like it since, such unsociable behavior is highly abnormal at a New England country and western event. One does not go to a New England country and western event just to watch or listen to the band, one goes to socialize to (and with) music, to interact with (and even make demands of) the audience, musicians, and music alike. Attendees may not always dance, but they nearly always socialize with other patrons, or they sell food, drinks, tickets, or CDs. To do otherwise is to create a source of tension—tension alleviated in this instance by the good-natured forcing of our participation. Having had their fun with us, many members of the audience approached us and asked where we were from, and they volunteered their thoughts, feelings, and reminiscences of or about the Hayloft Jamboree. I was overwhelmed by the gratitude expressed to me by audience members who were glad to find that someone from outside the community had finally deemed the Hayloft Jamboree worthy of serious inquiry.

Performance Frontier: Individual Expression versus Community Expression

Since my first night out as a working ethnographer, I have come to find what many before me have learned—that the first foray into the field can often be the most revealing. When Monica and I stepped into the light at the Legion Post 15, we witnessed nearly the full spectrum of expression between the self and the community inherent in the New England country and western community hall performance. Ostensibly, a performing group with microphones, amplifiers, and a PA system occupies the primary position of power in a room full of people, and yet the Hayloft Jamboree spent the evening using those tools of power to build an inclusive relationship with the audience by balancing the songs the band wanted to play with the songs the audience wanted to hear. In the process, nonparticipants like Monica and me were induced to dance and were drawn into full participation with the rest of the community.

The act of performers drawing audiences into participation of one form or another (not just dancing but also watching, listening, thinking, singing, and clapping) is not unique to country and western events, and yet the country and western ideal of performer-audience reciprocity has few counterparts with regard to mainly white American popular musics. For example, practitioners of rock music since the middle 1960s and punk music since the 1970s will likely note that the establishment of the parameters of any given rock or punk band's repertoire is hardly a democratic arrangement between the bands and their audiences. Significant American popular musics that evolved since the beginning of the rock era—such as rock, folk-rock, singer-songwriter, punk, country-rock, heavy metal, and alternative rock—have evolved from a model whereby performing groups maintain control over their own repertoire in order to deliver or develop a vaguely defined philosophical or political message (which the commercial industry has co-opted in the form of groups delivering a "brand" formed around their own content), and audiences turn out specifically to see such a delivery (Frith 1984; Garofalo 1987; Shank 1994). Allowing the audience to dictate repertoire on their own terms in the manner of the ideals of country and western events is a far cry from the ideals of artistic and philosophical autonomy that have been the hallmark of rock since at least the 1967 release of the Beatles' *Sgt. Pepper's Lonely Hearts Club Band* and of punk since its first rumblings in the 1970s. Despite the close association of rock and punk with idealistic democratic, socialistic, and anarchistic movements in both scholarly and popular publications, the manner in which the live performative event takes place—that is, with the band dictating the entirety of the repertoire to the audience and fielding requests only for their "own" material—is tightly controlled by the performers and hardly democratic, socialistic, or anarchistic.

Again, many groups will cater to varying degrees to the audience in any given environment, but an important difference here is the *ideal* of the performers themselves. While any rock band playing on the barroom circuit will make concessions to the audience at some point and play audience requests, they will often chafe at these outside demands for input on their repertoire. Indeed, this has been my own experience as a former full-time professional rock and alternative country musician. It is also a sentiment

I have heard echoed in the experiences of most other rock, punk, heavy metal, and singer-songwriter musicians I have known. In what was a typical journey for rock bands coming of age in the late 1980s and 1990s, my own group started out playing many covers when we were teenagers and subsequently spent several years honing our repertoire toward an entirely "original" (self-written) one and purging all covers from our sets. Only after establishing ourselves as an original band did we reintroduce cover songs, presented as artistic statements rather than as audience "requests." When I was a teenager, playing a cover of Van Morrison's "Brown Eyed Girl" at a high school dance was fun; when I became a professional rock musician performing in clubs, it was redundant and even detrimental to my artistic integrity. For the New England country and western performer, however, catering to the audience and seeking a balance between what the audience wants and what the performers want to play is central to the rhetorical foundation of the music.

This should not be misconstrued to mean that those in attendance at a New England country and western event want or expect the band to play only what the audience asks for. While audience members certainly place a high value on any performers' willingness to play their requests and to play a broad sweep of familiar songs, they are also in attendance for a show of individualism and innovation on the part of the performers. As such, the audience expects the band *not* to cater to their needs at various points. In other words, country and western groups are not there simply to put on a dance and play whatever the audience wants, whenever they want it, in the manner of a hired wedding band. Rather, the audience and the performers agree on a parameter of duality—a show and a dance—and the performance evolves accordingly in an act of band-audience reciprocity.

Country and western musicians regularly navigate this frontier between self-expression and community expression, and such navigation is a defining characteristic of the folk medium of country and western music. In New England, this frontier occupies a space between a show and a dance—what I refer to in this work as the country and western event, and which is a defining characteristic that distinguishes New England country and western from other regional variations of country and western music. At the country and western event, the performing group and the audience participate in negotiations between what the band wants to play and what the audience wants to hear (or, more accurately, what the audience wants the band to play). For the first thirty years of New England country and western—really until the mid-1960s—this was a formal distinction. Today, the line between the show and the dance is thoroughly blurred, though some vestiges of the old formal style hang on in places like the Canadian-American Club of Watertown, Massachusetts.

While in some respects the country and western group "works" for the audience by playing requested songs, the audience tends to grant the performing group a certain amount of autonomy in expressing themselves as individuals. The New England country and western event, as I see it, moves the musical event beyond an experience of "music appreciation" or "musical entertainment" and into a dynamic force of community integration and expression, commerce and neighborly gift giving, and reciprocal behavior between the performers and their audience. These in turn are hallmarks of *actual* communities built on social capital.

Defining "Community"

Community exists when a group of people share a set of dynamic, complex, and often complicated relationships that involve a moral commitment whereby individuals are obligated—by kinship ties or by social networks limited or bounded by physical and political geography—to work across differences in belief, taste, and opinion (Feintuch 2001, 149). Such a definition relies upon the theory of social capital—the idea that social contact and relationships increase human productivity (Putnam 2000). During times of economic stress, social capital increases in both value and visibility. Country and western music has facilitated the arc of this process in New England, drawing multiethnic working people into a dynamic sphere of sociability for the first time and forging a new community at New England country and western events. Preexisting commonalities of faith, occupation, and socioeconomic status had been obscured by ethnic differences magnified by ethnically segregated laboring, worshiping, and learning environments. A common interest in country and western music and dancing and an important cycle of gift giving (McCann 2001) between performers and the audience enabled community members to navigate across the boundaries of *difference* in order to establish what folklorist Henry Glassie (1995) terms "neighborliness" or what musicologist Helen O'Shea has characterized as "the pursuit of sameness" (2006–7, 17). The social capital built by this community became increasingly important as the region was deindustrialized over the latter half of the twentieth century, leaving many working-class New Englanders disenfranchised (Putnam 2000; Feintuch 2006; Temin 2000). In light of this, the New England country and western event has functioned as a tool of community building and of community sustainability.

Of course, the New England country and western event is not simply a celebration of neighborliness, it is also an openly commercial operation where admission is charged and recordings, food, and refreshments are sold. As such, the New England country and western event must be understood as a realm in which participants engage in a process of reciprocity that mixes both commerce and communalism. Efficient economic transactions are dependent upon the existence of strong social capital (Fukuyama 1999), and the gathering at the Legion Post 15 is evidence of that. The social capital that drives the country and western event is reinforced by the fact that it perpetuates the economic stability of the Legion Post 15, its employees, and the Hayloft Jamboree band. The blend of commerce and gift exchange fortifies social capital and strengthens community through acts of cooperation and reciprocity between the band, the audience, and the community hall.

The New England country and western event mirrors New England working-class community values in specific ways: the event demonstrates the value of balancing individualism and communalism; an event is always held in a community hall or other public place; it relies upon a cycle of reciprocity between the performers and the audience; and it features multigenerational family dynamics. To understand how these elements combine to build and reinforce a community rich in social capital requires a closer examination of how the New England country and western event is structured.

A Show and a Dance: Defining the New England Country and Western Event

The country and western event in New England mill towns in the early twentieth century coupled live concert performance with community participation. The country and western event itself consisted of a show for a seated audience who had paid for tickets and a dance for a standing (or dancing) audience, given freely by the band for the community after the show. This was a conscious pairing of halves distinct to New England country and western music. The show consisted of songs chosen by the performers. The dance consisted of the community dance repertoire and of songs requested by audience members. During the show the band was the primary focus of the seated—or "concert"—audience. During the dance the primary focus was on the scene of social negotiation on the dance floor.

Understanding the pairing of these two halves of the country and western event in the early twentieth century is important to understanding the function of country and western music in facilitating the social experience of a diverse mass and in helping to transform a segregated, multiethnic audience into a functioning—or socially integrated—community. Country and western events were promoted via the broadcast medium of radio. The show portion of the event provided a gathering place for a diverse mass of radio listeners who would not necessarily otherwise choose to congregate in the same physical space. (I stress radio listeners here—not record listeners—because of the relative unimportance of commercial recording in New England country and western during the barnstorming era. New England artists capable of using commercial recordings as a drawing force for live performance have been few and far between over the course of music's history in the region. This remains true today.) The dance that followed served to integrate normally clannish ethnic groups through the mixing caused by traditional square and round dancing. Over the course of the twentieth century, the country and western event has seen the gradual blurring of this formal distinction between the show and dance halves. Most of the older groups today, like the Hayloft Jamboree, intermingle show songs with dance songs. I know of one group—the Country Masters in Watertown, Massachusetts—who maintain a strictly dance portion of their overall show (although some audience members dance throughout). Among younger New England country and western audiences, couples dancing has become increasingly rare, and the country and western event appears to be moving in a decidedly concert-like (or entirely show-like) direction. In a parallel development, the country dance (or contra dance) event appears to have done away with the show and now focuses entirely on the dance.

Social dancing reflects the values or structure of the community (Feintuch 2001, 2006; Glassie 1995). The kind of square and round dancing done at most New England country and western events prior to the 1960s shows that working-class New Englanders valued "visiting." It was, to borrow a line from antebellum New England historian Karen V. Hansen (1994), a very social time—not romantic, social. Social mixing of the kind induced by a New England country and western square dance helped to break down barriers within ethnically segregated communities. The fast and frequent exchange of partners reflects an aspect of the New England custom of visiting, whereby early rural New Englanders would travel to make social calls (cider tasting, tea, maple sugaring, etc.), a custom some have credited as the means by which early New England community was built (Hansen 1994). Likewise, the multiethnic makeup of the performing groups—the result of a group's need for certain instrumentation rather than an agenda of social progress—embodied another aspect of the custom of visiting, whereby many hands made for light work, making sociable occasions out of hard communal labor (barn raising, midwifery, quilting, haying, cornhusking, etc.). A common interest in playing country and western music and any group's specific needs for musicians transcended ethnic and racial barriers for New England country and western musicians in the 1920s and 1930s.

If social dancing indeed reflects the values or structure of the community, it is plausible that the structure of the dance event also reflects those same values or perhaps other facets of community. Ethnomusicologist Jennifer Post (2004) shows that the overall setting of the New England "kitchen breakdown"—its social, musical, and dance components—is a reflection of rural New England community structure and beliefs. In applying that concept to the New England country and western event and New England working-class community, we find a value placed on both individual expression (as dictated by the band and their show) and community expression (as dictated by the community dance repertoire), as well as active negotiation of the two (through requests that modify the band's repertoire or innovations in local dance material as introduced by the band).

This is a significant way in which the New England country and western event differs from a contemporary New England contra dance or an early community orchestra dance. These other New England dance events were just that: music and calling were provided for people to dance to (there was no show). This was a difference that the audience and the musicians at New England country and western events were conscious of. As Angelo Boncore remembered:

> Well, actually, what we did is we performed. See, we were *actors as well as singers*. You know? We were entertainers. And we would do maybe a forty-five-minute show before we did the dancing. After the forty-five-minute show, then we'd go into the dance music: square dancing and general round dancing. But this is why the people liked us. Because not only did we play for dances, but we performed entertainment, which included comedy—comedy skits. You had to be acting. We did acting parts. We had lines that we had to do, back-and-forth comedy lines we had to do. And, basically, this is what they liked. So we kinda prepped the audience up for the dancing that was to come. (interview 2005)

This dynamic between individual innovation and community tradition embodies a kind of bargain between the performers and the audience. That the country and western event was, in part, innovative entertainment was part of its appeal to the audience. That this bargain between innovation and tradition can be read as part of the value system of the performers as well as the audience is reinforced by the very way the performers structured the event: playing the role of the "star" or the "artist" during the show and playing a subservient role—free of charge—to the audience during the dance. A powerful symbol of the fact that this bundle of values is central to working-class community identity can be found in the place where the New England country and western event is housed: the community hall.

Housing the Country and Western Event: The Community Hall

The New England country and western event is housed in community halls where a multigenerational audience is welcome. These centers—the town hall, the Grange hall, the local church, the YMCA, the Legion Post, the VFW hall, the fire department hall, and the ethnic social club (e.g., the Canadian-American Club)—are places where communities congregate to facilitate or negotiate legislative, economic, spiritual, and recreational matters. Locating the country and western event in community halls is significant, as it speaks of the role that social dancing and concert going have played in the development of New England community life. New England country and western musicians also make (or have made) personal appearances at locations such as bars ("beer parlors"), movie theaters (indoor and drive-in, and always between features), political rallies, and business openings. Though these events served as an important source of income and public exposure for performers, the music was secondary to the main attraction (the movie, the politician, the business opening), which is why they are not included here in the definition of the New England country and western event.

Part of the reason New England country and western events proved to be popular in the 1930s was that they provided a populist community model. Barnstorming New England country and western groups moved from town to town, performing in community halls, honoring a wide range of requests. As New England's population grew, well-known fiddlers, dance callers, and dance band leaders began establishing fixed dance halls and pavilions, making a dance an urban destination point for neighboring rural communities (Post 2004). Country and western groups took the music to the people. Many New England country and western performers from the barnstorming era either are self-effacing about their own popularity or speak disparagingly of small-town life (or perhaps both) when they explain the high turnout at New England country and western events in small community halls by saying there was nothing else going on in mill towns or rural New England. *Any* type of entertainment or *any* style of music was welcome—or at least provoked curiosity—and the people would attend the event just for something to do. Still, it should be remembered that country and western performers specifically targeted certain towns because of the amount of fan mail they had received from specific locations.

In the barnstorming era (roughly 1925–55), country and western acts would arrange with the manager of a community hall to "rent" the venue (i.e., pay the hall a certain percentage of the money taken in at the door—performers were not required to pay an up-front fee for rental). The performers would be responsible for preparing the hall for the concert with the cleaning of the hall, the setting up of chairs, and the preparation of the PA system (if there was one). Once the hall was prepared, the group would meet with a local family who had invited them for dinner, after which the performers would often give a performance in the kitchen. Most performers recall this being a rewarding personal experience that made them feel close to the host family and to the community for which they were playing. Some, like Bradley Kincaid and Grandpa Jones, waxed fondly reminiscent decades after the fact about the homemade pies that New England families would bake for them (Jones 1980; Jones and Wolfe 1984; Jones and Jones interview 1975; Boncore interview 2005; Gobers interview 2007; Smith interview 2007).

Upon returning to the community hall for the personal appearance, the group readied someone to "work" the door as a ticket-taker. The ticket-taker was almost always a woman traveling with the group either as a performer or as what contemporary musicians today would call a "road manager." The road manager's job entailed taking tickets, counting money, and tallying expenses. More often than not the ticket-taker was also married to—or related to—one of the band members and played a prominent musical role in the group as well. In this respect, the community hall functioned as the temporary "home" for the country and western act: community members were welcomed at the door by band members, who hosted them throughout the performance (Coté-Binette and Breau interview 2006; Boncore interview 2005; Calderone interview 2004; Maine Hall of Fame 1998). Admission came at a monetary price, but it should be remembered that radio performances drove attendance at the New England country and western event. Radio was, after all, a medium that was free to the public. Likewise, country and western performers on radio were often not paid (or paid very little) by their host stations. This "free" broadcast can be read as the first of a cycle of "gifts" between the performers and the audience.

Under the official order of business, the two-hour show portion of the personal appearance is what the band was paid for, while the two-hour dance portion was often arranged on the spot and was always performed gratis. While musicians of that era tend to recall each half taking two hours on average, the duration of country and western events varied. Sometimes the show only took forty-five minutes, or the dance took three hours. The point here is not to tout the stamina of the musicians but rather to show that the musicians and the audience tended to view these events as equal halves of a whole. The performers who hosted the New England country and western event would themselves shift the focal point of the show onto the audience for the dance. In doing so, the host performers would adopt a secondary role in which the musicians worked for the greater benefit of the community during the dance. During the dance there was no lavish attention given to the performers—as is indicated by the transformation from concert hall to dance hall with the removal of the chairs from the floor—despite the fact that the performers remained onstage. This act of moving the chairs is reminiscent of the dynamic of the New England kitchen breakdown, or "kitchen tunk," where family and friends would clear the kitchen of furniture for a dance after dinner.

This was not always a highly nuanced, polite, and idyllic arrangement. The musicians would occasionally try to maintain the attention of the audience during the dance. Audiences tended to be respectful of performers during the show, but band members were sometimes subject to harassment and ridicule during the dance. This harassment could sometimes lead to open fighting between performers and audience members. For instance, Rusty Rogers of the Down Homers tells a pair of stories about fights that broke out during dances in Connecticut. The first involves a man who told Rusty "you suck!" every time he danced past the small stage. Each time Rusty would smile and say, "Thank you!" Tired of the insult, Rusty knocked the headstock of his guitar into the man's teeth as he danced past. A similar tale involved another gentleman berating Rusty with insults as he danced by. (This was during the period in which Rogers was the bodybuilding champion of Connecticut; he did a strongman routine with weights during the show and lifted band members over his head with one hand for effect in the middle of songs.) The band could tell Rusty was tiring of the man's insults and warned him not to make trouble. When Rogers saw the perpetrator go to the bathroom during one dance number, he put down his guitar, followed the man in, grabbed the man by the hair, and flushed his head in the toilet before going back out to finish the dance. In both anecdotes, neither of the clashes with audience members interrupted the dance event. The focus of the performance had so shifted away from the Down Homers during the dance that one of the group's singers could step off the stage midsong, stick a man's head in a toilet, and walk back to the stage without disrupting the event. These moments were likely few and far between—though certainly memorable. More common is the kind of tension some performers have acknowledged feeling when the audience attempts to exert too much control over the content of the performance (Murphy 2005).

Clearly the "gift cycle" is not always graceful or nuanced, and it is interlaced with commercial transactions, and yet the presence of conflict is indicative of the reciprocity of both gift exchange and commerce used by participants to reach across boundaries of difference to build neighborliness or community. The cycle of reciprocity can be broken down into the following components:

1. radio performance by the band (free to listeners);
2. letters from listeners to the band and invitations to play locally;
3. renting of the community hall;
4. dinners for the musicians with host families;
5. after-dinner kitchen performances by the band;
6. paid admission to the show by the community/audience; and
7. a free dance given by the band.

The cycle of reciprocity is, of course, not limited to these items, but this is the cycle that emerges most frequently in interviews. In performances, it is not unusual for audience members to bring gifts—items as varied as pies, fine china, and oil paintings—for the band members. Likewise, it is not unusual to see the band celebrate the birthdays and wedding anniversaries of audience members, and while records, cassettes, and CDs are made by performers to be sold, it is not unusual for performers to give some audience members recordings for free. It is also commonplace for the New England country and western event of today to revolve around a fundraiser for various philanthropic causes, such as the American Liver Foundation, where the performers donate their time, and all proceeds go to charity or community organizations. This mixture of commercial exchange and gift cycle creates a cycle of reciprocity that shifts the focus of the event back and forth between the performers and the audience and embodies the felt need by the participants to assuage the tension between individual expression and community expression. Likewise, the gift cycle not only enables neighborliness but also fosters the kind of familial obligation that serves as the cornerstone of community in the building and reinforcement of social capital. This familial spirit pervades the rhetoric of New England country and western musicians and makes itself manifest in the behavior of the participants in the New England country and western event.

The Country and Western Event and the Family: Multigenerational Family Music

The country and western event and the family are inextricable parts of the same whole. Babe Jackson described the typical audience at a New England country and western event of the 1930s through the early 1960s as "mostly family": "There was *always* families with children. Country music was always a *family* show. Nothing rowdy. Nothing shady. It was always out and out family. And that's just what we did. We sang to the people, and we sang what they liked. And we sang before they had all these fancy amplifiers with all these different sounds. We had just a plain little amplifier with a speaker on the wall when we worked" (Jackson-Serio interview 2006).

The New England country and western outdoor "ranch circuit" provided family-style entertainment for working-class families every Sunday and every holiday weekend in warmer weather. Ranch performances tended to be the only shows that the performers' families would attend. Ranch managers expected good family manners onstage from the performers and dictated the stage rules to musicians: they were to be polite, mindful of improprieties, and professional in their stage demeanor and performance. And the audience would pack food for the musicians, who sat and ate with them during their set breaks.

Working for the Audience: Balancing the Show and the Dance

> It's up to the audience. You can be the greatest singer in the world and have no listeners, or you can be the worst sometimes singing the right song. To the people, you're the best singer.
> —Gene Hooper

As we have seen, the quest to strike a balance between innovation and tradition, self-expression and community expression, or a show and a dance can be fraught with tension. Musicians in any given group despise certain songs, establish boundaries for the type of country and western music they are willing to play, sometimes dislike the audience members making requests and in turn spurn them, and—in the event they do not feel like playing a particular request for any variety of reasons—often claim ignorance of songs they know how to play. And yet this rhetoric of audience accommodation is so fundamental to the ideal of the country and western musician that it can be hard to get the performers—particularly the older generations—to openly acknowledge the ideal's limitations even when this tension between the band and the audience is palpable to all participants. If it sounds as though I am pushing interviewees on this subject, I am. Having participated at country and western events as an accompanying musician and as a band leader, I am aware (after watching musicians balk at certain requests because they dislike the song, or the person requesting it, or the manner in which it was requested) that the rhetoric of accommodating "what the audience wants" has its limitations in practice.

Instead, New England country and western musicians are capable of virtuosic populist rhetoric when it comes to describing their roles as performers. For example, Ray Dixon, a country and western singer from Rhode Island who has been performing since the 1930s, believes that the role of the country and western singer is to accommodate a wide range of needs; he considers his ability to do so as the key to his longevity and success in the business:

> *Murphy:* Now, when you would play country shows, would you ever play French Canadian music during your set?
>
> *Dixon:* Yes. And I'd sing rock and roll. I'd sing that "you ain't nothin' but a hound dog" if they wanted rock. If they wanted Hawaiian, I'd do Hawaiian [sings "Beyond the Reef"]. I did 'em all: polkas, cha-chas, hulley-gulley. I feel that in the business, you should play a little bit of everything. That's how I feel. That's why I never loafed. Fifty years I never loafed. So it worked out good. (Beaudoyn interview 2006)

Singer Babe Jackson echoes Dixon's sentiment that a group's success depended on its ability to cater to a wide range of musical tastes and needs:

> *Jackson:* We played Greek weddings and Italian weddings. We played all kinds of wedding receptions.
>
> *Murphy:* When you would play a show at the German club, would you play polkas?
>
> *Jackson:* Oh, yes. Polkas, and I think there's a dance they call a mazurka. It's kind of a waltz? We played that. You *have* to kind of cater to the people. If they like waltzes, you give them more waltzes. If they like foxtrots, you give them that. Basically, though, the people that we played for were always very nice, and they would just enjoy the show and made us feel good. It was easy to do the show. (Jackson-Serio interview 2006)

Babe Jackson's qualified comment—"you *have* to kind of cater to the people"—is perhaps closer to the actuality of what the New England country and western performer does than Ray Dixon's unqualified suggestion that he would play what "they wanted." Johnny Smith makes the same claim Ray Dixon does—that it was the job of the country and western artist to play "whatever *they* wanted" during the 1930s (Smith interview 2007). And Babe Jackson, too, claimed, "We sang to the people, and we sang what they liked" (Jackson-Serio interview 2006). And yet, even when populist groups such as Jackson's, Dixon's, and Smith's played what *they* (the audience) wanted—the hully-gully, the fox-trot, the mazurka, the polka, or the blues—the groups did so on their own terms, and the end result was still a country and western sound.

A New England Working-Class Community in Action: Back at the Legion Post 15

In April 2004, when I first made contact with the Hayloft Jamboree, they were performing every Saturday night from 7:00 to 11:00 P.M. at Legion Post 15 in East Greenwich, Rhode Island. Richie Zack, the group's lead singer since its inception in 1946, was suffering from heart and kidney ailments at the time and had just been released from the hospital. The band was playing its first set of the night, but Richie left the stage after a few songs to take a break. He made a beeline for me. "I'm here because these people [gesturing to the audience] need me to be here," he told me. "I don't feel like playing a God-derned thing" (Murphy 2004a).

As we stood talking, well-wishers spun past in the midst of their dancing and asked about Richie's health. Despite his cantankerous comments about not feeling like "playing a God-derned thing," Richie appeared quite pleased to be there and was content to have his sisters—Babs and Maril—take over the band while he socialized. From the stage, Babs announced it was Maril's seventy-eighth birthday, and the one hundred or so attendees sang "Happy Birthday" with band accompaniment. As a birthday gift, Maril's three daughters came up out of the audience and sang several rockabilly standards and some folk-rock standards with band accompaniment.

The birthday environment of the East Greenwich Legion Post 15 was in many ways a typical moment in the New England country and western music community. The rise of country and western music as a meaningful form of music in New England was predicated on a series of gift exchanges, the first being that live country and western radio performances were free to the community and often at no charge to the radio station. Country and western groups promoted commercial products on their appearances only when their time slot was "sponsored" by a company (or companies). Commercially sponsored time slots were desirable to performers because they ensured the musicians a small income. However, based on the testimony of New England country and western performers from the barnstorming era, shows with commercial sponsors were the exception rather than the rule. Beginning performers rarely had commercial sponsorship, generally only securing sponsorship after becoming “known.” Unlike their famous southern and southwestern counterparts, like Roy Acuff's Krazy Tennesseans (sponsored by Krazy Water Krystals) and Bob Wills's Light Crust Doughboys (sponsored by Light Crust Flour), New England groups with commercial sponsorship did not hawk their sponsors' products onstage at personal appearances. They also rarely named their groups after their sponsors. (The Circle C Ranch Boys—a play on the initials of commercial sponsor Community Opticians—are the only known example in New England, dating from 1938.) These “free” radio performances triggered a cycle of gift giving, whereby local families provided musicians with free dinners and lunches, and performers often reciprocated by performing free dances after their shows. Such an exchange during the heyday of the country and western event—the 1930s to the 1950s, when the New England working class was burdened with the collapse of the textile industry—helped to cultivate what Burt Feintuch (2006) calls “community mindedness,” whereby the social capital generated at such music-centered events enables the participants involved to transcend “longing for” communities into a state of *actual* community where the members come to depend on one another.

At the Legion Post, the outpouring of support for Richie combined with Maril's birthday celebration and the musical gift from Maril's daughters gave the event the air of a large family gathering. During a set break, Tony Poccia, the group's steel player for fifty-seven years, told me that the close-knit Zackarian family encompassed more than blood relatives: “Eddy and Richie and the two girls, Babs and Maril, were a very, very close family. And it seemed like I got to be part of the family. Because being with them since 1947 [laughs]. What does that make me, part of the family, right [laughs]?” (Murphy 2004a).

The multiethnic makeup of Rhode Island's white working class mirrors that of the Hayloft Jamboree. Band members consist of Rhode Islanders of Armenian, Italian, Quebecois, Irish, and English extraction, and over the course of a half-century together they have melded as one family. Many in the audience had been attending the band's shows for as long as Tony Poccia had sat behind the steel alongside Richie, Babs, and Maril. In this room, the group was less like the focal point of a concert than it was like the core members of a large family gathering. The family dynamic of the event went deeper than the symbolism of the sheet cake and the pile of gifts audience members had brought for Maril Albro. The homecoming event was more than a polite "nice to see you again, Richie, how are you feeling?" This was a community that had grown up together, socialized together, coalesced during a time of ethnic segregation, celebrated the band's *Billboard* and television triumphs, witnessed and mourned the passing of several band members (a framed picture of the late Eddy Zack was placed prominently near the band table), endured the financial collapse of working-class life in Rhode Island, and done so *together*. As Richie Zack said, "These people need me to be here." Without the Hayloft Jamboree, the traditional continuity of the community would be jeopardized.

Some months later, this was put to the test: Richie Zack died on June 16, 2004, just over two months after I had seen him perform. The band went on hiatus for six months until Babs and Maril took over the group and resumed the Hayloft Jamboree shows every Saturday night. I had an opportunity to sit down with them before their first show following Richie's death. It was the first interview they had ever given in the forty-eight-year history of the group. What the interview reveals is that Babs and Maril were initially uncomfortable with the idea of continuing the band after Richie's death but that ultimately the community demanded that they keep the weekly Saturday night show going:

> *Babs White:* Right now, we are just staying here, working every Saturday night right here. And we haven't done any shows since Richie has been gone. This'll be the first year, if we decide to do anything, I'm not sure if we're gonna do a lot. We're not sure if we want to travel around without them [Richie and Eddy]. Because what we had was our act. You know? So we've been just waiting to see what kind of jobs are offered and if they're worth it. We've done a few wedding jobs. Things like that. But it's different, you know? It's just getting used to this now. And it hasn't always been that easy, has it?
>
> *Maril Albro:* No. Not easy. When you work with somebody for sixty years, and they're gone, well, it really has changed. You know? Things aren't there that used to be there.
>
> *Babs White:* You keep looking over at the side of the stage, always looking, waiting for the next thing to happen. And when he's not there, it's just difficult. But we feel like he's there in our heart. We feel like he's with us. Because it's important. And the people here, a lot of them just loved him. And they missed him, but they've been supportive of us. You know? We thought they were all going to just leave.
>
> *Cliff Murphy:* Oh, of course not!
>
> *Babs White:* They said, "No, we want to keep this going." So here we are. We gotta keep hoping that we can keep it going [laughs]. (White and Albro interview 2004, 16–17)

What the Hayloft Jamboree band displays here in yielding to the wishes of the community to continue after the death of its lead singer and brother is a deep commitment to sustaining community. The Hayloft Jamboree's weekly country and western event had created an *actual* community complete with the felt, familial obligation by the participants to transcend crisis and to seek continuation after profound loss. After the death of its key vocalists, the Hayloft Jamboree continued to play every weekend at the Legion Post 15 until 2013, when they moved to a part-time schedule. Such dedication demonstrates powerful evidence of reciprocity, whereby the New England country and western event fortifies community while also being fortified *by* it.

4

HOME ON THE GRANGE

The Frontier between "American" and "Immigrant" Worldviews in New England Country and Western

Imagine for a moment entering into the following setting: A roughhewn cattle ranch gate stands over the archway of the entrance to the community hall. You may have just walked in past a real live horse, resplendent in decadent tack, hitched up outside. Though it is Waterville, Maine, in 1942, the hall is filled with men and women in frontier dress—men in cowboy clothes and hats, boys in overalls and kerchiefs, girls and women in homemade calico dresses—and the floor is strewn with hay bales and wagon wheels. Across the room is a stage, decked in the same shambling frontier flotsam, and on the stage is a band dressed exactly like the audience—though maybe a little better, excepting the toothless comedian—surrounded by their instruments and equipment. The room is filled with the distinctive sound of country and western music—its swinging gait, its loping emphasis on the offbeat, its eagerness to be one with the audience, and its simultaneous push to stand apart from it. A young man and woman stand at the front of the stage—clearly the leaders of the group and married—and they have the rapt attention of the crowd. The man is tall and would be considered handsome even without the assistance of his expensive, hand-tailored cowboy suit. The woman, although petite, fills the stage with her impish grin, flashing dark eyes, and elegant beauty, and her shapely handmade dress sways wonderfully as she moves to the music. The man steps to the microphone and sings:

> Come out and listen while I sing and play for you
> I am the Lone Pine Mountaineer
> Come out and listen while I sing for you
> Those songs you love to hear
> I hope I please you, and if I do
> Please tell your friends to listen too

> Come out and listen while I sing for you,
> I am the Lone Pine Mountaineer

Yodeling fills the hall. The audience—each person partnered off and dancing—cheers spontaneously. This is what they've come for. The band continues its welcoming song as the singer steps again to the mic and speaks directly to the crowd: "Well, howdy folks, I'm your old friend Lone Pine. The whole gang is here today to entertain you for the next couple of hours. We'll play songs by yours truly here, plus some others by the folks in the band. We've also got some fine singing from little Betty Cody, and Little Abner is on guitar. We hope you enjoy it."

The group resumes its welcome song and closes with a cheer. "Now here's a song," says Lone Pine, "called 'The Old Chisholm Trail.'"

With that the band is off again, and the dancing resumes in full. Everyone seems to be dancing. Partners change freely during square dances. You join in on the dance floor, and in short order you spend a few fleeting moments with many others, changing partners freely and constantly.

The frontier world you have stepped into is an alternate world to the one you engage in at home, at work, and at church. In that other world, you do not engage at all with the multitudes you've met here on the dance floor. In the world of home, work, and worship, everyone speaks the same language as you. Their families came from the same regions of the same home countries together. And they work in the same rooms of the mill as you. And they likely discourage you from straying too far from the fold.

But the multitudes from the mills, from the churches, and from the nearby towns have all been drawn together in this frontier space because they are all devoted listeners of Lone Pine and Betty Cody's radio shows. And, for a change, it feels like the rules can bend. It is, after all, a space into which everyone arrived for the same reason and at the same time, welcomed here by a group whose faces look just like the ones seen every day at the mill.

Alternation, Inclusiveness, and the Imagined Frontier

Rules that governed New England working-class sociability changed dramatically at country and western events. This was not the West, of course, but the cowboy names, the clothing, the décor, and the music worked in concert to suspend everyday rules. Sociologists would call this phenomenon "alternation." Normally used to explain how groups of people—particularly religious cults—construct alternate symbolic universes, alternation relies on the use of name change, different dress, and different music in order to radically change individuals' worldview (Berger and Luckmann 1990; Pilarzyk 1978). Alternation describes the constructed frontier space of the country and western event and helps to explain how New England country and western fans of different—and normally segregated—ethnic backgrounds came to share the same space and work across difference to create a new community.

Historians have long posited theories about the transformative effects of the American frontier. Most notable among these historians was Frederick Jackson Turner, whose frontier thesis initially claimed that Americans became less European the farther they traveled west across the continent. Though such theories have come under intense criticism, even by Jackson himself (Turner 1984; Bogue 1998; Steiner 1995; Turner and Faragher 1998), he, perhaps like those in attendance at a country and western event, recognized that America's strongest and most culturally distinctive communities were multicultural ones where people had to work across difference. The transformative powers of the frontier remained strong in the American imagination.

New England mill workers at a Lone Pine and Betty Cody show in 1942 would not be thinking of Turner and his frontier thesis. But this idea had taken hold of the American imagination and bore powerful, popular fruit in the western novels and films that gripped the nation, including even its newly arrived immigrants like Betty Cody. Powerful politicians like Theodore Roosevelt and popular singers like Gene Autry espoused the transformative—and even morally cleansing—effects of the frontier. The frontier's hold on the American imagination remained strong even into the Space Age of the 1950s and 1960s in both popular culture (e.g., *Star Trek*) and politics (the "space race"). Before *Star Trek* brought Americans to "new life and new frontiers," President John F. Kennedy took the pioneering spirit of Turner's thesis to new realms when he dubbed his 1961 administration the "New Frontier." The aims of the New Frontier included space exploration, battle along the Asian Pacific frontier of Communism, development of the Peace Corps in the Third World, and the passage of civil rights legislation (Bernstein 1991). So while critics including Turner himself have rendered the frontier thesis questionable, history shows that these themes have remained a powerful part of the American imagination over centuries. In Turner's frontier, vastly different people arrived on the frontier together, worked together against shared hardships, and became Americans together. This was true of the "old" frontier as well—it produced American archetypes like the Appalachian frontiersman, the blackface minstrel, and the rustic Yankee who disdainfully tells the effete (more European) city slicker "you cayant get theyah from heyah." These distinctly "American" old frontier archetypes rolled into one on the imagined western frontier in the form of the singer in the cowboy hat. Real or imagined, the frontier space of the country and western event helped transform ethnic New England working-class sociability.

The Use of Frontier Stage Names

Most New England country and western performers choose a "frontier" (or "cowboy") stage name. Country and western stage names tend to be chosen because of their alliterative qualities (they "sound good"), and they aim to represent a western cowboy, southern Appalachian, or Yankee frontier persona. New England performers have tended to choose a western cowboy stage persona over a southern Appalachian or Yankee persona. Around 1935 New Englanders began changing their names to project a cowboy image. New England country and western musicians explain that a name change served four functions. First and foremost, country and western music is about entertainment and performing a role, and the use of a fictional name is standard practice in most stage productions (musical or otherwise). Second, a stage name like "Rusty Rogers" simply sounds good and is easy for promoters to remember and spell correctly. Third, the adoption of a stage name was a means by which performers would self-authenticate by associating themselves with a perceived site of country and western authenticity. Fourth and finally, "ethnic" musicians found it easier to get gigs if they had "western" (read: English, or, more to the point, "American") sounding names and personas. Hence Russell Kempton became Rusty Rogers, Vinnie Calderone became Jimmy Cal (Calderone interview 2004), Jackie LeBlanc became Johnny White (LeBlanc interview 2004), and Raymond Beaudoyn became Ray Dixon (Beaudoyn interview 2006).

New England country and western groups tended to be multiethnic ensembles from the very beginning. Stage names create the false impression that these groups were of uniform ethnicity or agents of Americanization. The process of name change bears close examination to see how this self-fictionalizing tradition was further utilized by "ethnic" New Englanders to gain entrance into mainstream "American" venues while also perpetuating their own ethnic traditions. Ethnic New Englanders did not simply seek to Americanize themselves through the use of a cowboy persona and stage name; instead, name change was used as a tool to build a bridge between traditions, to reshape ethnic boundaries, and to navigate or resolve the frontier tension between American and immigrant worldviews.

For ethnic New Englanders—ostensibly, community outsiders from non-Protestant (Roman Catholic and Greek, Russian, and Armenian Orthodox) backgrounds—adopting an Anglicized frontier stage name came with distinct advantages. First-generation American performers tended to be well known in the rather parochial or clannish ethnic communities from which they emerged. As a result, their new stage identity did not obscure them from their home community, and their group continued to be booked for country and western performances (which generally included a good deal of immigrant music, both traditional and popular) at ethnic social clubs, church-related social gatherings, and other social events that tended to be of homogeneous ethnic composition. According to many performers—many of whom insisted we speak of these matters off the record—ethnic clubs would only book ethnic performers, whether of the club's home ethnicity or not. This practice was extended to all ethnicities *except* Anglo-Saxon Americans. Ethnic communities were made aware of other ethnic country and western musicians by their appearance at other ethnic social clubs. For example, a performer of known Italian extraction (with the requisite frontier stage name) was made known as ethnic to other ethnic communities by his or her performances at Italian baptismal parties, parish suppers, or weddings. Other ethnic fraternal organizations (such as the German Club or the Polish American Club), parishes, or private persons would then be more inclined to hire that country and western performer for their event(s). To the general radio public, ethnic country and western performers using frontier stage names were assumed to be American (not ethnic), giving them entrée to American clubs as well as ethnic ones. So while an Anglo-Saxon performer like Yodelin' Slim Clark was known for being friendly and open-minded to matters of ethnic integration, he was booked almost exclusively into Anglo-Saxon-dominated venues and events in the first few decades of his career. In other words, ethnic musicians working under frontier stage names actually had greater ability to move within the broad socioethnic spheres of the New England country and western world than did "insider" Anglo musicians.

Choosing a Stage Name

Several of New England's most prominent country and western figures were first-generation Americans performing under Americanized pseudonyms: Eddie Zack (Zack is truncated from the Armenian Zackarian), Johnny White (Jean LeBlanc), Flo Cody (Florence Coté), Sleepy Willis (Taso Golios), and the Lane Brothers (Frank and Pete Loconto). Although ethnic performers would occasionally make their ethnicity the focus of a live performance, they did not choose to make ethnicity their calling card with regard to their stage name. In other words, an ethnic performer would not seek to identify himself as "the Greek cowboy" with a name like Hopalong Cassadeseus, nor did performers always truncate, translate, or Americanize the spelling of their name, like Eddy Zack(arian), Johnny White (Jean LeBlanc = John The White), and Flo Cody (Coté). Generally, names were chosen because they had a cowboy or frontier "sound" or association and sounded compatible with the dominant language of country and western music (English). For instance, John White—no relation to the aforementioned Johnny White—was one of the first prominent singing cowboys, recording extensively in the 1920s and 1930s. Likewise, performers never chose frontier names that evoked the Native American, French, or Spanish heritage of the western frontier.

Rhode Island country and western singer Ray Dixon is another example of this phenomenon. He grew up in Johnston, Rhode Island, speaking, reading, and writing French but was irritated by confusion over the spelling and pronunciation of his name by non-French-speaking people in the music business: "Yeah, well, my name is Beaudoyn. B-E-A-U-D-O-Y-N. But they used to call me Bo-deen, Bo-dine, and Iodine. And I said, 'Let me change this'" (Beaudoyn interview 2006). Note that Dixon did not choose to adopt one of the common misspellings of his last name (e.g., Bodeen), instead choosing a name intended to associate his stage persona with country and western authenticity by way of Dixie.

Fledgling country and western performers chose a stage name (or had one chosen for them) very early in their professional careers. New England country and western legend often points to this event taking place just moments before an entertainer's first public performance or chosen well in advance. I had a conversation with Maine country and western singer Robert Wincapaw—a self-described "mixed bag" of German and French ancestry—in which he explained the story of how he has become known to most people as Bob Elston:

Murphy: Tell me about the decision to change your last name.

Elston: Well, that all goes back to a lifelong friend that I've had, I guess, since age ten. We kind of grew up together, and we're neighbors. And his father was a great . . . great writer of baseball and reporter for baseball. And of course, his team was the New York Yankees. And when I first got into show business, he said, "Well, if you're gonna be in that business, you gotta have a stage name." And he said, "Well, let's call ya Bobby Berra," for Yogi Berra, catcher of the Yankees. Then he said, "Nope, nope, nope. Wait a minute," he said, "how about Elston?" for Elston Howard, catcher of the Yankees. And

> I said, "Yeah, I guess. *Sounds* good." And I never used it. Went along about a year or two. When I joined the Curley O'Brien show and I did my first 45, he said, "Do you have a stage name?" And I said, "Yeah, I was *given* one, but I never used it." He said, "What is it?" I said, "Elston." He said, "Hmm, sounds pretty good." He said, "Use it from now on." So I've used it. Ever since 1958 I've used that name. And a lot of people don't even know what my real name really is! (Wincapaw interview 2006)

Interestingly, the fact that New York Yankee catcher Elston Howard was an African American did not matter to Wincapaw. What mattered instead was that the name "sounds good."

Frank and Pete Loconto of Cambridge, Massachusetts, employed a method different from Wincapaw's. Frank Loconto recalled searching for a stage name by thumbing through the L section of the phone book, settling on Lane. Later in life, Frank regretted his choice—not on account of a resurgence of pride in his Italian heritage but because he realized that Lane Brothers had a certain "generic" sound to it (Frank "Lane" Loconto, e-mail message to author, July 21, 2005).

Anglo-Saxon, Scottish, and Irish American performers in New England also chose frontier stage names. Such was the case with Yodelin' Slim Clark (originally called Wyomin' Buck), Dick Curless (the Tumbleweed Kid), and Russell Kempton (Rusty Rogers—Rusty was Kempton's nickname as a boy, and Rogers was meant to conjure up associations with Roy Rogers). Name change was accompanied by a fictional frontier biography, and performers completed their persona with an army of accessories, including tailored rodeo clothes, holsters, guns, chaps, cowboy hats, and—with surprising frequency for a mostly urban-based musical form—horses.

Establishing Frontier Authenticity

Along with a stage name, performers often cultivate a fictional background rooted in one of country and western music's accepted sites of frontier authenticity. At the height of western music's popularity in New England, the "West" of the New England imagination appears to be somewhat differently defined from the "West" that plays out in a Texas beer joint, a Marty Robbins gun ballad, or a Bakersfield, California, country song. Based on the press materials and song book biographies of western musicians in New England during the barnstorming era, the West of the New England imagination was located in Colorado, Wyoming, Montana, the Dakotas, Iowa, Missouri, Kansas, Nebraska, and the Canadian provinces of Alberta, Saskatchewan, and Manitoba. Radio promoters regularly fabricated stories of western birthrights, and in the early decades of the music, performers were generally willing and enthusiastic participants in these fabrications. For instance, WBZ radio and television regularly stated in press releases that cowgirl yodeler Georgia Mae, who was born in Connecticut and raised in Dedham, Massachusetts, was from Colorado ("Radio's Wake-Up Girl" 1945). When the performing rights agency known as SESAC (Society for European Stage Authors and Composers) recorded a series of transcription discs in 1945 featuring Georgia Mae, the accompanying program notes also trumpeted her Colorado ancestry: "Georgia Mae was born in Denver, Colorado, and began singing when she was six years old. She went East with a kiddie review and decided to stay there when an opportunity was offered to her to have a radio program" ("Radio's Sweetest Personality" 1945, 2). On February 6, 2007, Georgia Mae sent me an e-mail in which she explained the Colorado references: "The article stating I was born in Colorado was not right. I think it was put in to make me seem more of 'A Cowgirl singing western songs.' The truth!!—I was born in Bridgeport, Conn[ecticut], my Mother was from Stratford Conn[ecticut], and my Father was born in Springfield, Ma[ssachusetts]. My Grandfather moved to Colorado when I was very young and a mention of him may have seemed a good idea to make me seem more authentic. So—'I am a Born Yankee.'"

SESAC's transcription series was aimed at a national and international radio market, and as such it sought to tailor its artist biographies toward audience expectations. The Down Homers were another New England group in the 1945 SESAC transcription series, and the accompanying biography states that Rusty Rogers—born and raised in New Harbor, Maine—was from Missouri. St. Louis, Missouri, has been called the gateway to the West (as symbolized by the Gateway Arch, located in the Jefferson National Expansion Memorial park in St. Louis), but it is hardly thought of as *being* the West. Still, SESAC deemed it close enough to make Rogers a more authentic cowboy singer. As Georgia Mae implied in her explanation of the origins of her fictional Colorado birthplace, she and Rusty Rogers were willing and active participants in the cultivation of frontier personas, and their purpose was twofold. First, that persona provided an imaginary center for country and western performance within New England, and second, it allowed New England performers' background sites of authenticity to be more in keeping with the expectations of audiences outside of New England.

A complete disavowal of New England roots would have been difficult in Georgia Mae's case. Her affiliation with Massachusetts was well known far outside the region, as can be seen in detailed WBZ reports tracking the geographic origins of her fan mail (in order to better target advertisers). WBZ's powerful fifty-thousand-watt clear channel signal meant that Georgia Mae—and the *New England Farm Hour* program on which she appeared on a daily basis from 6:00 to 7:00 A.M. throughout the 1940s—could be received well beyond New England. Twenty-five percent of her listeners tuned in from outside of New England (Pennsylvania, New York, West Virginia, Virginia, Maryland, Ohio, Michigan, North Carolina, and Ontario—in that order—represented a full 21 percent of her letter-writing fan base), and some were from locations as far away as Puerto Rico and Independence, Missouri (Westinghouse 1943). Closer examination of Georgia Mae's press materials circulated *within* New England by her promoters at WBZ radio in Boston shows that they, too, trumped up the yodeler's Colorado connection, and she would occasionally reference Colorado in her on-air banter between songs. Yet like many of the cowboy and cowgirl singers working in New England as "authentic" westerners, Georgia Mae had never set foot in the West—and still has not to this day (Harp interview 2004). New Englanders had close contact with Georgia Mae at her personal appearances and were well aware that she was a New Englander. (Radio listeners were also familiar with her mother and brother, who would periodically appear with her on her radio broadcast, and their accents made their New England heritage patently obvious to any listeners in New England.) Her Colorado background was understood as fictional by New Englanders and can in turn be understood as a device used in concert by both Georgia Mae and her audiences to orient their imaginations toward the frontier.

Since the rise of Nashville as a powerful country music business center in the 1950s, Tennessee and Texas have become the norm for fictional biographies of New Englanders today. Prior to that time, New England country and western performers claiming to be from the South always used the old colonial frontier from which the mythology of Davy Crockett and Mike Fink emerged (both men were real-life persons from the old frontier around whom a significant number of "tall tales" developed): Kentucky, eastern Tennessee, West Virginia, or eastern Ohio. Interestingly, few—if any—appear to have claimed Virginia, the Carolinas, Georgia, Alabama, Louisiana, Arkansas, or Mississippi. Given the popularity and continuing influence of Jimmy "The Mississippi Brakeman" Rodgers in New England, the exclusion of Mississippi as a fictional birthplace is the most surprising of the bunch and lends credibility to the idea that New Englanders sought to associate themselves specifically with frontier regions.

An important exception to these tendencies is the particularly popular and influential minority of performers who self-consciously position themselves *against* those accepted sites of authenticity by foregrounding their Maine roots. The western cowboy/cowgirl, the southern Appalachian backwoodsman, and the woodcutting or potato-digging Mainer are personas intended to ground the imaginative site of their performance firmly on the frontier.

Authenticity in New England: Maine as a Frontier Region

Performers who acknowledge their New England birthplace in their press materials tend to be Mainers. Maine's association with the frontier had long been rooted in its booming lumber industry of the early to mid-nineteenth century, producing folkloric figures like Paul Bunyan and a prodigious body of balladry memorializing the hardship and death encountered by woods workers on river drives. In the late 1830s, the border of Maine and the Canadian province of New Brunswick had been the last site of American-Canadian military conflict (the bloodless Aroostook War), and in the late nineteenth century, Aroostook County (Maine's largest and northernmost county) became the site of what was then the most productive potato-growing region in the United States. Between the folklore spawned by northern Maine's lumber industry, its characterization as a rugged wilderness region in Henry David Thoreau's *The Maine Woods* (1864), its status as one of the few remaining places where eastern Native American tribes remained unmoved from their ancestral lands, and its boom-or-bust potato industry, northern Maine developed a reputation (in New England as well as the rest of the nation) as one of America's few remaining frontier spaces. With the publication of *In Fair Aroostook* (Pullen 1902) the Bangor and Aroostook Railroad began promoting Bangor, Maine, as the edge of modern civilization and celebrating Aroostook County's reputation for fruitful game hunting and its history as a place of agrarian Acadian and Scandinavian settlement. The B&A Railroad called Aroostook County the "entrance into Maine's great game and garden country" (7). Maine had been promoted as a frontier region (both Penobscot County, where Bangor, Maine, is located, and Aroostook County) in the popular imagination as early as 1908 with the publication of Holman Day's popular novel *King Spruce*, and Aroostook County's frontier reputation is the centerpiece of Charles Morrow Wilson and Alden Woodworth's *Aroostook, Our Last Frontier* (1937) and Helen Hamlin's *Pine, Potatoes, and People* (1948). Although the Hamlin book (written by a native of Aroostook County) speaks more flatteringly of Aroostook County's multiethnic heritage and shows women to be equal partners in the well-being of its inhabitants, Wilson and Woodworth's *Aroostook, Our Last Frontier* captures the outsider's perspective of Aroostook County as one of the last remaining vestiges of Frederick Jackson Turner's western frontier:

> Aroostook talk is lusty with a rare, breezy optimism, suggestive of the once unbounded West. There is spontaneous comradeship of men at work or at adventure; men who rub elbows, spit, and sweat, rather than men who fondle palms, sniff, and doubt. It is West, an earlier and more free-spirited West gone pell-mell and boundlessly East. Whatever the maps may show you, Aroostook

> towns are Western towns—the same amazingly broad streets, new buildings, some of them undisciplined and spontaneous architecture; new automobiles, bright fronts, loud band music, the backslamming fellowship of a great frontier. (1937, 12)

Authenticity and Maine: Hal Lone Pine and Betty Cody

The first and most important New England group to capitalize on situating their biography within the context of Maine as a frontier region was Hal Lone Pine and Betty Cody. Lone Pine and Betty are considered by New England and Atlantic Canada country and western musicians and historians to be the most significant pioneers of country and western music in eastern Canada and New England. Lone Pine and Betty were significant in terms of establishing standards of professionalism and musical style and expanding the boundaries of New England country and western into eastern Canada and for retaining their regional accent and style on major-label recordings made for RCA Victor between 1951 and 1954. A legend of frontier authenticity was crafted around Lone Pine and Betty that draws from Appalachian, western, and Maine frontier legends, popular culture, and stereotypes.

It is possible that the origin of Hal Lone Pine's public association with the state of Maine is rooted in his debut appearance on radio. In 1932 Lone Pine (Harold Breau) and two friends performed on WABI in Bangor, Maine, as the Lone Pine Mountaineers. Their first song—sung by Lone Pine—was Jimmie Rodgers's "Brakeman's Blues" (1928), which features the opening line "Portland, Maine, is just the same as sunny Tennessee." From that point onward, Hal Lone Pine never felt the need to justify his place of origin in relation to his profession as a country and western musician. If anything, Lone Pine developed a knack for exploiting Maine as an exotic and authentic frontier region through the creation of his own legend.

The legend of Lone Pine's name takes on various forms in biographies issued by his various record companies and song publishers. Several facts are consistent throughout each, and, summarized, the story takes the following shape: Harold Breau was born in tiny Pea Cove, Maine, on June 5, 1916. He grew up exploring the woods in nearby Old Town, Maine—home of the famous canoe company of the same name—and befriended many of the Indian people in that area. One day when young Harold was about eleven years old, one of his Indian playmates fell through the ice and began to drown. In an act of selfless bravery, young Harold ventured out onto the thin ice and rescued the Indian girl. The Penobscot Indian Council was so grateful to Harold for his act of selfless bravery that they bestowed upon him the honorary Indian name "Lone Pine" in recognition of his towering height over the Native people.

Four facts about this story are indeed accurate:

1. Harold Breau was born in Pea Cove, Maine, on June 5, 1916.
2. Pea Cove is near Old Town.
3. Old Town Canoes have been manufactured in Old Town, Maine, since 1898 (Audette and Baker 1998).
4. One of Maine's largest Native American reservations is located at Indian Island, Maine, where the Abenaki people—primarily members of the Penobscot Nation—have made their home for centuries. Indian Island is located next to Old Town, and many Abenaki people (the People of the Dawn—the Penobscot, Passamaquoddy, Mic-Mac, and Maliseet tribes) who choose not to live on the reservation make their home in Old Town (MacDougall 2004).

Living in such close proximity to Old Town and Indian Island, Maine, it is likely that Harold Breau had interactions with Native Americans either in casual play or through arenas related to the Roman Catholic Church, and it is possible—although not remembered by his ex-wife or youngest son—that he was friends with Native Americans living in the area despite strained relations between the Abenaki people and government agencies (on both the state and federal levels) actively seeking to "break" the Abenaki of their Native languages and customs (MacDougall 2004). Breau's formal interaction with the Penobscot Nation in a "naming" ceremony is pure fabrication. Not only were relations between Native peoples and Americans strained at best, but no Abenaki tribes conveyed descriptive names like Lone Pine on *anyone*—Abenaki or otherwise. Traditional precolonial Abenaki names had long given way to Christian names derived from Jesuit Roman Catholic French influence, like Louis, Jean, Gerald, Francis, and so forth. The Abenaki never used descriptive names such as Sitting Bull—or, in this case, Lone Pine—famously used by western tribes.

However, the name Lone Pine is significant in its symbolism, as it is evocative of the place where Harold Breau was born and raised. Maine is known as the Pine Tree State on account of that tree's prevalence on the state's landscape, the importance the pine industry of the early nineteenth century had in building Maine's frontier economy and identity, and the important role Lone Pine's home region (the greater Bangor, Maine, area) played in processing the fruits of the lumber industry. Yet the word "lone" implies the kind of self-reliant, naturalistic loner celebrated in western novels, films, and songs. Coupling both the "lone" ranger identity of the West and the "pine" identity of Maine conjures up an image of a native Mainer out alone on the frontier. Lone Pine created an elaborate cowboy stage persona built on this Maine Lone Ranger—type legend of a boy who grew up with Indians. He wore tailored cowboy clothes, bought a trick horse, and produced a batch of press photos of himself astride a rearing stallion named Champ. Lone Pine's family members and former band members recall the singer's persona to be charismatic, convincing, and thoroughly irresistible; yet they also believe the legend of Lone Pine to be entirely fabricated. Lone Pine's son Denny Breau believes the name Lone Pine was actually derived from an old Hopalong Cassidy movie:

> Yeah, the story goes that he used to have friends on the reservation in Old Town. And apparently he saved a little boy from drowning. And they named him Lone Pine as a result of that, because he was so much taller than all the other kids for his age. So supposedly that's how he got the name. But I often wonder, because it was just maybe six months ago I was watching an old Hopalong Cassidy movie, and a lot of the things that were indicative to my dad's realm were in that movie, like there was a town called Lone Pine, and there was a horse called Champ. I started wondering, "Hmmm. Wonder if Dad was watching this one time?" You know, "That's what I'm going to call my . . ." It was as if there were too many coincidences not to have affected him at one time. (Breau interview 2005)

Denny Breau's observations drive closer to the truth behind the myth of Lone Pine. A great many western movies—from the silent film era onward—were shot on Lone Pine Ranch in Lone Pine, California. These included the Hopalong Cassidy films. Incidentally, these also included the films of cowboy actor Charles "The Durango Kid" Starrett, who grew up in the same town (Athol, Massachusetts) as Yodeling Kenny Roberts. And while Hopalong Cassidy's horse was actually named Topper, Roy Rogers's horse was named Champion, which is likely why Breau chose the derivative Champ for his own horse.

Still, the legend of Lone Pine graces most of Harold Breau's songbooks, LP jackets, and RCA Records press releases. Though his legend is embroidered, the association with the Abenaki people of Maine is clearly meant to convey a raw frontier existence. Lone Pine is a name that evokes the masculine self-reliance of the nomadic cowboy. The romantic association of cowboys with Indians was remarkably strong in the popular imagination at this time, and the appropriation of Indianisms was likely good for business. But there are aspects of Lone Pine's story that go beyond simple cowboys and indians: country and western singers have a long history of associating their musical upbringing with an inspired indifference to the social construction of race. It is a long list that includes most of the major figures in the music: Hank Williams and Tee Tot in Montgomery, Alabama; Bill Monroe and Arnold Shultz in Rosine, Kentucky; Jimmie Rodgers and African American railroad workers in Meridian, Mississippi; Wilf Carter and "The Yodeling Fool" in Canning, Nova Scotia; A. P. Carter and Lesley Riddle in Clinch Mountain, Virginia. Though some of these tales show that a mutual interest in music can help transcend racial tension in even the most violently segregated parts of North America, they also serve the romantic agenda of promoters (and musicians) who seek to exploit the frontier image of the country and western singer who fraternizes with the "other" and lives along the fringes of "decent" society.

Despite the debt many country musicians owe African American musicians, racial integration on country music stages graced by Nashville recording artists was virtually unheard of until the emergence of singer Charlie Pride in the late 1960s. New England and Atlantic Canada were unusual for featuring a handful of groups with one or two African American or Native American members who traveled as equal members of the band and regularly played at personal appearances in community halls. At the height of his popularity in 1965, the Dick Curless Show Band included Buddy Johnson—an African American—on bass, and Johnson plays bass on the recorded version of one of Curless's most popular Maine-themed recordings from the mid-1960s ("Tater Raisin' Man"). In the early 1950s Allerton "Al" Hawkes and an African American singer/guitarist named Alton Myers formed Allerton and Alton, the Cumberland Ridge Runners in Portland, Maine. Allerton and Alton performed five days a week on WLAM radio in Lewiston, Maine, until they were both drafted during the Korean War. And a number of country and western groups in Maine featured Native American members, most prominently "Indian Gerry" Slaggert, who was a member of Curly O'Brien's group in Bangor, Maine, in the 1950s and 1960s. Hal Lone Pine and Betty Cody played with African American fiddle and banjo players in Atlantic Canada in the 1950s, but none was ever a full-time member of the group, and the group never featured Native American musicians.

However, the association of Lone Pine with Native Americans was strong enough in the regional imagination that many New England and Canadian fans of the group misinterpreted Betty Cody's strong Quebecois accent on Indian-themed songs such as "Tom Tom Yodel" as a Native American accent and arrived at personal appearances expecting her to be a Native American. Betty Cody was born Rita Coté in Sherbrooke, Quebec, in 1921, and though she never fictionalized her birthplace, she adopted a stage name that was a decidedly western frontier variation on Coté (Cody, as in Buffalo Bill Cody). She hand-stitched all of her stage costumes, choosing styles that were evocative of the western frontier and that matched her husband's tailor-made rodeo suits. Lone Pine and Betty's amalgamation of a Maine and western frontier identity proved simpatico with an Appalachian frontier image upon their signing of a record contract with RCA Victor in 1952. One of the first RCA singles recorded and released by Hal Lone Pine and Betty Cody in 1952 was an old popular song called "On the Trail of the Lonesome Pine." The song is a romantic piece of vaudeville minstrelsy set in the Blue Ridge Mountains of Virginia. In 1908 author John Fox Jr. published a best-selling novel titled *The Trail of the Lonesome Pine*. The book spawned the aforementioned song in 1913, was made into a silent film by Cecil B. DeMille in 1915, and was made again with color and sound in 1936 by Henry Hathaway and starring Henry Fonda and Fred MacMurray. A version of the song as sung by Laurel and Hardy appeared in that comic duo's 1937 western *Way Out West*. Despite the prominence of "On the Trail of the Lonesome Pine" in the popular imagination, the repositioning of Lone Pine (from the western or Maine frontier) as the "lonesome pine" of Virginia's Blue Ridge Mountains was a seamless enough transition that many of Lone Pine and Betty's New England–based fans do not question the popular misconception that the group wrote "On the Trail of the Lonesome Pine" as their theme song. That Lone Pine and Betty positioned themselves on the western, southern Appalachian, or Maine frontier did not seem to matter so much, as long as they were positioned on *a* frontier.

Projecting the Frontier: New England Country and Western and the Legacy of Minstrelsy

Blackface minstrels have never participated in the New England country and western event. American literary critic Constance Rourke theorized that America's three comedic personas (the rustic Yankee, the backwoodsman, and the blackface minstrel) became amalgamated on the frontier (Rourke and Brooks 1980). If so, the first step toward amalgamation of this trio was when the rustic Yankee was subsumed under the mask of the blackface minstrel. Musicologist Charles Hamm's (1995) observations of what he believed to be the last minstrel show in the United States in Turnbridge, Vermont, in the 1980s certainly lend credence to the idea that by the twentieth century blackface minstrelsy in New England served as a vehicle for the ethnic (WASP) Yankee critique of encroaching (and increasing) multiculturalism in New England and beyond. At first glance, then, the minstrel's absence from the New England country and western stage is peculiar. However, closer examination of the hillbilly orchestra era in New England (1925–35) shows a preponderance of musicians with "uncle" names who doubled as hillbilly musicians and blackface minstrels. The ubiquity of popular culture's last rustic Yankee figures—Uncle Zed and Uncle Josh Weathersby—and their impact on the stage personas of New England and southern hillbilly musicians, the decidedly backwoods persona of the hillbilly, and the role these musicians played in New England as the last major wave of blackface minstrels indicate both that Rourke's theory of amalgamation played out as such in New England and that the rustic Yankee was still alive at the core of hillbilly orchestra performance practice.

It is difficult to say with certainty when multiethnic country and western music began in New England, but the emergence of Hal Lone Pine on WLBZ radio in Bangor, Maine, in 1932 provides the earliest known starting point. Lone Pine's 1930s groups (the Lone Pine Mountaineers, the Noisiest Gang in Radio) consisted of a mix of performers of Quebecois, Irish, Italian, and WASP ethnicity. By the end of the 1930s, Lone Pine had begun working with Uncle Ezra Jones, Bangor, Maine's most prominent rustic Yankee and blackface minstrel performer. In what was typical of interactions between multiethnic country and western groups and blackface minstrels like Uncle Ezra, Lone Pine employed Jones as an emcee and square dance caller at personal appearances, prohibited him from wearing blackface, and had him perform as Bozo the Tramp. Betty and Flo Cody recall that Lone Pine and the members of his group learned their stagecraft—microphone technique, makeup and costuming, comedic timing, pacing of repertoire, the creation of stage personas, and the ability to guide an audience through an evening's entertainment—directly from Uncle Ezra. The recollections of major figures in the history of New England country and western—Betty Cody, Grandpa Jones, Yodelin' Slim Clark, Gene Hooper, Ray and Ann Little, Betty Gribben, and Dick Curless—provide further evidence that multiethnic New England country and western groups owe a debt to blackface minstrelsy (and hobo, rube, Irish, Jewish, and other ethnic/racial minstrel forms, though to a much lesser degree) while also actively censuring blackface minstrelsy itself at country and western events. In short, blackface minstrels taught New England country and western performers how to create "authentic" stage personas and how to harness the imagination of the audience in order to produce an effective stage show.

From the very beginning, New England had no shortage of minstrelsy of all ethnic stripes—blackface minstrelsy (as performed by whites and blacks) was popular in urban centers and in rural stage productions in New England

and eastern Canada and played a prominent role in the development of the region's yodeling tradition in the 1920s. In Massachusetts in 1935, Grandpa Jones's "Grandpa" costume and persona were born on WBZ radio as an amalgam of elements of southern backwoods comedy learned in his home state of Kentucky with blackface minstrelsy (false whiskers, face makeup) learned from the blackface minstrels who originated the *Amos 'n Andy Show* on WBZ in Boston (Jones and Jones interview 1975). Betty Gribben explained that, prior to joining the Ken Mackenzie Tent Show in Portland, Maine, she learned her stage technique, comedic timing, and stage makeup from a local blackface minstrel. Gribben abhorred blackface minstrelsy, both for its demeaning nature and for the ability of burnt cork/greasepaint to unleash base and crude behavior in performers, but interactions with blackface minstrels at the amateur competitions where she got her start in the 1930s was unavoidable. "Once someone puts on that greasepaint," Gribben said, "there's no telling what they'll do" (interview 2007).

As Betty Gribben's quote shows, the costuming of minstrel performers enables them to behave in a manner contrary to social norms, engendering behavior that, without the costuming, would be considered bizarre, scandalous, embarrassing, subversive, or morally questionable. Eric Lott (1993) writes that blackface minstrelsy was a critical tool in the creation of "whiteness" and an engine in the social construction of race and the black/white color line that defines many discussions of American culture. Given Lott's assumption, it is possible that the tools of minstrelsy could be repurposed to redefine socially constructed ideas of racial, ethnic, and American identity. That multiethnic New England country and western groups utilized key aspects of minstrel performance practice while rejecting blackface itself stands at odds with Michael Rogin's (1992) characterization of blackface as the portal of the ethnic American's passage from immigrant to "white" American. If, as Hamm (1995) suggests, the tools of blackface minstrelsy could be utilized to critique multiculturalism in New England and the nation, could they not be altered to promote it?

Blackface minstrelsy persisted in most of New England through the 1950s, when the momentum of the civil rights movement made it difficult for many New Englanders to justify the practice. However, blackface minstrelsy continued in some places as late as the 1980s. The universal rejection of blackface minstrelsy in New England country and western performance from its very beginnings in the 1930s indicates that the content of blackface minstrelsy stood at odds with the vision of frontier America that New England's multiethnic country and western ensembles hoped to engender in their audiences. The tools of minstrelsy that enabled performers to construct racial, ethnic, class, regional, and national identities were used instead to construct an imaginary frontier space in which participants could reconstruct their boundaries of identity.

The Pros and Cons of Name Change: The Circle C Ranch Boys

The Calderone brothers—Vincent and Joseph—of Boston chose to Americanize their names in order to gain better acceptance among country and western audiences, going by Jimmy and Joey Cal. In 1936 Vinny—or Jimmy Cal—joined a western group based in East Boston named the Colorado Ramblers, playing accordion and accompanying singer and bass player Angelo Boncore. The group had named itself in honor of its banjo player, who hailed from Colorado. Like Calderone, Boncore chose an Anglo stage name—Al Blake—because he thought it made good show business sense. The group secured a regular radio broadcast on Boston's WHDH radio and a sponsorship from Community Opticians. The sponsorship, which paid the band a salary, coupled with the departure of their Colorado banjo player, prompted the group to rename themselves the Circle C Ranch Boys (the initials of Community Opticians were used to create a western "brand" in which the letter C appeared inside the letter O, which is the "circle") (Boncore interview 2005).

Angelo Boncore was well known in the Italian neighborhoods of Boston's North End and in neighboring Charlestown and East Boston. His family had been entrenched in the local business community, and Angelo owned and operated his own business, delivering range oil and ice by horse and wagon to Italian homes throughout Boston's North End. Vinny Calderone's family was also well known in the Italian communities of the North End and neighboring Charlestown. (Vinny's father and grandfather played accordion on street corners, and his mother supplied both neighborhoods with bootleg wine during Prohibition.) When the Circle C Ranch Boys hit the airwaves in 1938, Calderone's family was unfazed by his Americanized stage name. However, members of the Boncore family were dismayed to hear that Angelo was using the stage name Al Blake and took offense at what they perceived to be Angelo's shaming of his Italian heritage. The fallout over this issue within the family was powerful enough to prompt Angelo to raise the issue with WHDH's station manager. The station manager expressed reservations about a country and western group led by someone named Angelo Boncore, as well as doubts about the audience's ability to accept a name change in stride, but he conceded and allowed Angelo to return to his birth name. Al Blake became Angelo Boncore apparently without being a detriment to the group's popularity (Boncore interview 2005).

Americanized names were a handy tool for Italians in Boston, who were viewed with disdain by the greater population on account of their Roman Catholicism and by xenophobic fears that the ethnic heritage of New England was being diluted. Italians in Massachusetts were also suspected of being socialist, communist, and anarchist agitators and of being members of the Industrial Workers of the World—a fear exacerbated by the Sacco and Vanzetti trial, which began in 1920 and ended with both men's still controversial execution in 1927 (Puleo 2007). Owen Wister, who authored the best-selling western novel *The Virginian* in 1902 (*The Virginian* became the blueprint of the idealized American West from which the western film genre was built), saw the western frontier as an escape from the very immigrant hordes (what Wister called "encroaching alien vermin" [Scharnhorst 2002]) from which performers like Calderone and Boncore came. Wister wrote in an essay in 1895 that the immigrants who filled America's eastern cities "turn our cities to Babels and our citizenship to a hybrid face, who degrade our commonwealth from a nation into something half pawn-shop, half broker's office" (Scharnhorst 2002, xi). Historian Samuel Adams Drake—another New Englander—complained that the air around the Paul Revere House in Boston's North End "is actually thick with the vile odors of garlic and onions—of macaroni and lazzaroni. The dirty tenements swarm with greasy voluble Italians" (quoted in Conforti 2001, 209). Clearly, then, for Italian American country and western musicians in Boston in the 1930s, a switch to an Americanized "cowboy" name could potentially leapfrog these ethnic prejudices and greatly enhance the likelihood of landing a radio broadcast with commercial sponsorship. Though the matter of the Sacco and Vanzetti trial represents the extreme end of ethnic tensions in New England during the early twentieth century, many "ethnic" New England country and western musicians explained that their motives behind Anglicizing their names were to ameliorate power dynamics in the entertainment *business*; cowboy names helped "ethnic" musicians negotiate matters of business with powerful, potentially xenophobic gatekeepers.

Having navigated past xenophobic gatekeepers, performers utilized their frontier name and stage persona to ameliorate ethnic tensions that may have existed in the audience inside the performance venue. What is particularly noteworthy about the case of Angelo Boncore and the Circle C Ranch Boys is that Boncore's reversion from his stage name (Al Blake) back to his birth name in 1938 appeared to have no ill effect on the group's popularity with their existing audience, their ability to secure other sponsored radio broadcasts and schedule well-attended personal appearances, or their ability to win over new audiences—even in rural Maine, where Angelo was likely the first and only Italian American square dance caller. It is likely that the choice of a western band name like the Circle C Ranch Boys—a band name that did not mention the individual names of the performers—enabled audiences to be more accepting of "ethnic" musicians than they might have been otherwise.

Nonetheless, the use of Americanized or frontier stage names enabled ethnic Americans to assume the stage in many Anglo-dominated social arenas. This allowed ethnic audience members to hear "their" music at country and western events, with Italian, Irish, German, Greek, Portuguese, and French traditional dance music intermixing—upon request—with the standard country and western and popular fare. The ability of multiethnic country and western ensembles to satisfy a diverse audience was enhanced by the fact that where there was one ethnic musician in a group, there tended to be others. So while the Americanized names of country and western performers may give the appearance of an Americanizing leveler, it enabled the inclusion of ethnic musics in performances for the general public, exposed audience members to music that they were likely unfamiliar with (or perhaps suspicious of), and helped reinforce traditional musical values among specific participants. In other words, multiethnic country and western ensembles created a very real bridge between an American and an immigrant worldview—a frontier, if you will, between differing worldviews. Though the function of the country and western event aims at performers ameliorating tension between the band and the audience by honoring requests, requests that brought the ethnicity of the performers to the fore must have created tension and confusion in some settings. Some audience members were doubtlessly surprised—for better or for worse—to hear Betty Cody alternate verses of Hank Williams's "Hey Good Lookin'" in English and French. Yet the same audience members who had xenophobic fears of Italians were likely confounded by cowboys Al Blake and Jimmy Cal singing "Mala Femina" in impeccable Italian, only then to launch into a thoroughly convincing rendition of Johnny Bond's western standard "Cimarron." While old Yankees like Drake and Harvard professor and ballad scholar Barrett Wendell fretted about the changing face of New England, Italians living near Boston's Paul Revere House—like Vinny "Jimmy Cal" Calderone and Angelo "Al Blake" Boncore of the Circle C Ranch Boys—were busy making use of the frontier symbols and names of cowboy music to gain entrance to community halls and forge a more inclusive vision (or version) of America than that promoted by social Darwinists like Owen Wister.

Conclusion: Performance versus Reality along the New England Frontier

At first glance, the Americanized frontier image of Lone Pine and Betty Cody obscures their Quebecois ethnic heritage, and—if the recollections of other ethnic New England country and western performers are to be believed—intentionally so. Hal Lone Pine and Betty Cody, while ostensibly fronting an "assimilated" ensemble, were bilingual Franco American band leaders fronting a multiethnic group that actively performed songs in French for their New England and Canadian audiences; they were also likely the only major label country and western act from outside of Louisiana to have scored a Top 10 country and western hit with an audible French accent. As such, the adoption of an Americanized stage name and persona by the ethnic performer is not necessarily indicative of "Americanization" or abandonment of one's ethnic identity but rather is a means by which ethnic New Englanders subverted popular conceptions of American identity as understood through the frontier cowboy. New England country and western music promoted a vision of frontier multiculturalism, engendering a very real "alternation" between American and immigrant worldviews. While *alternation* is used here in the sociological sense, it is also a term used by New England's Franco American country and western musicians to describe the practice of translating English songs into their native tongue and alternating verses of the songs between French and English during their personal appearances, a practice popularized in New England by singers like Betty Cody in the late 1930s. Italian American alternation was also common, and American pop music fans know of it through hit songs such as "That's Amore," "O Solo Mio," and "Volare" as popularized by Louis Prima and Dean Martin (born Dino Crochetti). Dean Martin singing "That's Amore" is hardly subversive, but alternation as employed (and engendered in the sociological sense) by an Italian American New Englander under the wide brim of a frontier cowboy—the paragon of authentic American identity—in an environment normally closed off to ethnic performers constitutes what social constructionists would call a radical attempt at reorganizing everyday life (Pilarzyk 1978, 382). It is a reorganization of American or New England identity inclusive of multiculturalism.

5

"IT BEATS DIGGING CLAMS"

The Working Life of Country and Western Musicians in the Barnstorming Era

Gift exchange and the spirit of community are important elements of the country and western event. And yet, for the New England country and western musician, it (the event, the music) is also about the money. Country and western music has provided a way of making a living—or part of a living—for several thousand people in New England over the course of the music's history in the region and as such should be examined here as work.

Most contemporary country musicians entering into the professional marketplace today approach country music work in much the same way an aspiring professional athlete approaches his or her sport: an agent will develop and promote unknown and inexperienced talent for the purpose of securing a record contract for them, or musicians will spend years of preparation toiling in obscurity while incurring a financial loss, simply covering expenses, or earning spending money (as opposed to making a living) with the hope that one day an agent or scout will take notice of them and elevate them to the status of international "star." Modern-day New England country and western musicians who make a working-class or middle-class "living" do so by augmenting their earnings from a day job with money earned from music, or they work as musical chameleons ready to adapt to a wide variety of musical shades, working five to seven nights a week, like self-proclaimed "gig pig" Denny Breau (interview 2005).

This has not always been the case in New England, where country and western music once provided a means for a living for performers, owners and employees of country and western–only music venues, record companies, jukebox operators, and media outlets such as radio and television. For about four decades—roughly covering the duration of the barnstorming era—there were many full-time professional country and western bands working throughout New England who earned a higher income than the working-class wage earners, woodsmen, farmers, and fishermen who listened to their music and attended their shows. Country and western music provided a better income and a more cosmopolitan lifestyle than most working-class people could expect from factory, agricultural, woods, or maritime work. In fact, for many of the professional country and western musicians of the 1930s, it was this very real likelihood of making a better living that attracted them to making a life in country and western music—or, as Gene Hooper of Machias, Maine, says, "It beats digging clams" (Hooper and Hooper interview 2005).

According to Gene, one night's earnings from winning an amateur talent competition was far greater than what he could earn from an entire week spent digging for clams along the Maine coast during the Depression:

> And I was just lucky enough that I won that [amateur talent] contest and got five dollars. In 1937 or '6, whenever it was, I forget what year, that was a lot of money. 'Cause I'd been digging clams, you know, and clams then was twenty-five cents a bushel. And that was more than a bushel, because it was a basket. And I finally, that's the year I finally got this guitar and learned all of these songs. And that five dollars that I got from singing, why I'da had to work two or three months clamming to make that same kind of money, you know? So that kind of convinced me that maybe I—if I'm lucky—I can get into show business. (Hooper and Hooper interview 2005)

"Show business" is a term used frequently by the pioneer generations of New England country and western musicians. Jim Smalls, a country and western music promoter active throughout New England from the 1930s through the 1960s, groomed several aspiring musicians by teaching them the "business" side of show business before introducing them to what he called "the *other* side of show business," meaning the stage (LeBlanc interview 2004).

Starting Out in Country and Western Show Business: Amateur Competitions

Gene Hooper's introduction to the country and western profession by way of winning an amateur competition is a nearly universal experience among country and western musicians of his generation. Competitions were often staged by traveling entertainers who recognized that the promise of a cash reward would bring in many paying customers who would not otherwise attend; in particular, children and adolescents wishing to compete onstage guaranteed that entire families would attend a country and western event to see their children, grandchildren, nieces, and nephews perform onstage. Competitions featured a wide variety of curiosities—musical and otherwise—providing performance space for yodelers and contortionists alike. Rusty Rogers made fairly significant earnings by winning amateur contests in the mid-1930s near Damariscotta, Maine, winning as much as $25 and $30 on any given night. This was a substantial sum compared to his daytime earning potential: Rogers could earn a mere $2 per cord cutting pulpwood (and $3 per cord for peeling it)—hard, backbreaking labor conducted out in Maine's harsh winter and black fly–laden spring months. To Rogers, music appeared a more agreeable, exciting, and financially rewarding option (Rogers and Kempton interview 2005; Dennett 1991).

Until the onset of rock and roll in the late 1950s, amateur competitions hosted by country and western performers provided a significant career opportunity for aspiring professionals, as these competitions sometimes led to apprenticeships with the headlining act or to fifteen- to sixty-minute slots on regional radio stations. This, in turn, could lead to an income of between $280 and $400 (the salary for a sideman in the Down Homers) per month per musician (Roberts 1987; Roberts interview 2004; Rogers and Kempton interview 2005). Just as a matter of comparison, someone working forty hours a week in 1938—the year the Fair Labor Standards Act imposed the minimum wage at $0.25/hour (where it stayed for the next seven years)—brought home $10 a week, or $40 a month, or just 10 percent of what a member of the Down Homers earned each month.

Not all novice performers debuted at amateur competitions. Yodelin' Slim Clark made his debut at a Grange hall minstrel show in Petersham, Massachusetts, in 1929. Slim was just twelve years old at the time, and his family and friends were so impressed by his rendition of cowboy and hobo songs at the minstrel show that they began taking him to singing engagements in the surrounding area by Model A Ford in the summer and by horse-drawn sleigh in the winter (Cohen 1977). With a repertoire centered on cowboy and hobo songs, like "Little Joe the Wrangler," "Railroad Corral," and "Big Rock Candy Mountain," "I was making $25 a night," Slim said, at a time when most of New England was still deeply mired in the Great Depression. "I made so much that people called me 'the little rich brat'" (Ferriss 1996, 8E). By the age of fifteen Slim—the youngest of six children—was earning three times the amount earned by his widowed mother (Ferriss 1996). What this exact amount was is unclear, but Bradley Kincaid was earning $100 per week (with Grandpa Jones and Harmonica Joe Troyan earning $50 per week as his sidemen) while performing in the same region and at the same types of venues as Clark in 1935 (Jones and Jones interview 1975).

Song Specialist: Making the Jump from Amateur Contests to Barnstorming Ensembles

New England's most prominent country and western groups tended to employ a variety show–type ensemble cast. Most performers, like Rusty Rogers and Gene Hooper, made the transition from amateur competitions to barnstorming by securing a "specialist" role in a barnstorming ensemble, filling the role of a singer who specializes in a certain type of song. Specialists tended to stick to novelty songs, yodeling songs, slow romantic crooning, rockabilly (in later years), or old-time folk songs. John Reed, for instance, was a specialist in the Hank Keene Tent Show who only sang yodeling songs. There was a fixed pay scale in most bands that favored the bandleaders, then the musicians who played a full-time role, and then the specialists. There was generally room for advancement for specialists, though a major promotion tended only to happen when a specialist left one group for a more prominent role in another.

As an example of this transition process, singer Rusty Rogers started out on an amateur show circuit and joined up with an obscure band named Esther King and Pals of the Golden West from Newburyport, Massachusetts. After being fired from that group, Rusty hired on with Bud Bailey and His Downeasters to specialize in Sons of the Pioneers songs; he eventually became a featured singer and yodeler in the Down Homers. Rogers's story is a colorful one and exemplifies the types of narratives New England country and western musicians share about their rise to regional prominence. What we can see in Rogers's story is that the beginning wages of specialists in a country and western ensemble may have exceeded that of many mill workers, but specialists and teenage musicians still lived close to the financial edge. Living arrangements could be bleak and—relative to the pay scale—expensive, and bandleaders could be quite creative in cutting costs and in manipulating young musicians. In an interview, Rogers discussed how he came to join Bud Bailey and His Downeasters—a top-tier country and western group that worked out of Portland, Maine, and Portsmouth, New Hampshire, between the mid-1930s until the mid-1940s. Rusty's wife, Patty Kempton, was also present.

> *Rogers:* [The Downeasters were] on a station [in Portland], five thousand watts. So just before that, I had been with a group in Newburyport [Massachusetts] called Esther King and Pals of the Golden West, which I have pictures of and everything. And I was getting twenty dollars a week. So, pretty good [laughs]. Room and board. And [Esther King] kicked me out of the group.

Kempton: You didn't wanna pick the dump. [Esther King's family ran the town dump in Newburyport.]

Rogers: They woke me up one mornin,' said that "part of the job is pickin' the dump." And I says, "Whaddaya mean?" And they says, "Well, you gotta separate the papers and everything." And so I said, "Well, the hell with that." So they dropped me off at the Newburyport Bridge. And that was when the big hurricane—1938—came about. And I'm thumbin' in the middle of the damn hurricane; didn't have a dime in my pocket.

Kempton: Shoulda picked that dump [laughter]!

Rogers: Shoulda did better [laughter]! And I got a ride to Portland, and I spent my last dime to [get] back to the movie house where it's fifteen cents a night. And who should come on, but Lone Pine Mountaineer, who was . . .

Kempton: Betty Cody's husband.

Rogers: Betty Cody's husband. And with his group . . . Before the show I went up and I says, "I'm a yodeler and everything, and a singer." And he says, "Well, I don't need anybody yodelin'; I do that myself. But I'll put you on for a number." So he put me on for a number and he says, "You did very good." And he says, "I'll tell ya what," he says, "I can't use you, but I'll send you over to Bud Bailey of the Downeasters on WCSH. And," he says, "if you get a job with them," he says, "that's big time: that's five thousand watts," you know, compared to a little pissy-ass station [like the one in Newburyport]. So I went over, and [Bud Bailey] says, "Whaddaya do?" And I says, "I sing Sons of the Pioneers songs and yodel and everything." So he says, "Let's hear you." So he heard me, says, "Well, you're on." He says, "Do a Sons of the Pioneers song." I says, "Whaddaya want?" He says, "Well, here's one of their books." A 1938, '39 book. So I went out in the . . . well, it wasn't a dressing room, but anyway, it was part of the studio. And I looked through the music and I knew how to read music 'cause my father was a musician, and he taught me how to read. So I picked out a song. It was called "Ride, Ranger, Ride." A Sons of the Pioneers song. And I practiced it, and about five minutes later they put me on the air, and I walked into the studio that night—I didn't have a dime in my pocket—and they took me on the show. And the first place we played was Freeport. And, of course, this was about ten years before television, and we had a packed house and everything. And he give me *ten bucks* for the four-hour show; but I sold fifteen dollars worth of my pictures. . . . We used to sell pictures . . . and our pictures was twenty-five cents. And I sold fifteen dollars' worth of them, plus the ten dollars.

Kempton: Unbelievable [laughs]. They used to make so much money selling their pictures!

Murphy: Well, with that moustache [points to the picture featuring Rogers wearing an Errol Flynn–style moustache], how could they resist [laughter]?

Rogers: So I went back and I got me a [hotel] room. Four dollars a week [laughter]. Cheap shit.

Kempton: In Portland?

Rogers: Yeah! 'Course, I woke up in the middle of the night and there was . . .

Kempton: Cockroaches?

Rogers: Not bedbugs . . .

Kempton: Cockroaches.

Rogers: Cockroaches! All over the place. So after that I had to . . .

Kempton: He kept the light on so the cockroaches would stay away!

Rogers: . . . leave the light on [laughter].

Murphy: Now, you were living with Vinny Calderone at the time? [Vinny "Jimmy Cal" Calderone played accordion for Bud Bailey at this time.]

Rogers: No. This was, ah, maybe a few months before that. And then Jimmy [Cal] said, "Why don't you and I, you know, get a room together?" So I think we got in the big time. We paid ten dollars, I think, for a room. Ah, he's a hell of a guy. Great musician. Great showman. He played Vegas. He played everywhere.

Murphy: What was Bud Bailey like?

Rogers: [clears throat] Well . . .

Kempton: Tell him how he paid you.

Rogers: Very weakly. [This refers to a joke Rogers likes to tell about how he was paid "weekly. *Very* weakly."]

Kempton: He was very cheap.

Rogers: He said to us one day, he says, "Well," he says, "I got a new system. I been readin' a lot about health products, so I'm gonna give you these pills. These pills is like havin' a full-course meal." 'Course, we're dumb. We're only like—Jesus Christ—we're only . . .

Kempton: Teenagers, that's right.

Rogers: Teenagers, and he says, "This is equal to a *steak*." So he'd buy us a doughnut in the mornin' and a couple pills at night. He was really cheap.

Kempton: They were vitamins of some kind. They weren't speed or anything. (interview 2005)

Bandleaders like Bud Bailey hired musicians to work for weekly pay and a promise to cover meals. This deal worked in favor of the bandleader, who generally did not have to pay out for dinners; these were instead provided for free by locals at personal appearances. Though the anecdote about Bud Bailey feeding his teenage musicians vitamins instead of meals is fabulously extreme—or the requirement that members of Esther King's band sort trash at her family's Newburyport dump—it is representative of a business model whereby bandleaders held the purse strings and established pay scales that were both far from equitable and designed to benefit the group leaders, not the tenderfoot musician.

Dropping Out: Barnstorming as a Worthwhile Profession

In light of the potentially significant payday for aspiring professionals, working as a barnstorming country and western performer in the first half of the twentieth century could hardly be called "working class." Country music may be a working-class music (Fox 2004; Malone 2002b; Peterson and DiMaggio 1975), but it is not a working-class profession (Gilbert 2008; Gilbert and Kahl 1993; Zweig 2004). In fact, the barnstorming country and western profession in New England appeared to be such an unusually viable and lucrative form of self-employment in the 1930s through the 1950s—relative to other options like factory work—that it was not unusual for teenage musicians to drop out of high school in order to take up a life on the road. This was occurring at the very time New Englanders were placing a greater emphasis on the completion of high school: between 1910 and 1938 New Hampshire's high school graduation rates rose from 10 to 60 percent (Conforti 2001, 288). For Johnny Smith in Depression-era Maine, playing guitar in a hillbilly band was money in the bank for his family at a time when cash was in short supply; the tangible cash had significant value for the family over the intangible benefits of a high school degree:

> Well, this was back during the deep Depression. And I'd just started into high school, and I played guitar. And then Uncle Lem, he asked me to join the band, and I jumped at the chance, because, you know, for four bucks a night—which was really big money back in those days—it helped the family. I'd just started into high school, and I joined the band. And the daily schedule! We played all over the state of Maine. And the schedule would be: we had a six o'clock in the morning broadcast on the local radio station, and the broadcast served a purpose, because Uncle Lem could advertise where we were going to be. And I'd do the broadcast at six o'clock and then be in high school at eight o'clock until one o'clock. And [Uncle Lem] would be waiting to pick me up at one o'clock. They would pick me up at one o'clock, and we would drive anywhere. Twenty miles to fifty miles and do a program and play for a dance and drive back. [Smith is speaking here of the *average* drive the band would make for any given show. In the same interview, Smith recalled playing with Uncle Lem as far away as Lac-Mégantic, Quebec, some 185 miles due north from his high school in Portland, Maine. On modern roads with a modern car, this drive would take about eight hours round-trip. In 1938 roads between southeastern Quebec and Portland were narrow, infrequently maintained, and intermittently dirt and a (very bumpy) form of tarmac. As such, a drive from Portland to Lac-Mégantic would have taken longer and been considerably less comfortable than it would in the twenty-first century.] And a lot of times we wouldn't get back until the

> wee hours of the morning. And a lot of the times I was the only one that could stay awake. And I would *drive* a lot of times back—back to Portland. And with two or three hours of sleep I would be back to do the broadcast at six o'clock in the morning: and that's, well, five or six days a week. And that lasted all through high school, which accounts for the fact that I didn't graduate. (Smith interview 2007)

Dick Curless, too, never graduated high school on account of country and western music. In the late 1940s he had the choice between going on the road as a member of Yodelin' Slim Clark's Trail Riders and completing high school in Gilbertville, Massachusetts:

> Just before I graduated [in 1949], Slim Clark took off on tour and I either had to graduate—stay home and do my final exams—and get my diploma, or I could take the tour. So I took the tour. And the principal of the high school said, "Look, I've covered up for you pretty good this last year 'cause you've been touring and coming in late to classes. The school board's kind of come down on my ears here. You're either going to have to knuckle down and do your final exams to graduate high school." You know, one or the other, so I looked at him and said, "I think you know what my answer is." And he said, "Yeah. Good luck." And all I had to do was my final exams. I had my class ring, and my father and mother gave me a watch, my class trip. But [I bought new stage clothes] with my class trip money—I had to discuss this with my parents, and I said, "I want to tour with Slim. That's what I'm going to do the rest of my life. I know it." My parents knew I had the potential, too, just as Slim Clark did.
>
> I could make a good living at it then, too. You know, it doesn't sound like much, but ten dollars a night, twelve dollars a night, fifteen dollars a night was pretty good bread back then [in 1949]. Of course, I was a young fella, and I knew I was going to do that anyway, so I took off on tour with Slim Clark. Then I got the taste of the road, and I got the taste of the audiences outside of where I was acquainted. (Cohen 1977, 100)

The participation of both the Gilbertville High School principal and the Curless parents in the story of Dick Curless dropping out of school is striking; that both parties require Curless to talk the decision out suggests that both considered a barnstorming career versus a high school diploma a choice worth pondering. Curless's decision appears to have been accepted by both his principal and his parents without resistance. In light of the earnings he was bringing in at the time through music, it is likely that the principal and the parents were not being complicit in a reckless, irresponsible act on Curless's part.

Rusty Rogers also had a showdown with the school principal—only in his case, the principal was his father. The son was an eccentric youngster (some might say a delinquent) who regularly rode his pet bull into town and made a practice of skipping school by climbing out through the waste hole of the school outhouse. He ran away from home at age fifteen to play with the Katahdin Mountaineers and soon after returning was asked to leave school after punching a teacher. His father/principal was chagrined by the embarrassing circumstances of Rogers's departure from school but believed Rusty's earning potential as a professional musician made performing a responsible career path. Within a matter of months of dropping out, Rogers was earning a living through country and western music with Bud Bailey and His Downeasters (Rogers and Kempton interview 2005).

Not every musician had the same parental support as Curless and Rogers: Yodeling Kenny Roberts's widowed father was against Kenny's decision to drop out of Athol High School in his junior year to join the Down Homers full-time on nearby WKNE radio. Yet, according to Roberts, he discussed the matter at great length with his father and ultimately convinced him that the decision was a sound one. And it certainly was, financially: in his first year with the Down Homers (1943), Roberts averaged between $89 and $114 a week (Roberts interview 2004).

For Curless, Rogers, and Roberts, finishing school was an option. However, for the large Roman Catholic, immigrant, working-class families in New England in the 1920s, 1930s, and 1940s, quitting school can actually be seen as a part of the family culture of the times and a necessary fact of the family economy. For these families who served as the labor force and the economic foundation of the manufacturing industry in New England, universally low wages meant that large families often pushed their older children to quit school and work in order to help support the family. So important to the family was the wage-earning potential of older children that the "graduation" from school into factory work was a source of pride for young people in New England's mill towns and cities and a rite of passage into adulthood (Hareven and Langenbach 1995). As Flo Cody Hooper (born Florence Coté) recalled: "The day I turned sixteen, back then [in 1942], you know: 'Go find a job. You're sixteen years old today. No birthday party' [laughs]. Yup. And I did" (Hooper and Hooper interview 2005). Within the Coté family, the country and western profession was viewed as one option along with factory work; in other words, it was simply another opportunity to make money. In Flo's case, country and western music served as a second job, and in her sister Betty's case, it was a "living": "Well, all we wanted was to earn a living," Betty told me. "We never thought we'd get on recordings. We didn't try. We weren't trying."

Murphy: What did your parents think of your choice of profession?
Betty Cody: They wanted it.

> *Murphy:* Yeah?
> *Betty Cody:* Oh yeah. They were, "Hey, do whatever you have to do." But see, I didn't go on the road until I was married, you know? I'd come back every night. I'd perform and come back every night at home. But they were all for it. Oh yeah. (Coté-Binette and Breau interview 2006)

Many performers from the early era of New England country and western music who quit school to go professional later expressed regret or shame over not earning a high school diploma, but in light of the evidence, their decision to leave school was actually a financially sound one based on pure, hard cash that seemed in ample supply if the musicians were willing to work for it. The changes in the direction of national network programming that all but eliminated local musicians' access to broadcast media (and therefore their ability to subsist on earnings from country and western) beginning in the late 1950s could not have been predicted in the late 1930s. The decision of Franco-American musicians to drop out of high school and choose country and western over factory work—without resistance from their parents—is evidence that country and western music was considered a viable (and even lucrative) source of income that an extended family could depend on. This of course depended on whether or not the young person in question was successful. Franco-American musicians of Betty and Flo Cody's generation suggest that they would not have received their high school diploma regardless of whether or not they had pursued a career in music. For others like Dick Curless, dropping out of school and failing to succeed in music would have likely left them worse off than they would have been otherwise. Based on the stories of ex–professional country and western musicians who had trouble adjusting to working life after music, the travel and excitement of performing professionally would have made factory work even more distasteful to a failed professional musician.

Engine of Industry: The Personal Appearance in the New England Country and Western Profession

In New England country and western music, the personal appearance was the engine that drove the profession. Personal appearances were the single most important source of revenue for the professional New England country and western musician. Admittedly, there is a bit of a chicken-or-egg situation here: the ability of country and western performers to generate bookings for personal appearances hinged on their ability to secure a regular broadcast slot on local/regional radio. Radio was the primary means by which performers secured bookings and, in turn, advertised them. Nevertheless, personal appearances served as a profound shaping force in country and western as an expressive regional form. Sound recordings were viewed—at best—skeptically as a one-time money grab for musicians and a long-shot opportunity for a public relations boost. Generally, encounters with record companies were considered an inconvenience that came bundled in shiny promises for recording royalties. Vinny Calderone waved off my questions about a series of 78s his group, the Hy-Lo Trio, recorded in 1949 on Boston's Crystal label by saying "Record, record, record: no money, no money, no money!" (interview 2004). Though most histories of country and western music tend to reify recording artists, most New England country and western musicians considered a radio program with sponsorship at a fifty-thousand-watt radio station the gold standard in the profession and only had a passing interest in making records. A regular program on a station with a strong, clear signal translated into a fully booked schedule of lucrative personal appearances; making records was never lucrative for barnstorming New England country and western musicians.

Royalties earned from sound recordings have not enabled any New England country and western musicians to earn a living, with the possible exception of Dick Curless, contemporary country singer Jo Dee Messina, and—for a brief period—Hal Lone Pine and Betty Cody. Only a very small handful (Billy Hill, "The Last Roundup," "Empty Saddles," "The Glory of Love"; Paul Roberts, "There's a Star Spangled Banner Waving Somewhere"; and Al Anderson, "All You Ever Do Is Bring Me Down") earned a living from songwriting royalties. Monies earned from personal appearances, however, enabled barnstorming musicians to make a living in country and western, with sales of songbooks and pictures at personal appearances augmenting revenue earned from gate receipts or guarantees. Only the radio program itself was essential to earning a living from personal appearances; a wage earned from radio appearances was not. Though the most financially successful country and western acts in New England earned a living wage directly from radio appearances, many New England country and western musicians appeared on radio for little or no money and used their airtime to advertise personal appearances, which in turn generated enough revenue for them to live on.

The Work Schedule for a Barnstorming Country and Western Musician: 1920s–1960s

Most barnstorming musicians in the first half-century of country and western music in New England performed five to seven mornings and/or afternoons a week on live radio broadcasts and played five to seven nights per week of personal appearances, returning each night in order to play the next day at the radio station. Regional country and western acts were far-ranging; for instance, it is said that there is not a single town in Maine and Massachusetts that Yodelin' Slim Clark has not performed in (Clark interview 2005). Groups would travel up to four hundred miles round-trip in one evening. Keeping in mind that this was done in the days before the development of the interstate highway system, such a schedule was even more grueling and time-consuming than it would be today.

In 1952 the average work schedule for the Connecticut-based country and western group the Down Homers looked like this:

6:00–6:30 A.M.: broadcast live at WTIC, Hartford
6:30–7:30 A.M.: go out for breakfast
7:30–11:30 A.M.: sleep
11:30 A.M.–12:00 P.M.: prepare for the next broadcast
12:00–12:30 P.M.: broadcast live at WTIC, Hartford
12:30–4:00 P.M.: drive to a personal appearance
4:00–6:00 P.M.: prepare the hall for the personal appearance, set up gear, rehearse, eat
6:00–7:45 P.M.: show: perform songs and skits
7:45–8:00 P.M.: break
8:00–10:00 P.M.: dance: perform dance music
10:00–11:00 P.M.: sign autographs, sell pictures and songbooks, pack up gear
11:00 P.M.–2:30 A.M.: drive back to Hartford
2:30–5:30 A.M.: sleep
5:30–6:00 A.M.: wake up, go to the radio station (Rogers and Kempton interview 2005)

This schedule is representative of what the Down Homers did six days and nights per week for several decades and is not so different from that of the Hal Lone Pine Mountaineers, Ken Mackenzie, the Circle C Ranch Boys, Don Fields and His Pony Boys, Eddie Zack and His Dude Ranchers, Duke and the Swingbillies, Uncle Lem, the Katahdin Mountaineers, Jerry and Sky, Jimmy and Dick, Bud Bailey and His Downeasters, the Red River Rangers, and other full-time country and western groups working throughout New England from the mid-1930s through the late 1950s.

Marginalizing Aspects of Barnstorming

Rhetorically speaking, country and western music is a genre that reflects the values, language, and traditions of the working-class community (Malone

2002a, 2002b; Sample 1996; Fox 2004; Peterson and DiMaggio 1975). As in the case of Frank "Slim" Rego, tangible evidence that this is more than simple rhetoric can be found in the house that Rego bought with his income from barnstorming. Rego's multifamily home—like the triple-decker homes many of the "pioneer" generation of Massachusetts country and western musicians bought for their families and still live in today—served to house both his immediate and his extended family. But there is a significant downside to this work ethic that suggests a nonbusiness reason why New England country and western music has had difficulty sustaining itself. The very nature of itinerant barnstorming work removed working musicians from the home and their "home" community nearly all the time. As such, the "normal" domestic family life of the musicians suffered greatly.

Working as a full-time barnstorming musician meant spending more time away from home than otherwise. Barnstorming groups would generally work at a given radio station and tour heavily within a two-hundred-mile radius of that station for two or three years, after which the region was considered "played out." The musicians would then move to another broadcast area and work out of a different radio station. Though this was good for business, it meant that growing families such as that of Hal Lone Pine and Betty Cody were deprived of setting down roots in any given community for too long. Children were often left in the care of newly made friends or fans for extended periods of time.

For example, in 1948 Hal Lone Pine and Betty Cody deposited two of their children—seven-year-old Lenny and three-year-old Dickie—with fans Ida and Alphie Babineau on the Babineau family farm near Shediak, New Brunswick, in order for the Lone Pine Mountaineers to have greater mobility for barnstorming. The Breau boys lived on the Babineau farm for five years; during this time they saw their parents about twice a month (Forbes-Roberts 2006, 11). It was during these years that Lenny Breau learned to play guitar and later claimed to have done so in order to secure a job in his parents' band so that he could be with them instead of on the farm (14). Says Dickie Breau of this kind of upbringing: "It wasn't your typical family life. We never really did much together as a family. I don't remember picnics or cookouts or going to an amusement park together. Our parents were always on the road. Sonny [a nickname for Dickie's brother, Lenny] grew to know my parents better than I did, but until he started playing with them, it would have been a similar thing: he really wouldn't have had much time with them" (14).

However difficult this arrangement may have been for the Breau family, such a nomadic existence had a romantic appeal for the would-be country and western professional. Many New England country and western musicians—young and old—describe themselves as loners, misfits, or persons with a restless curiosity that a small-town existence could not satisfy. For these self-described (or self-made) outsiders, the itinerant lifestyle of the barnstorming musician had a self-reliant allure, one most certainly enhanced by the drifting, romantic life of singing cowboys as portrayed on film (Peterson 1997). For a teenage Gene Hooper, seeing Hal Lone Pine perform between cowboy Tom Mix features in 1935 in a Machias, Maine, movie theater proved an irresistible combination, and within months Gene had left his home in Machias for Lewiston, Maine, for a career as a barnstorming country and western musician (Hooper and Hooper interview 2005).

Once on the road, however, most musicians learned quickly that barnstorming was a grueling existence. The uprootedness inherent in the life of the barnstorming musician initially held a great deal of romantic allure for would-be country and western musicians in New England. But this kind of schedule severely impacted the ability of full-time professional musicians to maintain a so-called normal life. The emotional demands of being apart from friends and family for extended periods of time, coupled with the physical demands of constant travel and energetic performances, led many performers to medicate their physically and emotionally strained existence with alcohol, drugs, and extramarital sex. To sit with New England country and western pioneers as they page through their photo albums and scrapbooks and recount tales of the musicians who populate those pages is to know that many of New England's most well respected singers, fiddlers, accordion players, comics, and steel guitarists died of alcoholism. Hal Lone Pine died of alcohol poisoning in a Lewiston, Maine, flophouse in 1977. Guitarist George Moody, who was a mentor to former Merle Haggard lead guitarist Redd Volkaert and whose aggressive Telecaster guitar style was derived in part from transposing fiddle tunes to the electric guitar, died of alcoholism in Bangor in the 1980s. Gene Hooper, Dick Curless, and Johnny White had their promising music careers repeatedly derailed by alcoholism but found sobriety in newfound spirituality and brotherhood with one another. For itinerant country and western singers like Gene Hooper, the road itself drove him to drink in an effort to take the edge off the exhaustion. A teetotaler all his life, Hooper only began drinking after he joined the *Wheeling Jamboree*; ironically, he says that the major stars of the show—Hawkshaw Hawkins, Doc and Chickie Williams, and Big Slim the Lone Cowboy—never drank:

> *Hooper:* They wasn't drinkers. For me, I was the only one that had trouble with booze in Wheeling. I guess it's why I didn't get too many bookings

[chuckles]. I know it was, now, but I couldn't know it [then]. You're drinking, you know, you're giving everybody the dickens.

Murphy: Is it just because it's around so much, or just that road life is hard?

Hooper: There was an old guy named Lazy Jim Day [on the *Wheeling Jamboree*]. They called him "The Singing Newsman." And he always acted the same to me. I never thought of him [as an alcoholic]. No, I kicked more drunks out of halls before this. I *despised* anybody drinking. But Lazy Jim Day, he'd read the newspaper every morning before he'd broadcast. And he'd find different things where he could rhyme it. Instead of talking the news, he sang it and made it funny on top of that, you know?

I'd been up in Ontario working, and that's a long ways from Wheeling, West Virginia. And we was way up in the timberlands and Back Bay. Way up in that area, you know? And we was supposed to be back every week. But they let us have one week off a month after awhile. But anyway, I had to come back into Wheeling from way up in Ontario. And times I got back and we worked every night. One nighters. And they was quite a ways apart, you know, each night. And I's settin' in the Wheeling Hotel, and I never drank. And Lazy Jim was there, and he says, "Well?" I told him that I had a broadcast I had to do at WWVA that afternoon. And I says to him, "I'm played right out, Jim." He says, "You wait just a minute, Gene, and I'll get you something. Fix you right up, and you'll be able to do it."

Now, I don't know what he brought back, but he went to the bar and brought me back a drink. And he had it mixed with something where it didn't taste too bad, and I felt that *feeling*, you know, where I come alive, you know? So I figure, "This is the only way to do it. I'll just get me a fifth, take [it] with me, when I feel tired, I'll take a sup of it." But I never's a supper.

I never knew about alcoholism. I thought people done it on purpose. But it's a sickness. 'Cause if I took a drink right now, Cliff, I wouldn't stay here talking to you. One drink, I'd go right to town and get me a bottle. And I know that. I learned that along the hard way.

And anyway, this Lazy Jim, they found in the back seat of a car. Drinking so much, dead. That's how he died. See, he was drinking right steady, but I thought he was a comedian. I just thought he acted that way, paid no attention. So this is how I got started on the stuff. From that time I never quit 'til a number of years later. (Hooper and Hooper interview 2005)

Hooper's story is a powerful narrative of a man who felt dead from the road ("I'm played right out, Jim") and was revived ("I felt that *feeling*, you know, where I come alive, you know?") by alcohol. And in that regard it is not unlike John Lincoln Wright's song "One Drink Closer to Heaven," which perceives alcohol as a step toward salvation. Yet Gene's narrative—only partially included above—shows alcohol to be the great deceiver, feigning sustenance (the "feeling" of coming alive) while stealing what truly sustains him (music, career, family) and leading toward *actual* death (instead of the *feeling* of death—"I'm played right out") in the manner of Lazy Jim Day.

Hooper's drinking not only jeopardized his ability to make a living in music but also threatened to break up his marriage. In the early 1950s Hooper was touring with Hal Lone Pine's group, and the Coté sisters (Flo Coté was married to Gene, and Betty was married to Hal) insisted the men stop drinking. As Lone Pine and Betty's son Denny recalls:

> My dad didn't start drinking until he was in his forties. He wouldn't allow booze in the band *at all*. There were stories my mom was telling me about Uncle Gene [Hooper] and Dad, and the wives being pissed off about them drinking and didn't want them to drink. So they made real sure that they didn't have any booze with them. But yet, by the time they got to the gig, guys would be hammered. And apparently they were putting vodka in the windshield wiper thing. And about fifty miles or so, they'd say, "Geez, you know, do you hear a funny tick in there? We'd better go check that out." And lift the hood up and [makes slurping noise]. And they were getting hammered that way [laughs]! (Breau interview 2005)

Denny Breau believes that "the road equates drinking":

> It's about just about every music genre. Even in the folk music thing there's plenty of booze going around. Maybe not on the gig itself—certainly after when you're all recanting your stories. And I think alcohol's a pretty big part of our [culture], no matter how you cut it, you know? . . . I think it's that self-destructive tendency for the great geniuses that do that. And then I think for everybody else it's *just there*. And it becomes part of your everyday regimen where people wanna buy you a drink, you know? And you take it. (interview 2005)

For men like Gene Hooper, alcohol had been present at shows even before he became a country and western musician—his mother had discouraged him from attending local barn dances because liquor was known to flow at such events (Hooper and Hooper interview 2005). But alcohol wasn't always an albatross around the neck of the barnstorming musician. For some, like Johnny Smith—the only teenage member of Uncle Lem's Hillbilly Orchestra—it was a kind of pleasant rite of passage into manhood: "[Uncle Lem] would pick me up from high school, and we would stop and get an Italian sandwich to eat on the way and also a bottle of beer. And that's what I kind of remember: the good Italian sandwich and a bottle of beer" (interview 2007). For others, alcohol has served as a way to medicate the pain of separation from loved ones at home while on the road playing shows. Dick Curless recalled:

> I had hit bottom. I was on two fifths of vodka a day, and that was just for *me*. I was having a terrible time with blackouts and things I couldn't remember. It just wasn't right, and I couldn't believe it when I wouldn't come to my senses.
>
> So I begged to die. But when I felt death, I had a *long* talk with God, boy, and he's a good listener. I said, "I've changed my mind and I don't want to die. If you'll spare me, I have a lot to make up for to the people that I love."
>
> I stopped drinking in the summer of 1971. I was going to buy a Rolls Royce that year, an egotistical status symbol. But I bought this farm instead at the urging of my dear wife. I'm awful glad, boy, I listened to her that time. (Hughes 1984, 3E)

As told in personal narratives such as Curless's and in lyrics like those of John Lincoln Wright's "One Drink Closer to Heaven," alcoholism, whether transcended, as in the stories told by Hooper and Curless, or succumbed to, as told in Wright's song, is viewed as a gateway to spiritual salvation, a problem transformed into a solution.

Likewise, the mobile nature of barnstorming country and western acts made it easy for the musicians to carry on extramarital affairs. But as we can see in this particularly salty tale of life on the road for the Down Homers as told by Rusty Rogers, those on the home front were not necessarily fooled:

> Well, we were playing in upstate New York. Guy [Campbell, the group's fiddle player] liked to flirt around a lot, and he was quite a ladies' man. And he had bought his wife a brand new convertible. And one time while we was playing there, he met this girl. Like there was a two-hour show and two-hour dance. And he said, "We'll have a little date after the show."
>
> So I'm loading the trunk up with the instruments, and Campbell come out with the girl. He says that he was gonna walk around to the back of the building because it's about one o'clock or so. And he says, "Now, the wife doesn't trust me. And I don't think she'd ever come here, 'cause this is New York State, and she's in Hartford [Connecticut]. But she's so damn jealous and everything." And he says, "If you should see her while I'm out back, give me a nice warnin.' Yodel, will ya?" And I says, "Well, okay. You're the boss." [Guy Campbell and Shorty Cook "owned" the Down Homers.]
>
> So, about ten minutes later the car comes up and screeches to a halt. And it's his wife in the convertible. And I started to go "Yo-lo-lo-dee-dee, oh-lo-lo-lo-lo-dee-dee, hi-ho-lo-lo-dee-dee!" And she comes up and she says, "Shut up, Rusty!" She says, "You're tryin' to warn him!"
>
> So she goes out back, and we're all followin' her. And there was Campbell standin' up [makes a gesture to indicate fellatio], gettin' it on with the chick. And they didn't even see [her]. They didn't even see [her] when [she] come up on [them]. And she tapped him on the shoulder, and she says, "Is it good?" And he turned around to her, and he said, "You're damn right [laughs]!" And that ended it, and then she took off. (Rogers and Kempton interview 2005)

Infidelity could also be problematic for married couples performing on the road in the same group. Betty Cody and Hal Lone Pine met by way of country and western music, and when they were married in 1938, their honeymoon was a tour into the Deep South as a part of a traveling tent show(Coté-Binette and Breau interview 2006). For the next fourteen years they were constantly on the road. Though Lone Pine was considered a "straight arrow" and a morally upright gentleman by all who knew him early in life (including his wife and her family), he became a heavy drinker and an accomplished philanderer. Given the nature of barnstorming, it was generally difficult to find time away from fellow band members, and the fact that Lone Pine managed to carry on multiple extramarital affairs was a rather remarkable logistical feat—so much so that his infidelity came as a complete shock to Betty:

> *Cody:* Well, sometimes he was pretty shrewd [chuckles]. I remember. We'd come home from the show sometimes, you know? Like we were playing in St. John, New Brunswick, in a hall. And in town. . . . We'd come home, and he'd say, "Well," somebody would call him and he'd say, "I gotta go. I gotta go Betty. They want me at the station." And all the time it was to leave to wander around. And I trusted him. I trusted him. I *used* to [laughs]. I never thought, because *we were the ideal couple,* I thought. He was good to me and all that, but he was a roamer.
>
> *Murphy:* And you said that you would sometimes see that he had mistresses in the crowd sitting up front?
>
> *Cody:* Oh yeah.
>
> *Murphy:* How would you address that, or would you address that, or would things just sort of blow up eventually?
>
> *Cody:* Well, sometimes he had, you know, two, three in one town. You know? That were friends with him. But they were mistresses at the same time. And I'd have to cope with it. That was it. And they were friends with *me.* Those girls, they *admired* me [laughs]. But at the time . . . I didn't know what was going on. I was very innocent about the whole thing until I discovered what was happening. It was painful. Very, very painful. And I hate it. Divorce and all that. Mmm. (Coté-Binette and Breau interview 2006)

As a practicing Roman Catholic (she and Lone Pine never missed church while on tour, unless there was not a Catholic church nearby), Betty was hesitant to divorce Pine. Divorce was severely frowned upon by the church, and getting divorced—especially when children were involved—not only subjected one's family to the scorn of the religious community but was considered to jeopardize one's ability to gain salvation. Betty and Pine continued as husband and wife for several years, but Pine continued to have affairs—often with friends, devoted fans, and acquaintances of Betty's.

For one group in New England, at least, the exhausting schedule of the barnstormer led to a significant professional breakthrough. When Bradley Kincaid was working on WBZ radio in Boston with Marshall Jones and Harmonica Joe Troyan, Jones was run ragged by the group's barnstorming schedule: "I was dressed ordinary dress at first, and then we got to playing so much and a-coming back so late at night and then have to get up in the morning, I was always tired, you know. Bradley would say—now, this was 1935. Bradley would say, 'Come on up here to [the] microphone. You're just like an old grandpa'" (Jones and Jones interview 1975). From that point on, Jones became known as "Grandpa" Jones, a dynamic and memorable stage persona that secured him successive spots on the *Wheeling Jamboree*, the *Grand Ole Opry*, and, much later, the television show *Hee-Haw*. But Jones's road to fame on the *Grand Ole Opry* stemmed directly from his distaste for the barnstorming life: the *Wheeling Jamboree*, the *Grand Ole Opry*, and *Hee-Haw* provided Jones with a living wage, a means to advertise new sound recordings to a national audience, and the luxury of dictating how busy his touring schedule would be while maintaining some semblance of a home life (Jones and Wolfe 1984; Jones and Jones interview 1975). That Grandpa Jones had to leave New England in order to achieve a semblance of stability in his home life is significant: New England lacked a wide-ranging omnidirectional transportation hub on the scale of Chicago, Atlanta, Nashville, St. Louis, Dallas, Wheeling, and other southern and midwestern cities that played host to a number of major and nationally syndicated country and western radio barn dance programs where a home life was a distinct possibility. (This would have been roughly between the debut of the first radio barn dance program in 1924 on WLS out of Chicago and the closing of the *Louisiana Hayride* show out of KWKH in Shreveport in 1969, after which point the *Grand Ole Opry* was the only functional "home base" for a cast of regular performers.) Also, New England lacked a powerful broadcasting base with a commitment to a regular country and western variety show: only New England's smaller-wattage stations were committed to regular country and western variety shows like WCOP's *Hayloft Jamboree*. As such, the weekly stipend for regular performers on New England radio barn dance programs was minimal at best.

Chicken One Week, Feathers the Next: Keeping Your Day Job

Though country and western music may have been enough to sustain many musicians financially, it did not always provide emotional sustenance; most barnstorming country and western musicians in New England were not as fortunate as Grandpa Jones. Music made Frank "Slim" Rego popular in school, and his group was successful enough to lead him to believe that this was his future career. But ultimately he arrived at the same conclusion as Grandpa Jones: a barnstorming career could not sustain him emotionally:

> *Rego:* I'm ashamed to say this, but I never graduated [high school]. So I went through junior high and then the first year of high school, but then I went to work.
>
> *Murphy:* Doing what?
>
> *Rego:* I thought I was going to make music a career at that time, but, ah, even though I made a lot of money at it. Helped pay for this house.
>
> *Murphy:* What changed your mind?
>
> *Rego:* It's a grind. It's a real grind. It's too many ups and downs. Emotionally you have to have the right temperament for it. And you go out and do a show, and one audience will love you. You go out and do the same thing in front of another one, and it's not so great. And it's a downer. It's a downer. (Rego interview 2004, 5)

Note that Rego considered country and western both "work" and a "career." It should be pointed out that the decadent lifestyle of the professional musician celebrated in exhibits at the Country Music Hall of Fame and Museum (through prominent exhibits of performers' extravagant personal artifacts, such as singer Webb Pierce's gold-plated automobile), the Stax Soulsville, U.S.A. Museum in Memphis, Tennessee (soul singer Isaac Hayes's gold-plated and fur-trimmed Cadillac), Elvis Presley's Graceland (more gold-plated Cadillacs, two airplanes), and the Rock and Roll Hall of Fame and Museum in Cleveland, Ohio (too many examples to list here) perpetuates the impression that people choose a career in music in order to accumulate wealth and *avoid* work. Indeed, a standard quip among working musicians I have known is the joking insistence that they began their music careers in order to avoid work or to avoid "growing up." Quite to the contrary, Rego says that country and western *is* work. His references to country and western music paying for his house—in which he still lives and which has appreciated forty times its original $12,500 value—provides tangible evidence to others that a musical career was not such a poor choice after all.

Many country and western musicians like Frank "Slim" Rego performed music full-time but also maintained a full-time day job on the side to provide them with some semblance of emotional balance to their life. Others, like Flo Cody Hooper, who worked in a Lewiston, Maine, shoe shop, did so because it provided additional financial security and stability: "We used to work at the shoe shop during the day, and we'd get very tired, you know [laughs]? Shoe shop, then we'd go play with Pine and Betty, and come back home late at night, and get up at six o'clock in the morning, go to work" (Hooper and Hooper interview 2005). Likewise, Bob Elston—who was coming of age during the last years that local musicians held a prominent place on regional television in the 1960s—recognized early that relying on country and western music to sustain his family financially over the long term might put them in jeopardy:

> I started out on a part-time basis as a "weekend warrior" is what I used to call it. And of course, when you're young, things look different to you than when you get a little age on you. And of course you always have visions of making the big time and all this and that. And after you been in the business for a few years you suddenly realize, "This just ain't gonna get it." It's chicken one week and feathers the next, you know? And of course as I grew older and had responsibilities, why, I had to make money. And so I always had a regular job. And it was, we'd work three, four nights a week [playing music] on the side but always had a full-time job besides. (Wincapaw interview 2006)

Interestingly, those regional country and western performers who maintained a day job outside of music did not hide that fact from their fans in order to cultivate mystique. Frank "Slim" Rego recalled with some bemusement the adulation he and other local stars received when performing on the ranch circuit:

> *Rego:* Yeah, people would come just to see you. That's who they came to see.
> *Murphy:* And were you like stars to them?
> *Rego:* Well, they thought we were [laughs]. It was strange, in those days people were a lot simpler. I don't mean simple-minded. Their lifestyle was a lot simpler than today, and they thought because you were on the radio, you were wealthy [laughing]. And you weren't making a dime [from the radio station], but they thought you were wealthy. So you didn't want to say too much to burst the bubble.
> *Murphy:* So you wouldn't mention that you were working at Jordan Marsh or anything like that? [Jordan Marsh was the largest department store in downtown Boston when Rego worked there from the 1930s through the 1950s. The department store building still stands, though it has been renamed Macy's following a series of corporate buyouts.]
> *Rego:* Oh, I would tell them. I would tell them. I've never been ashamed of working for a living. No. I always worked very hard. When we were entertaining, I worked five days on my regular job, seven nights singing, and weekends installing stuff on the side.
> *Murphy:* How many years did you do that?
> *Rego:* I did that for about eight years.
> *Murphy:* And did you have kids at the time?

Rego: I had my son. Yeah, my son was alive. Well, that's how I bought this house. (interview 2004, 2)

What is enlightening about Rego's account is that the boundaries of the show business mystique only extended as far as personal income. Rego was proud of the fact that he worked in the flooring department at the Jordan Marsh department store in downtown Boston. Within the context of the New England working class, fans who perceived him as rich but choosing to "work for a living" anyhow were reassured that Joy and Slim was an act that truly embodied the work ethic of the working class. In other words, work wasn't important simply as a means to an end but as a way of life. This same kind of work ethic can be found in the world of Rust Belt polka music, where that genre's biggest stars like Eddie Blazonczyk continued to lug their own gear and set up their own sound systems long after they could have afforded to hire someone else to do it (Keil, Keil, and Blau 1992).

The key to maintaining a semblance of long-term financial stability in country and western music was to diversify one's sources of income beyond just the personal appearance. In Bob Elston's case this meant working in the grocery business while performing as a regular member of the Curley O'Brien Show (WLBZ-TV and WVII-TV, both in Bangor, Maine). For Flo Cody Hooper it meant working in a shoe shop, Babe Jackson in a jewelry shop, Ray Dixon as a landlord, Frank Rego in flooring, Judy Carrier in a precision tool factory and as a recurring member of *Clyde Joy and the Country Folks* on WMUR-TV out of Manchester, New Hampshire. Those groups such as the Lone Pine Mountaineers and the Down Homers who chose to make a living *solely* through country and western music did so by moving every few years, securing song publishing and recording deals, and pushing ever farther into regions that most barnstormers avoided. In doing so, they earned far greater money per appearance and had significant brushes with national stardom, but they were beholden to the unpredictable nature of fickle radio stations and audiences.

Whether musicians kept their day job or not, the occupational lifestyle of a barnstorming country and western musician in New England was not an easy one. These musicians who kept their day jobs lived with the frustration of never achieving the kind of national fame that most young country and western musicians aspire to at some point, but they tended to maintain some semblance of a home life to balance out their road life, even when they were performing most nights of the week. Full-time country and western groups rarely spent longer than two or three years living in any given area; over the course of twenty years this type of lifestyle often had devastating effects on the lives of the musicians and their families and loved ones.

6

THE NEW ENGLAND COWBOY

Regional Resistance to National Culture

Dying of stomach cancer, his prodigious talent mishandled by an industry that twice danced with him, Dick Curless ambled into a Brookfield, Massachusetts, recording studio in 1994 with an eclectic crew of musicians behind him. There was Duke Levine, a native of Worcester, Massachusetts, and former lead guitarist for 1990s pop-country sensation Mary Chapin Carpenter, on electric guitar. Tim Bowles and Michael "Mudcat" Ward, stalwarts of New England country-rock bands of the 1980s, were on pedal steel and bass. On the drums was Billy Conway of the rock band Morphine and Boston's protocowpunk band Treat Her Right. Rounding out the group on acoustic lead and rhythm guitar was Denny Breau. The youngest son of Hal Lone Pine and Betty Cody, Denny Breau grew up playing in rock bands in Lewiston, Maine, while worshiping his mother and older brother Lenny, who was tragically murdered in 1984. Unaware at the time that he was dying but substantially weakened by a lifetime of stomach ulcers brought on during the Korean War, Curless was taking a long look at his life, sizing it up, and pouring his guts out one last time. Remembered Denny Breau: "He called me, said, 'Denny, I'd like you to play on my album, 'cause your father's the one that gave me my start when I got back from Korea,' and I felt he was paying back a debt almost" (interview 2005).

Curless was also making sense of the world he had traveled through. The session, recorded in a converted farmhouse studio, took place close to the town of Petersham, where, as a young boy, he learned to sing, yodel, and play guitar at the knee of Yodelin' Slim Clark. Cowboys, particularly yodeling cowboys like Slim Clark and Kenny Roberts, flourished in this part of the state. And it is in regions like this—regions that have never recovered from deindustrialization and demilitarization—that the spirit of self-reliant libertarian resistance persists. To live in such a place—a place much like northern New England—is a choice, an act of stubborn resistance to material comforts and a commitment to the perpetuation of community memory. Old cowboys—like Old Yankees—are not out of place on this landscape. Rather, they serve as interpreters of place, guides who enable outsiders to explore the inner workings of a people actively negotiating their way through changing times—a theme engaged directly on Curless's last recording in the song "Changing Times," penned by his son-in-law Bill Chinnock:

> Maybe I'm holdin' on to the good old days
> When every cowboy could make his play
> Holdin' on in changin' times.
> Maybe I'm holdin' on to the things I know
> Too stubborn to change, too scared to let go
> I'm just an old cowboy livin' in changin' times.
> (© Bill Chinnock, lyrics reprinted by permission, Bill Chinnock Egg Custard Music, ASCAP.)

Curless's performance of the song reflects a sense of loss, the feeling of being a relic of a forgotten heritage. The New England country and western musician's important place in New England social history has been obscured for over fifty years now by the same industrial forces that obscure its place in the continental story of country and western music, where the sanctity of regional identity is crushed by the industrial weight of country music's southern thesis. What remains is a sense of loss and disenfranchisement as well as a rich social capital toward which New England country and western contributes a significant sum. Curless and others sing of industrial abandonment—in their case, the music and media industries they helped to build. This drama plays out against a larger, darker backdrop of industrial exploitation and abandonment of New England working people, visible in the crumbling stone walls, rotting piers, and empty mills whose ghosts speak of the region's agricultural, maritime, and manufacturing past.

"Log Trucks and Snowmobile Trails": The Backlash against Authenticity from Away

Historians Edward Ayers and Peter Onuf (1996) observe that regionalism tends to gain momentum at times when belief in the nation is weakest. Periodically, New Englanders have lashed out in frustration against a system that pretends to be devoted to the working class, to the local, to the home place but that demonstrates no interest in *this* home place, *these* working-class people, *this* locality. Likewise, the kind of self-authenticating-by-pretending-to-be-from-away that takes place in New England country and western periodically grates on New England performers and audiences who deem their own region to be perfectly authentic, thank you very much. The earliest example of this kind of anthem that I have found is a radio transcription from 1949 of a song performed by Massachusetts's yodeling cowgirl Georgia Mae. The lyrics were written by an anonymous fan and then mailed to Georgia Mae at WBZ, where she set it to music (Harp 1949). The song is called "The Hills of Old New England":

I've been around an awful lot,
I've had a lot of fun,
But when it comes to settling down,
There's only one place under the sun.
You can keep your western prairies
And your famous old cowhands
Because I love the hills of Old New England.
I've heard stories about the West,
But the places I love best
Are up among the hills of Old New England.
The Golden Sunset it thrills me,
The pine and the hemlock too,
For I was born and raised here,
I'm a Yankee through and through.
You can keep your boots and saddles
And all the gold you've panned
Because I love the hills of Old New England.
(© Georgia Mae Kingsbury, lyrics reprinted with permission)

The origin of "The Hills of Old New England" comes from the audience. The song is representative of the dynamic relationship between the audience and the performer inherent in country and western music and provides evidence that both the performer and the audience share a pro–New England sentiment. Over the years a backlash has begun to build in New England as an act of resistance against (or a critique of) nationalizing forces that appear to dictate sites of authenticity and power for country and western music. This is made explicit in "Log Trucks and Snowmobile Trails," an ode to Maine country authenticity by Mark Farrington of the band Cattle Call from Portland, Maine:

You can take your Texas prairie,
And your Louisiana swamp,
You can talk about the Southland all you want.
Sing songs about Old Dixie,

You can wear your cowboy hat,
I don't claim to know a thing about all that.

Log trucks and snowmobile trails,
Wind and snow and sleet and sometimes hail.
I don't expect you rebels to understand,
But I'll live and die in this winter wonderland.
(© Mark Farrington, lyrics reprinted with permission)

Farrington's song is a humorous jab at the Dixiefied country music of the "outlaw" era when "rebels" like Hank Williams Jr. and Charlie Daniels carefully cultivated images as unreconstructed Confederate good ol' boys. It should be noted that while the Internet has enabled Cattle Call to sell their music nationally and internationally, they have never performed outside of New England, let alone below the actual Mason-Dixon Line. As such, "Log Trucks and Snowmobile Trails" can be understood as an *imagined* kiss-off to those southerners and country music industrialists who claim ownership over country and western music and as a direct challenge to those New Englanders who adopt a southern worldview when performing or listening to country music.

Working from the idea that regionalism grows during times of disillusionment with the nation, the growing symbolic power of Maine as a region of authenticity within New England deserves closer scrutiny. When we discuss "country" music we are as often talking about music of pastoral nostalgia as we are about a national (and nationalistic) music of and about the United States (Malone 2002a; Malone and Stricklin 2003; Tichi 1994; Fox 2005). It is this swing term, in fact, that provides the key to understanding why the "country" music industry no longer had a need for "western" music beginning in 1958 with the creation of the CMA and country format radio (Kingsbury et al. 1998, 149). In this new world order, there was no longer room for regional variations of country music on playlists or in historical narratives. This is why many New England country and western musicians—under the guise of the cowboy—have entrenched themselves so deeply in their stance *against* "country" music and all it represents to them. At the very same time that the CMA rebranded country and western music as "country music," New England's working class was plunged into a very deep economic crisis, one that, it could be argued, still plagues much of the region today. Significantly, the resistant figure in Dick Curless's "Changing Times" chooses to clothe himself in the garb of the western cowboy: both the singing cowboy and the New England working class were effectively disenfranchised at the same time, and the nationalizing and globalizing forces of Nashville's country music industry have never looked back.

New England country and western music was a style—and an industry—developed by local and regional musicians. This is the story chronicled in this work. In the 1940s nearly all of the country and western musicians performing on New England radio came from New England. By 1970 local music of any style was rarely heard on radio, and what could be heard of country music were CMA-backed releases originating almost entirely from Nashville, Austin, or Los Angeles. With the exception of the occasional recording by Dick Curless, whose major label country music recordings (made in Nashville and Los Angeles) stripped him of his guitar, his touring band, and much of his agency to choose his own material, there was no New England country and western content left on major regional radio broadcasts and very little on low-power stations. Some remnants of local music appeared on television, and there was the occasional rare exception up through the early 1980s when a locally produced single would become a "hit" for several weeks on country format stations. But the bargain that the region had struck with the nation had backfired badly.

We can see a similar pattern develop in the textile industry of the early part of the twentieth century. Industry is built in the North and moves to the South and the West: what is left behind is the New England working class without enough jobs to go around. Powerful corporations choose to import southern goods rather than employ locals to develop local resources. The music industry was no different with regard to both its geographic migration south and its remaining infrastructure. By the 1960s the exceptions proved the rule, consisting of a few holdovers from the 1950s like Curley O'Brien, Ken Mackenzie, Rex Trailer, and Yodelin' Slim Clark, all of whom had migrated from radio to television.

The twist here, of course, is one pointed out by Jimmy Barnes: in the textile industry, resources were extracted from the South, processed in the North, and resold globally, but in country music, cultural values of working people in New England and elsewhere are extracted, exported south for production in Nashville, and resold back to their home regions as authentically southern cultural imports.

So Why Not Country Music from Maine?

Given the amount of resentment New England's traditional country musicians and fans feel toward Nashville, it is no wonder that the idea of "alternative country" has taken root here. Since the 1990s Maine artists like Jimmie Barnes, Dick Curless, and Cattle Call have emerged as varying forms of alternative country. In a critical analysis of the emergence of the alternative country music movement of the 1980s through the wake of 9/11, Aaron

Fox writes that "emplacement"—or the connection to particular places—is critical in the development of "alternative" products and cultures: "Thus ice cream from Vermont, medicine from China, and music from Texas are important components of the suite of alternative commodities" (2005, 165). Fox points out that the alternative movement hinges on perceptions of "purity" and "naturalness" as alternatives to the "contaminated, artificial character of modern mass culture" (165). By and large, the narrative of the alternative country music movement is that musicians and fans have a choice to make between mainstream Nashville country music or "real," "pure," and "insurgent" alternatives from elsewhere (usually Austin or Chicago). The alternative country music debate swings on aesthetic and industrial points, not on the functionality of the music. Alternative country pays homage to its antecedents, while Nashville wallows unabashedly in a pop heritage that begins with the Eagles and Lynyrd Skynyrd. Alternative country tends toward what Fox calls "bourgeois romanticism," which may be true with regard to middle and upper-class Americans' romanticized trip through rural poverty and working-class culture in much of the alternative country catalog. Nevertheless, this paradigm of alternative country, where indie labels such as Bloodshot in Chicago and New West in Austin seek to reestablish a sense of cultural authenticity about country music, ultimately presents consumers, fans, and listeners with a false choice. With regard to alternative country in Maine, a truer alternative can be located whereby people are choosing community country music as an alternative to industrial country music. Fox's critique of alternative country shows a class divide, with upper- and middle-class tastes coalescing around alternative country while working-class people choose Nashville. Yet the evolution of Maine country and western music as an alternative to Nashville country music is one that cuts across class lines. Interestingly, in southern New England, where the working-class has arguably fared better than in northern New England, many of the local and state-level country music organizations appear to have evolved toward being vehicles of promotion for local working-class artists who are seeking record deals in Nashville. Yet in Maine, due to the rich musical legacy of Slim Clark, Dick Curless, and Lone Pine and Betty Cody and of those individuals' success in building on romantic popular (bourgeois and otherwise) notions of northern New England (and Maine in particular) as a "pure" and "natural" alternative to southern New England and beyond, a Maine country music identity for both musicians and fans appears to be an "alternative" identity that cuts across class divisions.

Today, many New Englanders who wish to continue making a full-time living exclusively as country and western performers feel compelled to go to country music industrial centers (Nashville, Austin, and Los Angeles) in order to realize their goals. This pattern was already in place by the 1960s, when Dick Curless moved alternately between Nashville and Los Angeles, but he maintained his home and family life in the state of Maine. Many of the young musicians who would have arguably been New England's leading lights of a new generation of country and western musicians have moved elsewhere, like Slaid Cleaves and Rod Picott of South Berwick, Maine.

Cleaves and Picott were part of a wave of neotraditional country and western musicians who had come to the music by way of Bruce Springsteen, punk rock, and rock and roll. Though both performers were raised in Maine in families who enjoyed local country and western music (Rod Picott and his brother Richard remember with excitement the week in 1976 Dick Curless spent in a South Berwick, Maine, trailer recording his *Maine Train* LP; Richard Picott married a woman whose father was a trucker who died while driving through the Haynesville Woods), their departure from New England does not mark a direct break in local tradition in the way other departures have—particularly those of Jo Dee Messina and Mike Preston.

Jo Dee Messina was born in Framingham, Massachusetts, in 1970 and raised in Holliston, Massachusetts. As a young teenager she began apprenticing with the John Penny Band. At this time, the John Penny Band was backing Curless up regularly, and Penny was the musical director, an occasional booking agent for Curless, and a part-time local record company executive for Belmont Records (which released Curless's *The Great Race* LP in 1979). Messina spent several years learning the intricacies of the music, the business, and the stage from Penny. As Penny recalled, Messina aspired to a career as a country singer and told Penny she was willing to do what it took to make it in Nashville (interview 2004). In 1989 she left Massachusetts for Nashville and eventually landed a record deal with Curb. Her 1996 single, "Heads Alabama, Tails California," was produced by Nashville superstar Tim McGraw and represents what is likely the top-selling country music recording ever made by any native New Englander. Messina's recordings are sung with a pronounced and affected southern drawl—both a symbolic and a tangible representation that the New England region has been fully obscured from the national identity of the American working class as put forward in country music.

In the early 1990s Yodelin' Slim Clark began teaching his distinctive New England/Atlantic Canada singing style to a teenager named Mike Preston.

Preston's grasp of traditional country music (including New England artists) stunned the New England country and western community. He possessed a rich voice of impressive expressive quality well beyond his years, and the two recorded and released an album called *Passing It On* (Clark interview 2005). Within a short time, however, Preston would grow restless under the weight of local expectations. By the late 1990s Preston had left New England for Nashville to "make it" as a country singer, and those who had looked to him with hope for the future of the music in this region were left despondent. He has not been so fortunate as Jo Dee Messina with regard to securing a record deal or a hit single. In 2008 he finished recording his first album in ten years. It includes the John Lincoln Wright song "Lonesome Rainin' City," a song as much about the mythical powers of the city to transform the rural dreamer as about the disillusioning experience of the individual's encounter with the industrial:

> You can take a dreamer,
> Beat him in the ground,
> Lonesome rainin' city,
> Sure 'nuf beat me down.
> (© John Lincoln Wright, lyrics reprinted with permission)

The decisions of leading New England country and western talent to relocate to industrial centers like Nashville and Austin indicates what has become the norm in this region, which is if someone is interested in "making it" in the business, they must do so by accommodating the whims of the Nashville country music industry like Jo Dee Messina or seek an alternative route and move to Austin, Texas, like Slaid Cleaves. And who can fault them? Not all move there, but the dream is an important piece of an imaginary puzzle of success in the age of nationalized playlists and tells us a great deal about what New Englanders think their prospects are of "making it" in New England and what an alternative to Nashville's industrialized form of country music is considered to be. Singer-songwriters and instrumentalists from New England who do not necessarily identify themselves with country and western music but rather with "folk music" or bluegrass—performers such as Dave Mallett (Maine) and Dan Tyminski (Vermont)—have also sought out careers as songwriters and session musicians in Nashville. Some, such as Mallett, have returned home after some success (his songs have been recorded by Emmylou Harris and John Denver, among others), while others like Tyminski have found considerable success as a member of Alison Kraus's band, Union Station. Dan Tyminski is also the lead vocalist of the group the Soggy Bottom Boys, providing the singing voice of Ulysses Everett McGill (played by George Clooney) on the song "Man of Constant Sorrow" in the 2000 film *O Brother Where Art Thou?*

A survey of New England–based country music associations shows that each state has at least one organization whose mission is geared toward landing local musicians recording opportunities in Nashville. New England, which was once considered fertile ground for lucrative touring, drawing prominent outsiders like Bradley Kincaid, Elton Britt, and Jud Strunk to relocate here and others like Doc and Chickie Williams, Hawkshaw Hawkins, Hank Thompson, and Ernest Tubb to tour here as regularly as "home," all the while sustaining a plethora of local musicians (prominent or otherwise), has instead become viewed as a backwater of limited professional possibilities. Not only that, the music industry mission of local country music associations shows how much country music making has been transformed in the image of the industry. In New England, country and western music developed in response to a felt social need by the community; it was never about making records, even fifty years after Mellie Dunham first recorded his fiddle tunes. Indeed, country music as a job was never the point; rather, it was a happy opportunity for many from 1938 to 1958 (and only occasionally afterward) who would otherwise be working as minimum-wage millhands. When Betty Cody sought out an alternative to Nashville and the grind of full-time barnstorming away from her family, she did not move to Wheeling to make records that sounded different from Nashville: she quit professional music altogether, went home to Maine to work at the local mill, and played music only when the local community demanded it. Her choice marked a functional alternative (a return to the community) rather than the strictly stylistic one presented by the alternative country movement.

That New Englanders who self-identify as country and western or "traditional country" musicians and fans place themselves in opposition to country music from Nashville is significant not only because it tells us that the region of the New England working class no longer sees itself valued in contemporary country music but also because it serves to show that working-class New Englanders have very real criticisms about what this new country appears to value. Cowboy yodeler Wade Dow of Brooklin, Maine, is of the opinion that national network television and radio programming is demeaning in its laugh-track sitcoms, shock-jock radio shows, and pop-country programming. Dow believes today's country music hedges its financial success on its ability to sell sex (interview 2007). Bob Elston too believes that the country music industry is simply trying to sell sex (Wincapaw interview 2006). Jimmy Barnes—he of racy double entendre songs such as "Big Boat Becky"—believes that country music's agenda seems focused on selling sex by marketing someone who looks good and trying to develop a computerized sound around that person in order to make money. Barnes does not hear "real" family values or stories; he hears an industry that panders to family values through fully contrived songs made palatable to the masses through computerized "pitch control" machines (Barnes and Rice interview 2007). Yodelin' Slim Clark expressed concerns about the emasculating qualities of contemporary country music prior to his death (Cohen 1977), and Gene Hooper laments the fact that today's country music—and the line dance music of the 1980s and 1990s—simply tries to "sing a dance" (Hooper and Hooper interview 2005).

"Changing Times" and the other songs on Dick Curless's swan-song album, *Traveling Through*, were directed squarely at a New England audience hanging onto the threads of remembrance. The Rounder Records executives who funded and released the album did so with the expectation that country radio would not play the album and that those who purchased it would primarily be New Englanders who recalled the lanky singer's baritone voice with nostalgic pride (Marian Leighton Levy, e-mail message to author, January 31, 2008). Ultimately, Curless's *Traveling Through* encapsulates and embodies a message: the true alternative is a redirected focus on home and community.

Retreat to the Maine Woods

The story of how two of Maine's country and western icons—Yodelin' Slim Clark and Dick Curless—came to live in Maine encapsulates the draw of northern New England as an alternative way of life for self-reliant individualists. Originally from Scots-Irish and Acadian families from the Canadian-American border region of Aroostook County, the Curless family moved to Massachusetts when Dick's father was in search of work generated by the devastating effects of the hurricane of 1938. Their arrival in Boston's North Station was a bewildering introduction to city life. In time, the Curless family moved to Gilbertville in north-central Massachusetts near the rural factory towns of Petersham, Greenfield, and Athol. It was while living in Gilbertville during Prohibition that Dick's father befriended Yodelin' Slim Clark, who mentored the two Curless boys in music and oil painting while sampling Phil Sr.'s homebrew (Curless interview 2007).

To the Curless family, Slim Clark appeared to be both the quintessential down-home Yankee and a fascinatingly eccentric character. A seemingly rural horseman who was both a virtuosic yodeler and a sensitive oil painter of natural scenes, Clark was born in Massachusetts's second largest urban center (Springfield) and made a habit of wearing full cowboy gear—with spurs—wherever he went (Gobers interview 2007). As a boy growing up in western Massachusetts, he was smitten by radio broadcasts of cowboy singers, hobo singers, and tragic folk songs. It was a musical style—and a lyrical message—that spoke to the deepest fundamental aspects of Clark's personality:

> I suppose I was like all kids, either want to be a fireman or a policeman or a cowboy. And I liked the outdoors and the rough side of life—simple, plain. I wouldn't care if I became a millionaire tomorrow. I wouldn't dress any different. I wouldn't live any different. I'd still be the way I was brought up and the way I like to live, more or less free like a horse or a deer or something. And that kind of music had that kind of flavor, that appeal to me. (Cohen 1977, 49)

When Curless reached high school age, he became a member of Clark's touring band, the Trail Riders, and the group barnstormed throughout New England and eastern Canada. After a run of dates around Bangor in 1950, Curless and Clark took a week off to fish in Sebago, Maine. For both men, Maine held an allure that was drawn from its distance from the urbanity of Massachusetts and from the quality of hunting and fishing (not only on account of it being easier to hunt legally in Maine but also because Maine had cultivated its fish and game stocks for several decades at this point to attract out-of-staters like Curless and Clark) and because the response to their cowboy music in Maine was powerful and lucrative. Curless recalled that he said to Clark, "This is the life," and the two men began planning to relocate to Maine. Curless moved to Maine in 1950, Clark in 1951 (Cohen 1977).

Although both Dick Curless and Slim Clark spent their formative years in the state of Massachusetts (Curless lived in Gilbertsville, Massachusetts, from age seven until age twenty-four; Clark was born in the city of Springfield in 1917 and lived in Petersham, Massachusetts, until age thirty-four), they have both become considered the quintessential Maine cowboys. The annual Dick Curless Memorial Scholarship Fund Event in Union, Maine, features a stage flanked by oil paintings of Dick Curless and Yodelin' Slim Clark, both wearing cowboy hats, and both painted by Slim Clark. People in northern New England joke about how one is not a "native" even after decades of living in the area (and in some cases even if one was born there). Yet Slim Clark and Dick Curless are notable exceptions to this rule: Mainers are resistant to the suggestion that Slim Clark was "from away" or that Dick Curless has anything to do with Massachusetts. Mainers—and even fans from Massachusetts—are quick to correct me when I mention that Slim was from Massachusetts or that Dick Curless spent most of his youth there. When the facts are presented, this resistance gives way to a mixture of surprise and chagrin. In every case, however, any momentary disorientation or disappointment is quickly overcome, as though this new piece of information—that Clark or Curless left Massachusetts for Maine—is further proof that they were Mainers at heart.

Slim Clark and Dick Curless both performed the role of the old cowboy living in changing times so convincingly that their nativist, regionalist outlook is accepted as entirely home grown. Slim Clark, in particular, was possessed of the kind of self-reliant spirit that Mainers consider an innate characteristic: he claimed that record executives in the 1940s and 1950s were frustrated by his prioritization of hunting and fishing over making recordings. According to Slim Clark, he would regularly leave the Continental recording studios in New York City in order to go hunting or fishing back in New England. When record executives tried to track him down, he was unable to be reached at his distant hunting and fishing camps deep in the Maine wilderness (Clark interview 2005; Cohen 1977). Whether this is just romantic embroidery on Slim Clark's part or not, such claims appear to have been accepted wholesale by his fans (and his family) as being entirely true and indicative of Slim's free-spirited nature.

Slim Clark's creative process was equally free-spirited. Slim claimed that he wrote songs when it "just hits me, you know, it just comes along like a cold" (Cohen 1977, 57), and he made spontaneous—and often rambling—monologues a centerpiece of his personal appearances. His willingness to allow spontaneity to take its course endeared him to Mainers, who enjoyed Slim's ability to wring humor from even the most unlikely sources, such as "Send Me the Flower Money Now," in which he asks friends and family to advance him the cash they would spend later on his funeral arrangements. Such humor was not restricted to songs; for instance, Denny Breau tells the following story of standing at a urinal next to Slim during a bathroom break at the Maine Country Music Awards just months before Slim Clark died:

> I said, "How ya doin,' Slim?"
>
> "Well, the doctors tell me I'm dyin,'" he says. "Everything's shuttin' down," he says. "But I don't get it," he says. "I still get a good foam when I pee," he says.
>
> And that was probably one of the funniest things I've ever heard in my life. (interview 2005)

Yodelin' Slim Clark's repertoire consisted of songs about nature, cowboys, hoboes, Indians, and Swiss alpine romances. With the exception of the Swiss songs, which were really more of a vehicle for yodeling showcases and humorous wordplay, Clark did not sing many love songs. He also never sang overtly about the state of Maine or the New England region—with the notable exception of the Maine logging song "The Jam at Gerry's Rock." He stubbornly refused to modernize his sound or themes even when they threatened to harm his ability to earn his livelihood, choosing instead to subsist off hunting, fishing, and the sales of his paintings (Clark interview 2005; Cohen 1977). In Clark's opinion, the changing winds of the commercial country music industry had shifted too far into the realm of pop music and what he called "mushy" love songs (Cohen 1977, 59). Clark's opinion of country and western music in the modern era was that it had been emasculated by Nashville, and the "rough and barky" (49) and generally unfettered approach of unaccompanied cowboy singing was—to use Slim's word for it—more "man-ny" (59) than the post-CMA era of Nashville country music. "I play the way I sing," Clark said, "rough-edged, crude, western and folk songs" (51). Slim Clark believed that any attempt to polish up his music toward a Nashville "countrypolitan" sound would be "like hauling pulp in a Cadillac" (51). As an artist—both in song and on canvas—Slim Clark strove to create a vision of *masculine* self-reliance.

Masculine self-reliance and nativist regionalism are the hallmarks of Dick Curless's "A Tombstone Every Mile." This last—and perhaps greatest—New England country and western musician arrived after New Englanders were effectively locked out of Nashville and its network radio stations. Dick Curless's ascent to the *Billboard* Top 10 in 1965 is a story of legendary proportions, and deservedly so, as it encapsulates the single-mindedness and self-reliant spirit that dominates the culture of New England's working class and its cowboy musicians. For what Curless did was effectively force Nashville to pay attention to him (and the state of Maine) by winning over teamsters with his self-produced 45 rpm record and utilizing this grass-roots support by having truckers distribute his records to jukeboxes and radio stations along their routes. Dick Curless and songwriter Dan Fulkerson founded an independent record label called Allagash (an intentional reference to the Maine frontier), recorded "A Tombstone Every Mile" at a TV studio in Bangor in late 1964, and released "A Tombstone Every Mile" in 1965. The pressing plant in Philadelphia making Allagash's records also pressed records for Capitol Records. The company notified Capitol of the record's unusually strong sales figures, and Capitol gave Curless a contract and enabled him to be included in national print, radio, and television media alongside CMA-certified stars of the 1960s. All of Curless's virtuosic vocal talent notwithstanding, it was this transcendence of industrial barriers that transformed Dick Curless from local Joe to local legend. This transformation was cynically summed up in a conversation I had with Jimmy Barnes, who told me, "Nobody in Maine gave a shit about Dick Curless until his record got played on network radio." While the facts support the idea that Curless's music was important to plenty of Mainers prior to "A Tombstone Every Mile," Barnes's comment speaks of many musicians' perception that local people favor national acts over local ones regardless of quality. In any case, Curless's national hit song telling of Aroostook County potatoes and the natural power of the Maine Woods forever secured his place as *the* quintessential Maine country and western singer in the regional imagination. Curless scored twenty-one hits on the *Billboard* country charts over the course of his career (Kingsbury et al. 1998, 122), all of which occurred between 1965 and 1973, the year Curless chose not to renew his contract with Capitol Records. During that time, Curless's association with the state of Maine remained at the forefront of his national identity (as evidenced most dramatically by the press photos in which he is wearing his signature eye patch and is dressed as a Maine woodsman wielding an axe) and the Red Sovine hit recording "Freightliner Fever" (1970), which makes mention of Curless being "hung up on a hill in Maine."

Curless's notoriety as a country singer from Maine lingers to this day both within and without New England. Outside of New England, the first comment most people make upon hearing my research topic is "Oh, like Dick Curless?" According to Dan Fulkerson, who wrote "A Tombstone Every Mile," his quarterly royalty checks from BMI reflect that Curless's recordings of "A Tombstone Every Mile" and "'Tater Raisin' Man" receive steady airplay on satellite radio. Additionally, the song "A Tombstone Every Mile" remains in circulation among trucking enthusiasts, reserving a place for the state of Maine in the repertoire of country music's most aggressively "traditional" subgenre. (Massachusetts's country and western singer John Lincoln Wright recorded a version of the song in 1977; Bill Kirchen—arguably the most noteworthy national figure in contemporary trucking music—released a recording of the song on a CD titled *A Tombstone Every Mile* in 2006; British punk–new wave singer and American trucking song enthusiast Nick Lowe released a version of the song in 2005; and a multitude of bluegrass bands have covered the song in the past.) A CD of new recordings of trucking songs called *Rig Rock Deluxe—Tribute to the American Trucker* was released in 1999 and was dedicated to the memory of Dick Curless, who died in 1995. The CD featured new recordings from traditionalist country musicians Buck Owens, Marty Stuart, Billy Jo Shaver, Steve Earle, Don Walser, Dale Watson, and Kay Adams, as well as alternative country musicians BR549, Son Volt, Cherie Knight, and others; the dedication of the record to Dick Curless is a testament to his importance nationally among fans and performers of trucking music.

So Curless and Clark were both individuals who were persuaded by a perceived way of life, by natural surroundings, and by a steady stream of Maine-based musical bookings to leave Massachusetts for the state of Maine. Their migration north is representative of a broader shift in New England culture that prompted this same migration into a region for purely philosophical reasons. Perceived as being more raw, more natural, and less constrained by bureaucracy, modernity, and population, Maine's state slogan, "The Way Life Should Be," specifically targets those people who see it through that romantic lens. Two of Maine's other official and unofficial brands or slogans are "Vacationland" and "Life in the Slow Lane." The Maine license plate features the word "Vacationland" along with the image of a lobster, while "Life in the Slow Lane" often appears nearby in the form of a bumper sticker. Taken as a whole, "The Way Life Should Be," "Vacationland," and "Life in the Slow Lane" all imply that Maine is a place set apart. To visit Maine is to take an easygoing vacation away from the fast-lane pace of the rest of the nation. This fast-lane culture of the rest of the nation is, implies the state slogan, the way life should *not* be. Maine natives are not uncritical of their tourist-driven economy, nor are they uncritical of state government policies that make it difficult for outside businesses to move into the state. Southern Maine comprises the bulk of the state's middle class, and—based on the opinions of most persons interviewed for this work—residents in much of the rest of the state resent what they view as a two-class society of native people and wealthy newcomers and seasonal residents. One critic of the idealism of the state's tourism-driven slogan stated that Maine's real slogan should be "Maine: The Way Life Is."

Within a few years of their move to Maine, both Curless and Clark were firmly ensconced in the Maine image. Curless posed for press photos wearing the full regalia of the Maine woodsman and peppered his press releases with personal tales of quitting the music business in order to find physical and spiritual recuperation in the Maine woods. Maine is not only an imagined destination for those seeking recuperation or alternatives. Powerful evidence of this fact is the recent relocation to Aroostook County of Amish people who are fleeing rapid development and suburbanization of Lancaster County, Pennsylvania (Schweitzer 2005). The arrival of some one hundred Amish to the small town of Smyrna, Maine, since 1996 has aroused a sense of mutual respect for self-sufficiency among native Mainers and the newly arrived Amish. The resistant figure of the New England cowboy is not unlike that of the

Amish of Smyrna, Maine: a person who willingly withdraws from the way life is in a national culture and retreats into a region where life is the way it "should be," a place where the Slim Clarks of the world can live "more or less free like a horse or a deer" and unfettered with the heavy burdens of modernity, wealth, and urbanity.

Indeed, many of the traditional occupations that have sustained Mainers for centuries—fishing, woods work, farming—have been jeopardized by aggressive corporate industrial practices. The industrial base that had sustained Maine's working people for over a century—textile work, tannery work, paper mill work, shoe factory work, lumber camp work, and so forth—made a rapid departure from the state in the second half of the twentieth century. To remain in Maine—or, in the case of Slim Clark and Dick Curless, to *move* to Maine in the face of industrial collapse or, in the case of Betty Cody, to quit country music to work in a Lewiston, Maine, shoe mill while her songs were still in the Top 10—reflects the prioritization of a certain way of life over the pursuit of material comforts. Or to put it another way, to remain in Maine reflects an individual's prioritization of social capital over financial capital. To use and make country and western music in the manner that Mainers do can be read as an act of regional resistance to national culture.

EPILOGUE

"Oh, You're Canadian": My Night as a Canadian American in Watertown, Massachusetts

I had wanted to see the Country Masters perform for a while. Their tenure as the house band at the French-American Victory Club in Waltham, Massachusetts, was legendary in the local community. The group had recently moved from the Waltham Club to the Canadian-American Club in neighboring Watertown, Massachusetts, and they had just released their first CD after nearly forty years of performing. I saw on the club's website that they would be playing, but I couldn't find anyone to go see the show with me. So I went alone.

The Canadian-American Club sits on Arlington Street in Watertown with a dimly lit sign out front and no windows. It is a bleak and telling irony that the bright neon lights of a nearby Canadian-themed chain restaurant—the Bugaboo Creek Steakhouse—create an optical illusion that causes Arlington Street to be utterly blanketed in darkness.

Structurally, the club follows the pattern of old social halls where there is a public function room / dance hall / stage on the second floor and a private club room on the first floor. I climbed the concrete steps to the second floor and was greeted at the top step by a lady who looked rather startled to see me. I asked the admission price, and she shouted with a smile, "It says right there on the sign!" I paid my ten dollars and walked into a brightly lit hall. All forty occupants turned and took a long look at me, and I do mean a *long* look. I felt the physical sensation of getting caught—at what, I don't know—but a feeling of shock flashed across my skin not unlike the time in college when I got caught in a spotlight by park rangers while streaking at night on the Gettysburg battlefield. I was certainly the only person in the room not of retirement age.

With a slow gait I hoped would convey a casual awareness that I knew what I was doing there, I approached the bar, and the bartender said, "I've never seen you in here before." With a nervous laugh I explained that I'd come to see the band and that my plan to make a low-key entrance was an obvious failure. Chuckling, she said, "Normally I'm the youngest one here." She looked to me to be about sixty-five. We both had a good laugh.

I sat down alone in the back with a Coke and listened to the Country Masters. I noticed I was the only one *watching* the band. The rest only occasionally looked over: they had come to socialize to music, or dance to music, not to watch a concert. A woman thirty years my elder and trying to look my age in a tight-fitting cream sequined top came over and sat next to me. She introduced herself as Flossie and said she'd felt bad I was sitting alone. She explained—and not in an accusatory way—that she and her girlfriends wanted to know why I was there. Clearly I had a story. I told her I'd come to see the band, which is not what the girls had guessed.

"I'd guessed you'd walked into the wrong place and were trying to save face by staying for a drink," she laughed.

Flossie worked as a waitress in Lexington, Massachusetts, but was born and raised in Prince Edward Island. "Are you Canadian?" she asked, and I told her no.

"Not even any roots in Canada?"

"Well," I laughed, "I guess back in the 1800s my ancestors came to the United States from Ireland by way of St. John, New Brunswick. That was the cheap boat trip. They may have stayed in St. John a few days before settling temporarily in Bangor?" It was true, but in the brown, wood-paneled glow of the Can-Am Club it sounded painfully lame.

"Oh, you're Canadian then," she said matter-of-factly.

On that note, Flossie went back to her seat, and I turned my attention again to the band. It was fascinating to watch the Country Masters at work, as they covered a number of musical bases that I find interesting in streams of New England country music. They featured mostly honky-tonk songs that ranged in vintage from the 1940s through the 1990s (they cover a Vince Gill song on their CD). Lead singer Jimmy Spellman has a strong voice that falls into the stream of vocal style that I would attribute to Hank Snow, Dick Curless, and Gene Hooper. At various points the group broke out into different configurations, first to play traditional Cape Breton tunes (during which time they brought fiddler Ludger Lefort onstage, and steel player Frank Caruso sat out), then a bluegrass set (Jimmy Spellman switched to acoustic guitar, and Frank Caruso played bluegrass-style fiddle), then a traditional square dance set, then back to honky-tonk. Most of the audience danced at some point during this set; as this was an older crowd, it was dominated by women who at times danced with one another.

The square dance set featured a caller who had serious trouble getting the minimum of four couples needed to actually run the dances. The squares he called were akin to the squares Monica and I had danced the previous summer at a ceilidh in Baddeck, Cape Breton. For these, Jimmy Spellman played electric guitar, and there was no steel player. The dancers looked old but enthusiastic. What was curious about the dancing and the music over the course of the night was that most of the people in the club danced during the honky-tonk songs and the Cape Breton songs. The squares featured only eight people, but that seemed to be a problem, because not enough couples knew how to do—or appeared willing to do—the dances. The bluegrass set featured some confused dancing where groups either danced in pairs at half-time or tried painfully to keep up with the tempo of the song as though it was a country song. It is clear that—to paraphrase bluegrass historian Neil Rosenberg—bluegrass is a concert music, not a dance music.

During one of the set breaks, Ludger Lefort talked with me at the bar about growing up in Cheticamp, Cape Breton, and learning to play the fiddle from his brother. He reminisced about going to see the legendary Cape Breton fiddler Angus Chisholm play as a boy and then later playing with him at clubs in Watertown and Boston when both men had relocated there. Ludger talked about going to see Maine country and western performers like Hal Lone Pine, Gene Hooper, and others when they toured through Nova Scotia and about making a weekly habit of listening to the *Wheeling Jamboree*, even though it meant driving to the highest point on the mountain in Cape Breton to get reception on a Saturday night.

Ludger was kind enough to take me to the "club" part of the venue (downstairs), where Jimmy Spellman was having a cigarette with friends. Jimmy and I talked for about five minutes, and I learned he'd been inducted into the MCMAA (Massachusetts Country Music Awards Association) Hall of Fame in 2006. He let me know that he has a number of older recordings, all on cassette, some of which he'd recorded with Johnny White, which he would play for me when we got together to talk.

After meeting Jimmy, I headed upstairs, where a number of people, seeing that I'd become friendly with Ludger, approached me to ask what I was doing at the club. I explained that I was a fan of the Country Masters and that I'd come to see them play. They were intrigued—maybe "puzzled" would be a better word—to hear that I'd found their music on the Internet and even more intrigued that I'd found their schedule on the Canadian-American Club's website. It would appear that the Internet is still a marvel and a mystery to the members of the Canadian-American Club.

On this night, most of the patrons I met at the club were born in Canada—mostly PEI or Nova Scotia—and the expectation is that visitors to the club share the same heritage. I was asked again—multiple times—if I was Canadian. I told the same halfhearted story about how my great-great-grandparents had come to the United States from Ireland by way of New Brunswick.

"Oh, you're Canadian then," I was told (Murphy 2006).

What I experienced during my first night at the Canadian-American Club in Watertown was typical of my experiences at other country and western events in New England and the Canadian Maritimes. At the Can-Am Club I talked with others about my enjoyable visit the previous summer to Cape Breton and PEI, which produced big, proud smiles all around. The patrons who crowded around me at my Canadian American coming-out event talked with me about Hank Snow, Wilf Carter, Joe Cormier, Stompin' Tom Connors, and other Maritime legends with an ease and familiarity that is not readily found elsewhere in the United States, or New England, for that matter.

I was encouraged to return for the weekly Friday night pickin' party held downstairs—in other words, I was invited to participate in community activities. Though I was an outsider, my presence at the club was encouraged by all of the patrons, and I was heartily welcomed back in the future. And I'd achieved ethnic solidarity as a Canadian American. My tenuous connection to Canadian heritage was not lost on anyone; rather, it was plainly accepted as a symbolic point of inclusion. Today, ethnicity in the New England country and western world serves as a marker of awareness of community history, heritage, and traditions. It is more important to be aware that one is "ethnic" (Italian, French, Irish, Yankee, etc.) than to actually be *of* a given ethnicity. Awareness of ethnicity conveys an awareness of personal and community heritage and implies that one can be a productive community member and therefore worthy of inclusion. Time and again at New England country and western events, including this night at the Canadian-American Club, this enabled me to transcend "outsider" status—precisely because such events serve as a place where community heritage is maintained.

With the passage of time, and with the blurring of the firm ethnic community boundaries that existed in the early days of New England country and western barnstorming, an overt demonstration that one cares about maintaining community memories reveals an identity far broader than that of a single ethnicity, an identity consisting of many jumbled heritages with a common social bond. As the memory of New England working-class sociability and the central role that locally made country and western music played in that heritage wanes in the face of corporate narratives of American music history and the southern thesis of country music, New England cowboys living in changing times live out a sturdy and stubborn resistance.

REFERENCES

Interviews

Barnes, Jimmy, and Becky Rice. 2007. Interview by Cliff Murphy. Transcript, Northeast Archives of Folklife and Oral History, Maine Folklife Center, Orono.

Bean, Rose, and Wayne Bean. 1980. Interview by Deborah Kodish. Northeast Archives of Folklife and Oral History, University of Maine, Orono.

Beaudoyn, Raymond [Ray Dixon]. 2006. Interview by Clifford R. Murphy. Transcript, Massachusetts Traditional Arts Archive, Massachusetts Cultural Council, Boston.

Boncore, Angelo. 2005. Interview by Clifford R. Murphy. Transcript, Massachusetts Traditional Arts Archives, Massachusetts Cultural Council, Boston.

Breau, Dennis. 2005. Interview by Clifford R. Murphy. Transcript, Northeast Archives of Folklife and Oral History, Maine Folklife Center, University of Maine, Orono.

Brown, Gordon [Country Gordy]. 2004. Interview by Clifford R. Murphy. Transcript, Massachusetts Traditional Arts Archives, Massachusetts Cultural Council, Boston.

Calderone, Vincent [Jimmy Cal]. 2004. Interview by Cliff Murphy. Transcript, Massachusetts Traditional Arts Archive, Massachusetts Cultural Council, Boston.

Clark, Kathy [Doctor Kathy]. 2005. Interview by Clifford R. Murphy. Transcript, Northeast Archives of Folklife and Oral History, Maine Folklife Center, University of Maine, Orono.

Coté-Binette, Rita [Betty Cody], and Denny Breau. 2006. Interview by Clifford R. Murphy. Transcript, Northeast Archives of Folklife and Oral History, Maine Folklife Center, University of Maine, Orono.

Curless, Phil. 2007. Interview by Clifford R. Murphy. Transcript, Northeast Archives of Folklife and Oral History, Maine Folklife Center, University of Maine, Orono.

Devine, Sandy, and Aurora Devine. 2005. Interview by Clifford R. Murphy. Massachusetts Traditional Arts Archives, Massachusetts Cultural Council, Boston.

Dinsmore, Horace. 1975. Interview by Edward "Sandy" Ives. Northeast Archives of Folklife and Oral History, Maine Folklife Center, University of Maine, Orono.

Dow, Wade. 2007. Interview by Clifford R. Murphy. Transcript, Northeast Archives of Folklife and Oral History, Maine Folklife Center, University of Maine, Orono.

Fournier, Raymond. 2005. Interview by Clifford R. Murphy. Massachusetts Traditional Arts Archives, Massachusetts Cultural Council, Boston.

Gobers, Ramona Riggins Jones [Ramona Jones]. 2007. Interview by Clifford R. Murphy. Transcript, Massachusetts Traditional Arts Archives, Massachusetts Cultural Council, Boston.

Gribben, Elizabeth ["Windy" Betty]. 2007. Interview by Clifford R. Murphy. Transcript, Northeast Archives of Folklife and Oral History, Maine Folklife Center, University of Maine, Orono.

Hand, Reid. 1975. Interview by Edward D. Ives's Anthropology 123 class. Northeast Archives of Folklife and Oral History, Maine Folklife Center, University of Maine, Orono.

Harp, Georgia Mae. 2004. Interview by Maggie Holtzberg and Clifford R. Murphy. Transcript, Massachusetts Traditional Arts Archives, Massachusetts Cultural Council, Boston.

Hawkes, Allerton "Al." 2006. Interview by Clifford R. Murphy. Transcript, Northeast Archives of Folklife and Oral History, Maine Folklife Center, University of Maine, Orono.

Hooper, Gene, and Flo Hooper. 2005. Interview by Clifford R. Murphy. Transcript, Northeast Archives of Folklife and Oral History, Maine Folklife Center, University of Maine, Orono.

Jackson-Serio, Babe. 2006. Interview by Clifford R. Murphy. Transcript, Massachusetts Traditional Arts Archive, Massachusetts Cultural Council, Boston.

Jones, Marshall "Grandpa," and Ramona Riggins Jones. 1975. Interview by Douglas Green. Country Music Foundation Oral History Project, edited by J. Rumble, Frist Library and Archive, Country Music Hall of Fame and Museum, Nashville.

Kincaid, Bradley. 1974. Interview by Douglas Green. Transcript, Oral History Collection, Country Music Hall of Fame and Museum, Nashville.

LeBlanc, John [Johnny White]. 2004. Interview by Clifford R. Murphy. Transcript, Massachusetts Traditional Arts Archives, Massachusetts Cultural Council, Boston.

Little, Ray, and Ann Little. 1975. Interview by Edward "Sandy" Ives. Northeast Archives of Folklife and Oral History, University of Maine, Orono.

Littlefield, Eva. 1975. Interview by Lisa Feldman. Northeast Archives of Folklife and Oral History, University of Maine, Orono.

Makem, Tommy. 2005. Interview by Clifford R. Murphy. Massachusetts Traditional Arts Archives, Massachusetts Cultural Council, Boston.

Metivier, Paul Roberts. 2005. Interview by Clifford R. Murphy. Transcript, Northeast Archives of Folklife and Oral History, Maine Folklife Center, University of Maine, Orono.

Penny, John. 2004. Interview by Clifford R. Murphy. Transcript, Massachusetts Traditional Arts Archives, Massachusetts Cultural Council, Boston.

Poccia, Tony. 2004. Interview by Clifford R. Murphy. Massachusetts Traditional Arts Archives, Massachusetts Cultural Council, Boston.

Rego, Frank "Slim." 2004. Interview by Clifford R. Murphy. Transcript, Massachusetts Traditional Arts Archive, Massachusetts Cultural Council, Boston.

Roberts, Kenny. 2004. Interview by Maggie Holtzberg and Clifford R. Murphy. Transcript, Massachusetts Traditional Arts Archives, Massachusetts Cultural Council, Boston.

Roberts, Kenny, and Betty Ann Roberts. 1987. Interview by John W. Rumble. Oral History Collection, Country Music Hall of Fame and Museum, Nashville.

Rogers, Rusty, and Patty Kempton. 2005. Interview by Clifford R. Murphy. Transcript, Northeast Archives of Folklife and Oral History, Maine Folklife Center, University of Maine, Orono.

Senter, Jim, and Ruth Senter. 2004. Interview by Clifford R. Murphy. Transcript, Massachusetts Traditional Arts Archives, Massachusetts Cultural Council, Boston.

Smith, John "Johnny" Henry. 2007. Interview by Clifford R. Murphy. Transcript, Northeast Archives of Folklife and Oral History, Maine Folklife Center, University of Maine, Orono.

Snow, Schuyler "Sky." 2006. Interview by Clifford R. Murphy. Massachusetts Traditional Arts Archives, Massachusetts Cultural Council, Boston.

White, Babs Zackarian, and Maril Zackarian Albro. 2004. Interview by Clifford R. Murphy. Transcript, Massachusetts Traditional Arts Archives, Massachusetts Cultural Council, Boston.

Wincapaw, Robert [Bob Elston]. 2006. Interview by Clifford R. Murphy. Transcript, Northeast Archives of Folklife and Oral History, Maine Folklife Center, University of Maine, Orono.

Other Sources

Academy of Country Music (ACM). 2007. Academy of Country Music Website and History. Academy of Country Music. November 8, 2007. http://www.acmcountry.com/content/index.php.

Alden, Grant. 1996. "The Wilds, the Innocent, and the Grand Ole Opry." Review. *No Depression*, no. 4. http://www.nodepression.net/issues/nd04/wilds.html.

Algeo, John T. 1960. "Korean Bamboo English." *American Speech* 35 (2): 117–23.

Audette, Susan T., and David E. Baker. 1998. *The Old Town Canoe Company: Our First Hundred Years*. Gardiner, Maine: Tilbury House Publishers.

Awalt, Robert R. 2007. *Kenny Roberts* (downloadable Word document). www.kennyroberts.homestead.com, 2002. Accessed April 19, 2007, at http://www.kennyroberts.homestead.com/files/KENNY_ROBERTS_Bob_Awalt.doc.

Ayers, Edward L., and Peter S. Onuf. 1996. Introduction to *All over the Map: Rethinking American Regions*, by Edward L. Ayers, Patricia Nelson Limerick, Stephen Nissenbaum, and Peter S. Onuf. Baltimore, Md.: Johns Hopkins University Press.

Bassett, Lee Emerson. 1927. [Untitled]. *American Speech* 2 (7): 324–26.

Berger, Peter L., and Thomas Luckmann. 1990. *The Social Construction of Reality: A Treatise in the Sociology of Knowledge*. New York: Anchor Books.

Bernstein, Irving. 1991. *Promises Kept: John F. Kennedy's New Frontier*. New York: Oxford University Press.

Bogue, Allan G. 1998. *Frederick Jackson Turner: Strange Roads Going Down*. Norman: University of Oklahoma Press.

Boyd, Jean Ann. 1998. *The Jazz of the Southwest: An Oral History of Western Swing*. 1st ed. Austin: University of Texas Press.

Bronner, Simon J. 1978. "The Country Music Tradition in Western New York State." *Journal of Country Music* 6 (4): 29.

———. 1987. *Old-Time Music Makers of New York State*. A York State Book. Syracuse, N.Y.: Syracuse University Press.

Cohen, Bruce. 1977. "Country Music and the People of Maine: A Documentary Overview." B.A. honors thesis, Tufts University, Medford.

Cohen, Norman. 1965. "The Skillet Lickers: A Study of a Hillbilly String Band and Its Repertoire." *Journal of American Folklore* 78 (309): 229–44.

Conforti, Joseph A. 2001. *Imagining New England: Explorations of Regional Identity from the Pilgrims to the Mid-Twentieth Century*. Chapel Hill: University of North Carolina Press.

Cronon, William. 2003. *Changes in the Land: Indians, Colonists, and the Ecology of New England*. 1st rev. ed. New York: Hill and Wang.

Davis, Amy. 1998. "Local Oprys in Kentucky: The Grassroots Support of Country Music." In Kentucky Folklife Festival program book, Kentucky Historical Society, Frankfort.

Davis, Edwin B. 1944. "American Nasality." *English Journal* 33 (7): 387.

Dennett, Ruth E. 1991. "Rusty Rogers, One of the True Pioneers in Country Music, Still Enjoys Performing and Is Planning New Cassette Release." *My Country*, June, 19.

Dorson, Richard M. 1940. "The Yankee on the Stage: A Folk Hero of American Drama." *New England Quarterly* 13 (3): 467–93.

Douglass, Frederick. 2005. *My Bondage and My Freedom*. Barnes & Noble Classics. New York: Barnes & Noble.

Doyle, Bertram W. 1936. "The Etiquette of Race Relations—Past, Present, and Future." *Journal of Negro Education* 5 (2): 191–208.

Dunham, Alanson Mellen "Mellie." 1926. *"Mellie" Dunham's 50 Fiddlin' Dance Tunes*. Boston: Carl Fischer.

Eff, Elaine. 1978. "Truckstop: The Research, Presentation, and Interpretation of Occupational Folk Culture." Cooperstown Graduate Program, SUNY College, Oneonta.

Faragher, John Mack, ed. 1998. *Rereading Frederick Jackson Turner: "The Significance of the Frontier in American History" and Other Essays*. New Haven, Conn.: Yale University Press.

Feintuch, Burt. 2001. "Longing for Community." *Western Folklore* 60 (2/3): 149–61.

———. 2006. "Revivals on the Edge: Northumberland and Cape Breton—a Keynote." *Yearbook for Traditional Music* 38:1–18.

Feintuch, Burt, and David H. Watters, eds. 2005. *The Encyclopedia of New England: The Culture and History of an American Region.* New Haven, Conn.: Yale University Press.

Feld, Steven. 1984. "Sound Structure as Social Structure." *Ethnomusicology* 28 (3): 383–409.

Ferriss, Lloyd. 1996. "A Hit 78: Slim Clark Headed for Nashville." *Maine Sunday Telegram*, September 29, 1E, 8E.

Forbes-Roberts, Ron. 2006. *One Long Tune: The Life and Music of Lenny Breau.* Denton: University of North Texas Press.

Fox, Aaron A. 2004. *Real Country: Music and Language in Working-Class Culture.* Durham, N.C.: Duke University Press.

———. 2005. "'Alternative' to What? O Brother, September 11, and the Politics of Country Music." In *Country Music Goes to War*, edited by Charles K. Wolfe and James E. Akenson. Lexington: University Press of Kentucky.

Frith, Simon. 1984. "Rock and the Politics of Memory." *Social Text*, no. 9/10, 59–69.

Fukuyama, Francis. 1999. "Social Capital and Civil Society." In *International Monetary Fund Conference on Second Generation Reforms.* International Monetary Fund, Washington, D.C., http://www.imf.org.

Garofalo, Reebee. 1987. "How Autonomous Is Relative: Popular Music, the Social Formation and Cultural Struggle." *Popular Music* 6 (1): 77–92.

Gilbert, Dennis L. 2008. *The American Class Structure in an Age of Growing Inequality.* 7th ed. Thousand Oaks, Calif.: Pine Forge Press.

Gilbert, Dennis L., and Joseph Alan Kahl. 1993. *The American Class Structure: A New Synthesis.* 4th ed. Belmont, Calif.: Wadsworth.

Glassie, Henry H. 1995. *Passing the Time in Ballymenone: Culture and History of an Ulster Community.* 1st ed. Bloomington: Indiana University Press.

Green, Archie. 1965. "Hillbilly Music: Source and Symbol." *Journal of American Folklore* 78 (309): 204–28.

Green, Steve. 1998. *Uncle Joe Shippee and the All New England Fiddle Contest.* Orono: Northeast Archives of Folklore and Oral History, University of Maine.

Greenberg, Mark. 2004. *Liner Notes to Don Fields and His Pony Boys' Historic WDEV Broadcasts & Last Sessions.* Edited by M. Greenberg. Berlin, Vt.: Multicultural Media.

Guralnick, Peter. 1999. *Lost Highway: Journeys & Arrivals of American Musicians.* Boston: Back Bay Books.

Hall, Roger. 2007. "The Last Round-Up." A tribute to Billy Hill. http://www.americanmusicpreservation.com/billyhill.htm.

Halper, Donna. 2007. Some John Shepard History. http://www.bostonradio.org/essays/shepard.

———. 2008. The Boston Radio Timeline. http://www.bostonradio.org/timeline.html.

Hamlin, Helen. 1948. *Pine, Potatoes and People: The Story of Aroostook.* 1st ed. New York: W. W. Norton.

Hamm, Charles. 1983. *Music in the New World.* 1st ed. New York: Norton.

———. 1995. "Last Minstrel Show?" In *Putting Popular Music in Its Place*, edited by Charles Hamm. Cambridge: Cambridge University Press.

Hansen, Karen V. 1994. *A Very Social Time: Crafting Community in Antebellum New England*. Berkeley: University of California Press.

Hareven, Tamara K., and Randolph Langenbach. 1995. *Amoskeag: Life and Work in an American Factory-City*. Library of New England. Hanover, N.H.: University Press of New England.

Hilmes, Michele. 1997. *Radio Voices: American Broadcasting, 1922–1952*. Minneapolis: University of Minnesota Press.

Hubka, Thomas C. 2004. *Big House, Little House, Back House, Barn: The Connected Farm Buildings of New England*. Twentieth anniversary ed. Hanover, N.H.: University Press of New England.

Hughes, Michael. 1984. "A Comeback in Curless Country." *Portland Telegram*, November 11, 1E, 3E.

Ives, Edward D. 1964. *Larry Gorman: The Man Who Made the Songs*. Bloomington: Indiana University Press.

———. 1971. *Lawrence Doyle: The Farmer-Poet of Prince Edward Island; a Study in Local Songmaking*. Orono: University of Maine Press.

———. 1978. *Joe Scott, the Woodsman-Songmaker*. Urbana: University of Illinois Press.

Jensen, Joli. 1998. *The Nashville Sound: Authenticity, Commercialization, and Country Music*. Nashville: Country Music Foundation Press and Vanderbilt University Press.

Johns, Elizabeth. 1986. "The Farmer in the Works of William Sidney Mount." *Journal of Interdisciplinary History* 17 (1): 257–81.

Jones, Louis "Grandpa," and Charles K. Wolfe. 1984. *Everybody's Grandpa: Fifty Years behind the Mike*. Knoxville: University of Tennessee Press.

Jones, Loyal. 1980. *Radio's "Kentucky Mountain Boy" Bradley Kincaid*. Berea, Ky.: Appalachian Center/Berea College.

Keil, Charles. 1985. "People's Music Comparatively: Style and Stereotype, Class and Hegemony." *Dialectical Anthropology* 10 (½): 119–30.

Keil, Charles, Angeliki V. Keil, and Dick Blau. 1992. *Polka Happiness*. Visual Studies. Philadelphia: Temple University Press.

Kingsbury, Paul, Laura Garrard, Daniel Cooper, John Rumble, and the staff of the Country Music Hall of Fame and Museum, eds. 1998. *The Encyclopedia of Country Music: The Ultimate Guide to the Music*. New York: Oxford University Press.

Klymasz, Robert B. 1972. "'Sounds You Never before Heard': Ukrainian Country Music in Western Canada." *Ethnomusicology* 16 (3): 372–80.

Kroeger, Gerald. 1968. "The History of Boston Radio to 1941." Ph.D. diss., Florida State University, Ann Arbor, Michigan.

Lane, Brigitte Marie. 1990. "Franco-American Folk Traditions and Popular Culture in a Former Milltown: Aspects of Ethnic Urban Folklore and the Dynamics of Folklore Change in Lowell, Massachusetts." Ph.D. diss., Harvard University.

Leary, James P. 1983. "Ethnic Country Music on Superior's South Shore." *JEMF Quarterly* 19 (72): 219–30.

———. 2004. "Ethnic Country Music on Superior's South Shore." In *Exploring Roots Music: Twenty Years of the JEMF Quarterly*, edited by N. Porterfield. Lanham, Md.: Scarecrow Press.

———. 2006. *Polkabilly: How the Goose Island Ramblers Redefined American Folk Music*. American Musicspheres. Toronto: Oxford University Press.

Lewis, George H. 1993. "A Tombstone Every Mile: Country Music in Maine." In *All That Glitters: Country Music in America*, edited by G. H. Lewis. Bowling Green: Bowling Green State University Popular Press.

Lewis, George K. 1980. [Untitled]. *Geographical Review* 70 (2): 245–46.

Lomax, Alan. 1962. "Song Structure and Social Structure." *Ethnology* 1 (4): 425–51.

Lott, Eric. 1993. *Love and Theft: Blackface Minstrelsy and the American Working Class*. Race and American Culture. New York: Oxford University Press.

MacDougall, Pauleena. 2004. *The Penobscot Dance of Resistance: Tradition in the History of a People*. Revisiting New England. Durham: University of New Hampshire Press; Hanover, N.H.: University Press of New England.

Maine Hall of Fame (Members 3). 1998. http://www.mackenziewsd.com/member3 htm.

Majarian, Lynda. 2004. "Confronting Kake Walk." *View Online*, University of Vermont. http://www.uvm.edu/theview/article.php?id=1086.

Malone, Bill C. 1968. *Country Music, U.S.A.: A Fifty-Year History*. Publications of the American Folklore Society, Memoir Series, vol. 54. Austin: Published for the American Folklore Society by the University of Texas Press.

———. 2002a. *Country Music, U.S.A.* 2nd rev. ed. Austin: University of Texas Press.

———. 2002b. *Don't Get above Your Raisin': Country Music and the Southern Working Class*. Music in American Life. Urbana: University of Illinois Press.

Malone, Bill C., and David Stricklin. 2003. *Southern Music/American Music*. Rev. ed. Lexington: University Press of Kentucky.

Mark, Jeffey. 1930. "Recollections of Folk-Musicians." *Musical Quarterly* 16 (2): 175.

Martin, Frederick. 1921. "The Prevention and Correction of Speech Defects." *English Journal* 10 (1): 20–27.

Mayer, Leo V. 1993. "Agricultural Change and Rural America." *Annals of the American Academy of Political and Social Science* 529: 80–91.

McCann, Anthony. 2001. "All That Is Not Given Is Lost: Irish Traditional Music, Copyright, and Common Property." *Ethnomusicology* 45 (1): 89–106.

Mercer, Caroline G. 1967. "Adam Verver, Yankee Businessman." *Nineteenth-Century Fiction* 22 (3): 251–69.

Mulgrave, Dorothy I. 1937. What the English Teacher Should Know about Speech. *English Journal* 26 (8): 648–50.

Murphy, Clifford R. 2004a. Field notes on Hayloft Jamboree Show at Legion Post 15 in East Greenwich, Rhode Island, April 3. Massachusetts Traditional Arts Archives, Massachusetts Cultural Council, Boston.

———. 2004b. Field notes on Hayloft Jamboree Show at Legion Post 15 in East Greenwich, Rhode Island, December 4. Massachusetts Traditional Arts Archives, Massachusetts Cultural Council, Boston.

———. 2005. Field notes on visit with Rusty Rogers (Russell Kempton) and Patty Kempton. Northeast Archives of Folklife and Oral History, Maine Folklife Center, University of Maine, Orono.

———. 2006. Field notes on the Country Masters at the Canadian-American Club in Watertown, Massachusetts. Massachusetts Traditional Arts Archives, Massachusetts Cultural Council, Boston.

———. 2008. "New England Country & Western Music: Self-Reliance, Community Expression, and Regional Resistance on the New England Frontier." Ph.D. diss., Brown University, Providence, Rhode Island.

Nettl, Bruno. 1970. [Untitled]. *American Anthropologist* 72 (2): 438–41.

Nissenbaum, Stephen. 1996. "New England as Region and Nation." In *All over the Map: Rethinking American Regions*, edited by E. L. Ayers. Baltimore, Md.: Johns Hopkins University Press.

Northeast Archives of Folklore and Oral History. 1988. *Traditional Music of Maine*. Cassette tape. Northeast Archives of Folklore and Oral History, Orono, Maine.

O'Shea, Helen. 2006–7. "Getting to the Heart of the Music: Idealizing Musical Community and Irish Traditional Music Sessions." *Journal of the Society for Musicology in Ireland* 2:1–18.

Pecknold, Diane. 2007. *The Selling Sound: The Rise of the Country Music Industry*. Refiguring American Music. Durham, N.C.: Duke University Press.

Peña, Manuel H. 1985. *The Texas-Mexican Conjunto: History of a Working-Class Music*. Mexican American Monographs no. 9. Austin: University of Texas Press.

Peterson, Richard A. 1997. *Creating Country Music: Fabricating Authenticity*. Chicago: University of Chicago Press.

Peterson, Richard A., and Paul DiMaggio. 1975. "From Region to Class, the Changing Locus of Country Music: A Test of the Massification Hypothesis." *Social Forces* 53 (3): 497–506.

Pilarzyk, Thomas. 1978. "Conversion and Alternation Processes in the Youth Culture: A Comparative Analysis of Religious Transformations." *Pacific Sociological Review* 21 (4): 379–405.

Porterfield, Nolan. 1979. *Jimmie Rodgers: The Life and Times of America's Blue Yodeler*. Music in American Life. Urbana: University of Illinois Press.

Post, Jennifer C. 2004. *Music in Rural New England Family and Community Life, 1870–1940*. Revisiting New England. Lebanon, N.H.: University Press of New England.

Puleo, Stephen. 2007. *The Boston Italians: A Story of Pride, Perseverance, and Paesani, from the Years of the Great Immigration to the Present Day*. Boston: Beacon Press.

Pullen, Clarence. 1902. *In Fair Aroostook: Where Acadia and Scandinavia's Subtle Touch Turned a Wilderness into a Land of Plenty*. Bangor, Maine: Bangor and Aroostook Railroad Company.

Putnam, Robert D. 2000. *Bowling Alone: The Collapse and Revival of American Community*. New York: Simon & Schuster.

"Radio's Sweetest Personality—the Girl with the WHITE GUITAR and TRIPLE YODEL." 1945. In the Spotlight (Outstanding Musical Personalities). *SESAC Music* 4 (11): 2–4.

"Radio's Wake-Up Girl—Georgia Mae." 1945. *WBZ News Features*. Westinghouse Radio Stations, Boston.

Roberts, Roderick J. 1978. "An Introduction to the Study of Northern Country Music." *Journal of Country Music* 6 (4): 6.

Rogin, Michael. 1992. "Making America Home: Racial Masquerade and Ethnic Assimilation in the Transition to Talking Pictures." *Journal of American History* 79 (3): 1050–77.

Root, A. R. 1926. "A Survey of Speech Defectives in the Public Elementary Schools of South Dakota." *Elementary School Journal* 26 (7): 531–41.

Rosenberg, Neil V. 1985. "Big Fish, Small Pond: Country Musicians and Their Markets." In *Media Sense*, edited by P. and M. L. Narvaez. Bowling Green: Bowling Green State University Popular Press.

———. 1988. "Ethnicity and Class: Black Country Musicians in the Maritimes." *Journal of Canadian Studies* 23 (1/2): 18.

———. 1993. "Country Music—Popular or Folk?" In *All That Glitters: Country Music in America*, edited by G. H. Lewis. Bowling Green: Bowling Green State University Popular Press.

Rosenzweig, Roy. 1987. "Middle-Class Parks and Working-Class Play: The Struggle over Recreational Space in Worcester, Massachusetts, 1870–1910." In *The New England Working Class and the New Labor History*, edited by H. G. Gutman. Urbana: University of Illinois Press.

Rourke, Constance. 2004. *American Humor: A Study of the National Character*. New York Review Books Classics. New York: New York Review Books.

Rourke, Constance, and Van Wyck Brooks. 1980. *The Roots of American Culture and Other Essays*. Westport, Conn.: Greenwood Press.

Russell, Duncan "Skip," and Frank Pierce. 1976. *1976 New England Country Music Guidebook*. Vol. 1, no. 1. Wells, Maine: Country Company.

Russell, Tony, and Bob Pinson. 2004. *Country Music Records: A Discography, 1921–1942*. New York: Oxford University Press.

Ryden, Kent C. 2001. *Landscape with Figures: Nature and Culture in New England*. American Land and Life. Iowa City: University of Iowa Press.

Sample, Tex. 1996. *White Soul: Country Music, the Church, and Working Americans*. Nashville: Abingdon Press.

Sanderson, David. 2003. "Mellie Dunham: A Remembrance, Norway, Maine Summer Festival, 2003." Norway, Maine Summer Festival.

Sanjek, David. 1998. "Blue Moon of Kentucky Rising over the Mystery Train: The Complex Construction of Country Music." In *Reading Country Music: Steel Guitars, Opry Stars, and Honky-Tonk Bars*, edited by C. Tichi. Durham, N.C.: Duke University Press.

Scharnhorst, Gary. 2002. Introduction to *The Virginian: A Horseman of the Plains*. New York: Simon & Schuster.

Schweitzer, Sarah. 2005. "Putting Down Roots: Amish Find a Home in Rugged Maine." *Boston Globe (Online)*, February 2, 2.

Shank, Barry. 1994. *Dissonant Identities: The Rock 'n' Roll Scene in Austin, Texas*. Music/Culture. Hanover, N.H.: University Press of New England.

Smith, Judith E. 1987. "The Transformation of Family and Community Culture in Immigrant Neighborhoods, 1900–1940." In *The New England Working Class and the New Labor History*, edited by H. G. Gutman. Urbana: University of Illinois Press.

Stampfle, Peter. 1997. "Peter Stampfle, May 1997." In *A Booklet of Essays, Appreciations, and Annotations Pertaining to the "Anthology of American Folk Music," Edited by Harry Smith*, edited by P. Seitel. Washington, D.C.: Smithsonian Folkways/Sony Music Special Products.

"State Lawmaker Renews Call for Dividing Maine." 2010. *Boston Globe*, March 10.

Steiner, Michael. 1995. "From Frontier to Region: Frederick Jackson Turner and the New Western History." *Pacific Historical Review* 64 (4): 479–501.

Taft, Michael. 1974. "That's No More Dollars: Jimmy Linegar's Success with Country Music in Newfoundland." *Folklore Forum* 7:21.

Tallmadge, William H. 1983. [Untitled]. *American Music* 1 (1): 92–94.

Temin, Peter. 2000. *Engines of Enterprise: An Economic History of New England*. Cambridge, Mass.: Harvard University Press.

Thorson, Robert M. 2002. *Stone by Stone: The Magnificent History in New England's Stone Walls*. New York: Walker and Company.

Tichi, Cecelia. 1994. *High Lonesome: The American Culture Of Country Music*. Chapel Hill: University of North Carolina Press.

Titon, Jeff Todd. 1994. *Early Downhome Blues: A Musical and Cultural Analysis*. 2nd ed. Cultural Studies of the United States. Chapel Hill: University of North Carolina Press.

Tosches, Nick. 2001. *Where Dead Voices Gather*. 1st ed. Boston: Little, Brown.

Tribe, Ivan M. 1996. *Mountaineer Jamboree: Country Music in West Virginia*. Lexington: University Press of Kentucky.

Tucker, Bruce. 1989. "'Tell Tchaikovsky the News': Postmodernism, Popular Culture, and the Emergence of Rock 'n' Roll." *Black Music Research Journal* 9 (2): 271–95.

Turner, Frederick Jackson. 1984. *The Significance of the Frontier in American History*. [Madison, Wis.]: Silver Buckle Press.

Victor Record Company. 1916. "New Victor Records for July 1916."

Wells, Paul F. 1976. "Mellie Dunham: 'Maine's Champion Fiddler.'" *John Edwards Memorial Foundation Quarterly* 12 (43): 117–18.

Westinghouse Radio Stations WBA & WBZA Sales Promotion Department. 1943. "Mail Study Response to Calendar Offer Made by Georgia Mae, the Cowgirl Songstress during 'The New England Farm Hour' Broadcast over WBZ & WBZA December 21 to January 30." Westinghouse Radio Stations WBZ & WBZA, Boston.

Whisnant, David E., with Charles Camp. 1977. "A Voice from Home: Southern Mountain Musicians on the Maryland-Pennsylvania Border." *Southern Exposure* 5:80–89.

Wilgus, D. K. 1965. "An Introduction to the Study of Hillbilly Music." *Journal of American Folklore* 78 (309): 195–203.

Williams, Doc, with Barbara D. Smik. 2006. *Doc Williams: Looking Back*. Wheeling: James Thornton Creative Impressions.

Wilson, Charles Morrow, and Alden Woodworth. 1937. *Aroostook, Our Last Frontier: Maine's Picturesque Potato Empire*. Brattleboro, Vt.: Stephen Daye Press.

Wilson, John S. 1972. "Country Fiddler." *New York Times*, April 23, 1.

Wincapaw, Robert [alias Bob Elston and Friends]. 2002. *For the Record: A History of Maine's Country Music*. 1st ed. Clinton, Maine: Bob Elston (self-published).

Wolfe, Charles K. 1997. *The Devil's Box: Masters of Southern Fiddling*. 1st ed. Nashville: Country Music Foundation Press and Vanderbilt University Press.

———. 1999. *A Good-Natured Riot: The Birth of the Grand Ole Opry*. Nashville: Country Music Foundation Press and Vanderbilt University Press.

Zinn, Howard. 2003. *A People's History of the United States: 1492–Present*. New ed. New York: HarperCollins.

Zweig, Michael. 2004. *What's Class Got to Do with It? American Society in the Twenty-First Century*. Ithaca, N.Y.: ILR Press.

INDEX

CLIFFORD R. MURPHY was a member of the seminal New Hampshire alternative country bands Say ZuZu and Hog Mawl. He has a PhD in Ethnomusicology from Brown University and is Director of Maryland Traditions, the folklife program of the Maryland State Arts Council.

MUSIC IN AMERICAN LIFE

Only a Miner: Studies in Recorded Coal-Mining Songs *Archie Green*
Great Day Coming: Folk Music and the American Left *R. Serge Denisoff*
John Philip Sousa: A Descriptive Catalog of His Works *Paul E. Bierley*
The Hell-Bound Train: A Cowboy Songbook *Glenn Ohrlin*
Oh, Didn't He Ramble: The Life Story of Lee Collins, as Told to Mary Collins *Edited by Frank J. Gillis and John W. Miner*
American Labor Songs of the Nineteenth Century *Philip S. Foner*
Stars of Country Music: Uncle Dave Macon to Johnny Rodriguez *Edited by Bill C. Malone and Judith McCulloh*
Git Along, Little Dogies: Songs and Songmakers of the American West *John I. White*
A Texas-Mexican *Cancionero*: Folksongs of the Lower Border *Américo Paredes*
San Antonio Rose: The Life and Music of Bob Wills *Charles R. Townsend*
Early Downhome Blues: A Musical and Cultural Analysis *Jeff Todd Titon*
An Ives Celebration: Papers and Panels of the Charles Ives Centennial Festival-Conference *Edited by H. Wiley Hitchcock and Vivian Perlis*
Sinful Tunes and Spirituals: Black Folk Music to the Civil War *Dena J. Epstein*
Joe Scott, the Woodsman-Songmaker *Edward D. Ives*
Jimmie Rodgers: The Life and Times of America's Blue Yodeler *Nolan Porterfield*
Early American Music Engraving and Printing: A History of Music Publishing in America from 1787 to 1825, with Commentary on Earlier and Later Practices *Richard J. Wolfe*
Sing a Sad Song: The Life of Hank Williams *Roger M. Williams*
Long Steel Rail: The Railroad in American Folksong *Norm Cohen*
Resources of American Music History: A Directory of Source Materials from Colonial Times to World War II *D. W. Krummel, Jean Geil, Doris J. Dyen, and Deane L. Root*
Tenement Songs: The Popular Music of the Jewish Immigrants *Mark Slobin*
Ozark Folksongs *Vance Randolph; edited and abridged by Norm Cohen*
Oscar Sonneck and American Music *Edited by William Lichtenwanger*
Bluegrass Breakdown: The Making of the Old Southern Sound *Robert Cantwell*
Bluegrass: A History *Neil V. Rosenberg*
Music at the White House: A History of the American Spirit *Elise K. Kirk*
Red River Blues: The Blues Tradition in the Southeast *Bruce Bastin*

Good Friends and Bad Enemies: Robert Winslow Gordon and the Study of American Folksong *Debora Kodish*
Fiddlin' Georgia Crazy: Fiddlin' John Carson, His Real World, and the World of His Songs *Gene Wiggins*
America's Music: From the Pilgrims to the Present (rev. 3d ed.) *Gilbert Chase*
Secular Music in Colonial Annapolis: The Tuesday Club, 1745–56 *John Barry Talley*
Bibliographical Handbook of American Music *D. W. Krummel*
Goin' to Kansas City *Nathan W. Pearson, Jr.*
"Susanna," "Jeanie," and "The Old Folks at Home": The Songs of Stephen C. Foster from His Time to Ours (2d ed.) *William W. Austin*
Songprints: The Musical Experience of Five Shoshone Women *Judith Vander*
"Happy in the Service of the Lord": Afro-American Gospel Quartets in Memphis *Kip Lornell*
Paul Hindemith in the United States *Luther Noss*
"My Song Is My Weapon": People's Songs, American Communism, and the Politics of Culture, 1930–50 *Robbie Lieberman*
Chosen Voices: The Story of the American Cantorate *Mark Slobin*
Theodore Thomas: America's Conductor and Builder of Orchestras, 1835–1905 *Ezra Schabas*
"The Whorehouse Bells Were Ringing" and Other Songs Cowboys Sing *Collected and Edited by Guy Logsdon*
Crazeology: The Autobiography of a Chicago Jazzman *Bud Freeman, as Told to Robert Wolf*
Discoursing Sweet Music: Brass Bands and Community Life in Turn-of-the-Century Pennsylvania *Kenneth Kreitner*
Mormonism and Music: A History *Michael Hicks*
Voices of the Jazz Age: Profiles of Eight Vintage Jazzmen *Chip Deffaa*
Pickin' on Peachtree: A History of Country Music in Atlanta, Georgia *Wayne W. Daniel*
Bitter Music: Collected Journals, Essays, Introductions, and Librettos *Harry Partch; edited by Thomas McGeary*
Ethnic Music on Records: A Discography of Ethnic Recordings Produced in the United States, 1893 to 1942 *Richard K. Spottswood*
Downhome Blues Lyrics: An Anthology from the Post–World War II Era *Jeff Todd Titon*
Ellington: The Early Years *Mark Tucker*
Chicago Soul *Robert Pruter*
That Half-Barbaric Twang: The Banjo in American Popular Culture *Karen Linn*
Hot Man: The Life of Art Hodes *Art Hodes and Chadwick Hansen*

The Erotic Muse: American Bawdy Songs (2d ed.) *Ed Cray*
Barrio Rhythm: Mexican American Music in Los Angeles *Steven Loza*
The Creation of Jazz: Music, Race, and Culture in Urban America *Burton W. Peretti*
Charles Martin Loeffler: A Life Apart in Music *Ellen Knight*
Club Date Musicians: Playing the New York Party Circuit *Bruce A. MacLeod*
Opera on the Road: Traveling Opera Troupes in the United States, 1825–60 *Katherine K. Preston*
The Stonemans: An Appalachian Family and the Music That Shaped Their Lives *Ivan M. Tribe*
Transforming Tradition: Folk Music Revivals Examined *Edited by Neil V. Rosenberg*
The Crooked Stovepipe: Athapaskan Fiddle Music and Square Dancing in Northeast Alaska and Northwest Canada *Craig Mishler*
Traveling the High Way Home: Ralph Stanley and the World of Traditional Bluegrass Music *John Wright*
Carl Ruggles: Composer, Painter, and Storyteller *Marilyn Ziffrin*
Never without a Song: The Years and Songs of Jennie Devlin, 1865–1952 *Katharine D. Newman*
The Hank Snow Story *Hank Snow, with Jack Ownbey and Bob Burris*
Milton Brown and the Founding of Western Swing *Cary Ginell, with special assistance from Roy Lee Brown*
Santiago de Murcia's "Códice Saldívar No. 4": A Treasury of Secular Guitar Music from Baroque Mexico *Craig H. Russell*
The Sound of the Dove: Singing in Appalachian Primitive Baptist Churches *Beverly Bush Patterson*
Heartland Excursions: Ethnomusicological Reflections on Schools of Music *Bruno Nettl*
Doowop: The Chicago Scene *Robert Pruter*
Blue Rhythms: Six Lives in Rhythm and Blues *Chip Deffaa*
Shoshone Ghost Dance Religion: Poetry Songs and Great Basin Context *Judith Vander*
Go Cat Go! Rockabilly Music and Its Makers *Craig Morrison*
'Twas Only an Irishman's Dream: The Image of Ireland and the Irish in American Popular Song Lyrics, 1800–1920 *William H. A. Williams*
Democracy at the Opera: Music, Theater, and Culture in New York City, 1815–60 *Karen Ahlquist*
Fred Waring and the Pennsylvanians *Virginia Waring*
Woody, Cisco, and Me: Seamen Three in the Merchant Marine *Jim Longhi*
Behind the Burnt Cork Mask: Early Blackface Minstrelsy and Antebellum American Popular Culture *William J. Mahar*

Going to Cincinnati: A History of the Blues in the Queen City *Steven C. Tracy*

Pistol Packin' Mama: Aunt Molly Jackson and the Politics of Folksong *Shelly Romalis*

Sixties Rock: Garage, Psychedelic, and Other Satisfactions *Michael Hicks*

The Late Great Johnny Ace and the Transition from R&B to Rock 'n' Roll *James M. Salem*

Tito Puente and the Making of Latin Music *Steven Loza*

Juilliard: A History *Andrea Olmstead*

Understanding Charles Seeger, Pioneer in American Musicology *Edited by Bell Yung and Helen Rees*

Mountains of Music: West Virginia Traditional Music from *Goldenseal* *Edited by John Lilly*

Alice Tully: An Intimate Portrait *Albert Fuller*

A Blues Life *Henry Townsend, as told to Bill Greensmith*

Long Steel Rail: The Railroad in American Folksong (2d ed.) *Norm Cohen*

The Golden Age of Gospel *Text by Horace Clarence Boyer; photography by Lloyd Yearwood*

Aaron Copland: The Life and Work of an Uncommon Man *Howard Pollack*

Louis Moreau Gottschalk *S. Frederick Starr*

Race, Rock, and Elvis *Michael T. Bertrand*

Theremin: Ether Music and Espionage *Albert Glinsky*

Poetry and Violence: The Ballad Tradition of Mexico's Costa Chica *John H. McDowell*

The Bill Monroe Reader *Edited by Tom Ewing*

Music in Lubavitcher Life *Ellen Koskoff*

Zarzuela: Spanish Operetta, American Stage *Janet L. Sturman*

Bluegrass Odyssey: A Documentary in Pictures and Words, 1966–86 *Carl Fleischhauer and Neil V. Rosenberg*

That Old-Time Rock & Roll: A Chronicle of an Era, 1954–63 *Richard Aquila*

Labor's Troubadour *Joe Glazer*

American Opera *Elise K. Kirk*

Don't Get above Your Raisin': Country Music and the Southern Working Class *Bill C. Malone*

John Alden Carpenter: A Chicago Composer *Howard Pollack*

Heartbeat of the People: Music and Dance of the Northern Pow-wow *Tara Browner*

My Lord, What a Morning: An Autobiography *Marian Anderson*

Marian Anderson: A Singer's Journey *Allan Keiler*

Charles Ives Remembered: An Oral History *Vivian Perlis*

Henry Cowell, Bohemian *Michael Hicks*
Rap Music and Street Consciousness *Cheryl L. Keyes*
Louis Prima *Garry Boulard*
Marian McPartland's Jazz World: All in Good Time *Marian McPartland*
Robert Johnson: Lost and Found *Barry Lee Pearson and Bill McCulloch*
Bound for America: Three British Composers *Nicholas Temperley*
Lost Sounds: Blacks and the Birth of the Recording Industry, 1890–1919 *Tim Brooks*
Burn, Baby! BURN! The Autobiography of Magnificent Montague *Magnificent Montague with Bob Baker*
Way Up North in Dixie: A Black Family's Claim to the Confederate Anthem *Howard L. Sacks and Judith Rose Sacks*
The Bluegrass Reader *Edited by Thomas Goldsmith*
Colin McPhee: Composer in Two Worlds *Carol J. Oja*
Robert Johnson, Mythmaking, and Contemporary American Culture *Patricia R. Schroeder*
Composing a World: Lou Harrison, Musical Wayfarer *Leta E. Miller and Fredric Lieberman*
Fritz Reiner, Maestro and Martinet *Kenneth Morgan*
That Toddlin' Town: Chicago's White Dance Bands and Orchestras, 1900–1950 *Charles A. Sengstock Jr.*
Dewey and Elvis: The Life and Times of a Rock 'n' Roll Deejay *Louis Cantor*
Come Hither to Go Yonder: Playing Bluegrass with Bill Monroe *Bob Black*
Chicago Blues: Portraits and Stories *David Whiteis*
The Incredible Band of John Philip Sousa *Paul E. Bierley*
"Maximum Clarity" and Other Writings on Music *Ben Johnston, edited by Bob Gilmore*
Staging Tradition: John Lair and Sarah Gertrude Knott *Michael Ann Williams*
Homegrown Music: Discovering Bluegrass *Stephanie P. Ledgin*
Tales of a Theatrical Guru *Danny Newman*
The Music of Bill Monroe *Neil V. Rosenberg and Charles K. Wolfe*
Pressing On: The Roni Stoneman Story *Roni Stoneman, as told to Ellen Wright*
Together Let Us Sweetly Live *Jonathan C. David, with photographs by Richard Holloway*
Live Fast, Love Hard: The Faron Young Story *Diane Diekman*
Air Castle of the South: WSM Radio and the Making of Music City *Craig P. Havighurst*
Traveling Home: Sacred Harp Singing and American Pluralism *Kiri Miller*

Where Did Our Love Go? The Rise and Fall of the Motown Sound *Nelson George*

Lonesome Cowgirls and Honky-Tonk Angels: The Women of Barn Dance Radio *Kristine M. McCusker*

California Polyphony: Ethnic Voices, Musical Crossroads *Mina Yang*

The Never-Ending Revival: Rounder Records and the Folk Alliance *Michael F. Scully*

Sing It Pretty: A Memoir *Bess Lomax Hawes*

Working Girl Blues: The Life and Music of Hazel Dickens *Hazel Dickens and Bill C. Malone*

Charles Ives Reconsidered *Gayle Sherwood Magee*

The Hayloft Gang: The Story of the National Barn Dance *Edited by Chad Berry*

Country Music Humorists and Comedians *Loyal Jones*

Record Makers and Breakers: Voices of the Independent Rock 'n' Roll Pioneers *John Broven*

Music of the First Nations: Tradition and Innovation in Native North America *Edited by Tara Browner*

Cafe Society: The Wrong Place for the Right People *Barney Josephson, with Terry Trilling-Josephson*

George Gershwin: An Intimate Portrait *Walter Rimler*

Life Flows On in Endless Song: Folk Songs and American History *Robert V. Wells*

I Feel a Song Coming On: The Life of Jimmy McHugh *Alyn Shipton*

King of the Queen City: The Story of King Records *Jon Hartley Fox*

Long Lost Blues: Popular Blues in America, 1850–1920 *Peter C. Muir*

Hard Luck Blues: Roots Music Photographs from the Great Depression *Rich Remsberg*

Restless Giant: The Life and Times of Jean Aberbach and Hill and Range Songs *Bar Biszick-Lockwood*

Champagne Charlie and Pretty Jemima: Variety Theater in the Nineteenth Century *Gillian M. Rodger*

Sacred Steel: Inside an African American Steel Guitar Tradition *Robert L. Stone*

Gone to the Country: The New Lost City Ramblers and the Folk Music Revival *Ray Allen*

The Makers of the Sacred Harp *David Warren Steel with Richard H. Hulan*

Woody Guthrie, American Radical *Will Kaufman*

George Szell: A Life of Music *Michael Charry*

Bean Blossom: The Brown County Jamboree and Bill Monroe's Bluegrass Festivals *Thomas A. Adler*

Crowe on the Banjo: The Music Life of J. D. Crowe *Marty Godbey*
Twentieth Century Drifter: The Life of Marty Robbins *Diane Diekman*
Henry Mancini: Reinventing Film Music *John Caps*
The Beautiful Music All Around Us: Field Recordings and the American Experience *Stephen Wade*
Then Sings My Soul: The Culture of Southern Gospel Music *Douglas Harrison*
The Accordion in the Americas: Klezmer, Polka, Tango, Zydeco, and More! *Edited by Helena Simonett*
Bluegrass Bluesman: A Memoir *Josh Graves, edited by Fred Bartenstein*
One Woman in a Hundred: Edna Phillips and the Philadelphia Orchestra *Mary Sue Welsh*
The Great Orchestrator: Arthur Judson and American Arts Management *James M. Doering*
Charles Ives in the Mirror: American Histories of an Iconic Composer *David C. Paul*
Southern Soul-Blues *David Whiteis*
Sweet Air: Modernism, Regionalism, and American Popular Song *Edward P. Comentale*
Pretty Good for a Girl: Women in Bluegrass *Murphy Hicks Henry*
Sweet Dreams: The World of Patsy Cline *Warren R. Hofstra*
William Sidney Mount and the Creolization of American Culture *Christopher J. Smith*
Bird: The Life and Music of Charlie Parker *Chuck Haddix*
Making the March King: John Philip Sousa's Washington Years, 1854–1893 *Patrick Warfield*
In It for the Long Run *Jim Rooney*
Roots of the Revival: American and British Folk Music in the 1950s *Ronald D. Cohen and Rachel Clare Donaldson*
Pioneers of the Blues Revival *Steve Cushing*
Blues All Day Long: The Jimmy Rogers Story *Wayne Everett Goins*
Yankee Twang: Country and Western Music in New England *Clifford R. Murphy*

The University of Illinois Press
is a founding member of the
Association of American University Presses.

Composed in 10/13 Sabon
with Rosewood Display
by Lisa Connery
at the University of Illinois Press
Manufactured by Cushing-Malloy, Inc.

University of Illinois Press
1325 South Oak Street
Champaign, IL 61820-6903
www.press.uillinois.edu